NEW PLAYWRIGHTS
The Best Plays of 2002

D1308098

SMITH AND KRAUS PUBLISHERS
Contemporary Playwrights / Full-Length Play Anthologies

Humana Festival 1993: The Complete Plays
Humana Festival 1994: The Complete Plays
Humana Festival 1995: The Complete Plays
Humana Festival 1996: The Complete Plays
Humana Festival 1997: The Complete Plays
Humana Festival 1998: The Complete Plays
Humana Festival 1999: The Complete Plays
Humana Festival 2000: The Complete Plays
Humana Festival 2001: The Complete Plays
Humana Festival 2002: The Complete Plays
Humana Festival: 20 One-Act Plays 1976–1996

New Dramatists 2000: The Best Plays by the Graduating Class
New Dramatists 2001: The Best Plays by the Graduating Class

New Playwrights: The Best Plays of 1998
New Playwrights: The Best Plays of 1999
New Playwrights: The Best Plays of 2000
New Playwrights: The Best Plays of 2001

Women Playwrights: The Best Plays of 1992
Women Playwrights: The Best Plays of 1993
Women Playwrights: The Best Plays of 1994
Women Playwrights: The Best Plays of 1995
Women Playwrights: The Best Plays of 1996
Women Playwrights: The Best Plays of 1997
Women Playwrights: The Best Plays of 1998
Women Playwrights: The Best Plays of 1999
Women Playwrights: The Best Plays of 2000
Women Playwrights: The Best Plays of 2001

If you require prepublication information about forthcoming Smith and Kraus books, you may receive our semiannual catalogue, free of charge, by sending your name and address to *Smith and Kraus Catalogue, PO Box 127, Lyme, NH 03768.* Or call us at (800) 895-4331, fax (603) 643-1831. www.SmithKraus.com.

NEW PLAYWRIGHTS

The Best Plays of 2002

CONTEMPORARY PLAYWRIGHTS
SERIES

SK
A Smith and Kraus Book

A Smith and Kraus Book
Published by Smith and Kraus, Inc.
177 Lyme Road, Hanover, NH 03755
www.SmithKraus.com

First Edition: July 2003
10 9 8 7 6 5 4 3 2 1

The Library of Congress Cataloging-In-Publication Data

New Playwrights: the best plays of 2002. —1st ed.
p. cm. — (Contemporary playwrights series)

ISBN 1-57525-367-4
1. American drama—20th century. I. Series.
PS634.N416 2000
812'.5408—dc21   00-029707

CONTENTS

FOREWORD

This book, the third in this series I have edited for Smith and Kraus, contains an eclectic mix of new writing for the stage. You will probably have heard of few, if any, of these plays and their authors. But don't let that deter you. Most people have only heard of the plays that have had major success on a tiny island on the northeast coast of the United States (you know the island); when in fact many of the most interesting plays come from elsewhere, and may or may not ever have a significant production on this aforementioned island, for one reason or another.

Probably the best known of the playwrights whose work I have included herein is Tom Donaghy, whose plays often deal with the institution of the family, in an age long past what we might consider the traditional nature of this institution. *Boys and Girls* asks pertinent questions about what's the most effective family, and it does so from a unique perspective, dealing as it does with the topic of gay parenting. I think it is a funny, brilliant, and very courageous play — courageous for its conclusion, which seemed to confuse and even annoy some critics when the play was produced in New York by the inestimably valuable Playwrights Horizons. I am not going to give away the ending. I'll just say that it will surprise you unless your mind works outside the box of cultural expectations common to most urban theater people.

The West End Horror is a clever and highly inventive Sherlock Holmes play. Holmes is visited by none other than George Bernard Shaw, who enlists his services in solving the murder of a theater critic. This leads Holmes into the fascinating netherworld of London theater, where he meets the likes of Oscar Wilde, Richard D'Oyly Carte, and Sir Arthur Sullivan.

Birth, by Bless ji Jaja, was produced in New York City — in Brooklyn, which, for most Manhattanites, is Outer Slobovia. It was a great success at the Billie Holiday Theater, a non-Equity professional black theater in the heart of Bedford-Stuyvesant. It seems to be a requirement of black playwrights (since the 1960s) that their work be angry drama. What makes *Birth* a very unusual play is that it is an out-and-out comedy about two black couples in their sixties. It's a comedy about holding it together as you near the finish line, which will, I think, resonate with any audience, black or white, young or old.

Unequalibrium, too, was done in New York, but in a tiny theater in lower Manhattan, the Gene Frankel Theater. This sequence of character monologues by Alexander Lyras and Robert McCaskill (originally performed by Mr. Lyras), disparate in execution, culminates in a surprising and heartbreaking ending, in which all these people meet late one night on a dark Manhattan street.

Professional Skepticism is a realistic comic drama about skulduggery at a Big Five accounting firm. It's as topical as the headlines these days (and no doubt, for years to come).

Craig Wright's *Orange Flower Water* is also about marriage and family. It's a comic drama about the causes and effects of adultery, originally produced in Minneapolis at the Jungle Theater.

Finally, I decided to include a one-act play by a student, William Kuhn, whose *Absolving Buckner* won the prestigious Eleanor Frost Prize at Dartmouth College. It's a comedy about the chickens coming home to roost for four guys in a bar.

There is a *wealth* of new writing for the theater of interest to you and your audiences (if you're a theater person). You just have to know where to look for it. A good place to start is Smith and Kraus's anthologies.

D. L. Lepidus

INTRODUCTION

A few years ago I was in another city for rehearsals of a play of mine, and a professor from a local university asked me if I would speak with some students after a performance. They were to pay me a fee from something called the "Poets and Writers Fund." After the show, as his group was gathering for the talk, my friend the professor approached me, looking harassed and sheepish, and said, "We have a problem with your fee. After the longest and most bitter debate in the history of the Poets and Writers Fund, the committee has decided that they can't pay you because playwrights are not writers."

My first impulse was to go call Shakespeare and Chekhov to let them know we'd all apparently been operating under some serious misconceptions about what we've been doing, but the professor was a very nice man, and the students were all sitting there waiting, so I said I'd do it for free, and we had a decent enough time, although I could see several very stern looking old men standing in the back glaring at me and shaking their heads at everything I said. I figured this must be the committee.

I'm sorry to report that these gentlemen are not alone in their conviction that writing plays is somehow not the same sort of activity as writing a story or a poem, and there are of course people who believe that Shakespeare cared nothing about the written texts of his plays. I am not one of these people. There are other Shakespearean scholars who think that actually producing the plays somehow spoils them, that the dangerous mess of production can never be as rich an experience as reading them. I don't agree with these people, either, but it does seem fairly obvious to me that a play can be every bit as powerful and satisfying a work of literature as any novel or epic poem. I can't imagine that anybody who's read *King Lear* can seriously doubt this for a moment. So I can only presume that when the committee decided that playwrights are not writers, what they were really asserting was that while dead playwrights may have once produced literature, living playwrights, certainly living American ones, manifestly cannot.

And yet, what you have before you is a printed volume of new American plays. Whether you will judge any of them to be great literature is of course entirely up to you. What seems to me to be undeniably the case is that there is no inherent reason why a play cannot be as much a work of literature as a sonnet or *Moby Dick*. Like them, a play is an imaginative work meant to be read first of all, and re-imagined in the mind of the reader before it is anything else. That a play is also a blueprint for production adds a whole other layer of significance and power to it. It certainly does not diminish its potential value as literature. Only its own internal richness and complexity, or lack thereof, can determine that. I don't think Aristotle was having an off day when he ranked tragedy as the most powerful of all art forms.

But I'm not in the business of ranking genres. I just come introducing this collection of new American plays. What they will make happen in your head when you read them, I can't say. But the possibility that an American play can be a significant work of literature, and therefore worth reading for its own sake, is something I hope some day will not seem to be an eccentric or absurd position to take. My friends at Smith and Kraus are doing a great service by getting many new plays into print so people like you can read them and decide for yourself. I commend them for their courage, and their faith that a play, being that part of the theatrical event which endures when all else has been lost, is both a work of literature and the portal to that other dimension of experience which is its incarnation in flesh and blood.

Don Nigro

DON NIGRO lives in a small town in Ohio with many cats and writes many plays, which are produced regularly all over the world, even in the United States. Many of his plays are published by Samuel French, a couple by Smith and Kraus.

BOYS AND GIRLS

By Tom Donaghy

PLAYWRIGHT'S BIOGRAPHY

Tom Donaghy is the author of the plays *The Beginning of August, Minutes from the Blue Route, Northeast Local, From Above, Down the Shore,* and *The Dadshuttle.* The plays have been published in a collection by Grove Press, are archived on video at Lincoln Center Library for the Performing Arts, and have been produced by some of the most prestigious theaters in the country, including Atlantic Theater Company, Playwrights Horizons, Lincoln Center Theater, The Goodman Theater, Philadelphia Theater Company, and South Coast Repertory. For more information, please visit tomdonaghy.com.

ORIGINAL PRODUCTION

Boys and Girls was originally produced at Playwrights Horizons. The play opened on May 28, 2002. The cast was as follows:

REED . . . . Robert Sella

JASON . . . . Malcolm Gets

BEV . . . . Nadia Dajani

SHELLY . . . . Carrie Preston

CHARACTERS

REED: early thirties.
JASON: early thirties.
BEV: early thirties.
SHELLY: early thirties.

PLACE, SETTINGS

Various settings in and around any large American city.

Boys and Girls

ACT I

Late August. A bar. A martini shaker and two martinis sit on a café table flanked by two bar stools. As the lights come up, Jason arrives and greets Reed, who has been waiting for him.

REED: Hi.

JASON: Hi.

(They take each other in.)

REED: I've lost a little.

JASON: It looks good.

REED: No.

JASON: It's not too much.

REED: People say, "You look so skinny."

JASON: It's not.

REED: You don't want people to think there's something wrong! Which there isn't.

(They smile at each other. Jason looks around the place.)

JASON: This is nice.

REED: I found it.

JASON: This neighborhood is someplace I don't get.

REED: I was walking around one day. They have those Cuban drinks. And they have hummus on the tables. Which is gratis. It looks like.

JASON: Did you want to get dinner?

REED: I ate. Or I would.

JASON: I didn't, but I'm not hungry. Probably later. It's only — *(He looks at his watch.)* It's early.

(They sit.)

REED: Well.

JASON: I know.

REED: I'm glad we can do this!

JASON: Sure.

REED: I am.

JASON: I don't mean "sure" like "sure, whatever." 'Cause I'm glad.

REED: Good.

(They are silent a moment.)

JASON: What if we had dinner later?

REED: I don't —

JASON: Yeah.

REED: Yeah, I don't know. I've got to be cracking early tomorrow, get going.

JASON: You're right.

REED: Maybe if we weren't —

JASON: Right.

REED: — hadn't planned this —

JASON: Dinner is so huge!

REED: It is!

(They laugh.)

REED: It's a real — you can't get out of dinner once it's in motion!

(They laugh.)

REED: You know, in spite of all our, mm, trouble —

JASON: Trouble?

REED: — the troubles, what we are — this — is very rare. This.

JASON: Me too.

REED: And it kills me. It kills me. It always —

JASON: Let's not —

REED: Right.

JASON: We don't have to get into all that —

REED: I don't want to either.

(They smile. Reed pours them drinks from the shaker.)

REED: It's my birthday.

JASON: Oh, God, I'm so bad.

REED: That's all right.

JASON: I'm so bad.

REED: What're you supposed to — ?

JASON: I am the worst!

REED: — remember since — please!

JASON: No. Happy birthday.

REED: I'm very old.

JASON: Well.

REED: I got carded last week, so I thought fuck it.

JASON: Well, who knows what's old anymore? Plans?

REED: There's a, ah, festival, a music festival up by the house.
Ravel. Lots of strings.

JASON: Happy birthday.

REED: Please.

JASON: Hardly old.

REED: It's an outdoor festival. On a, uh, lawn. You bring a picnic dinner, wine. Cheeses.

JASON: It's supposed to be nice this weekend.

REED: It's sunny all weekend, they're saying.

JASON: I saw the news before I came, yeah. *(Beat.)* There's maybe *some* chance of —

REED: — small chance of late afternoon —

JASON: — showers —

REED: — drizzle. *(Beat.)* Only tomorrow, though. So Sunday I'm gonna try and organize everyone up at the house, which will be a challenge because they are constantly stoned. They're growing it in the garden. And it's going in all the food! Everyone's walking around, toppling things. All the crockery's broken. Pieces of everyone's dead grandmother's china. There's all this ice cream, eating it from the box with spoons, too stoned to put it in bowls. There's pot in the salad, everyone's lost their mind. — These are PhDs and they are baked! No one's paid a bill in ages. And I don't understand the books. When we all got the place I was like, "I don't want to be den mother. That's all I ask, I'm through with caretaking!" *(Beat.)* That wasn't directed at you. Or us. None of that was meant to have significance.

JASON: I know.

REED: I'm *just* —

JASON: I didn't take it that way.

REED: I wanted to see you.

JASON: I just heard it.

REED: That's the thing. Not settle scores.

JASON: I just heard it without subtext.

REED: *(Beat.)* That's forever ago and I don't want to do anything but — for us to be nice —

JASON: OK.

REED: — and treat each other as well as we always —

JASON: Good.

REED: I feel — I want us to be — nice.

JASON: *(Beat.)* My father finally died.

REED: I know. I heard through people and I —

JASON: It's OK —

REED: — didn't know what to —

JASON: — you know.

REED: Send something — ?

JASON: No, come on. He's been dying forever. And I hated him. *(Beat.)* Come on, please.

REED: No, I —

JASON: I mean — please. I just wanted it noted.

(They take sips of their martinis.)

REED: Ok, look, I don't want to be disruptive by calling, but there are so many things that happen, unaccountable, a wrench gets in and all that goes on — and I wonder if — if when we see each other, if we can't feel that together? That thing nothing that's happened to us, our failure, can touch. I'm blathering.

JASON: No.

REED: Do you know?

JASON: It's not like you abandoned me.

REED: Of course.

JASON: No one's abandoned me. I'm not a child.

REED: I didn't. I certainly didn't. It was your choice. You can arrange it any way in your head you want.

JASON: What was?

REED: And I'm sure you have. Self-protectively. But you have had the choice.

JASON: No, it wasn't.

REED: You could've come up to me any moment, at any moment and said, "I've decided to be responsible. I've decided we are grown-ups."

JASON: It was *your* choice.

REED: "I've decided you know, some cliché, "Love saves the day," or some other bumper sticker. Something. You had that choice.

JASON: Fine.

REED: You don't believe it.

JASON: And what would you say?

REED: Well.

JASON: If I did? If I came and said just blah, just all that. You'd say what?

REED: *(Beat.)* I'd say I'd consider it.

JASON: You suck.

REED: No, you do. You really do.

(They laugh at themselves.)

JASON: I have a present for you. It's just a little —

REED: I thought you forgot.

JASON: I did, but maybe I knew somewhere in the back of my head —

(Jason takes a gift-wrapped book out of his pocket and puts it on the table.)

REED: What is it?

JASON: It's a biography.

REED: Can I open it later?

JASON: *(Nods.)* I know you're off biographies, but I think you'll like it. It has perspective.

REED: Someone I admire?

JASON: One of your icons. I know you're off them, but this one I thought —

REED: Did you read it first?

JASON: Too many pages. There's no time lately, the hours, I'm stuck dawn to dusk, beyond dusk. A car comes to drive me home, though. And there's always food, ordering in, expense accounts.

REED: Good.

JASON: And I'm being praised for my work. They're being very good to me. And there've been raises. So I can get this.

REED: No.

JASON: I want to.

REED: That's silly.

JASON: No, I'm getting it. It's your birthday, let me pay the fucking bill at least. Please. Come on.

REED: *(Beat.)* I want to talk about something. I don't know how to bring it up gently. Your — sadness, your sadnesses. In the past, your struggles. I'm not with you on a daily basis anymore so —

JASON: You're not.

REED: No, I'm sure —

JASON: *(Over next line.)* If you were, you'd know —

REED: — you're fine, you're better, I hope.

JASON: You're not and if you were —

REED: You seem better and I don't know, I know this is presumptuous, but your last call.

JASON: *(Beat.)* Oh.

REED: You'd been drinking a lot. You said it.

JASON: I know.

REED: You said it and I thought, I don't want him to.

JASON: I know. And I appreciate it, I do.

REED: That's why I sent that letter.

JASON: I appreciate it I do. Your concern. I do.

REED: That's why I sent it.

JASON: You're right to — to — to think of me. You are, but —

REED: No.

JASON: — but no, you are. As hard as that sounds — to hear. For me.
(*Jason takes another sip of his drink.*)

REED: I always wanted us to understand each other.

JASON: I do.

REED: And if there's any way, if there's some way you could see there's help. From sadness. There's help.

JASON: It just happens I don't believe in help. Or therapy. Or whatever you're suggesting. And I'm surrounded by people who feel the same way.

REED: And I'm —

JASON: Fine.

REED: — surrounded by —

JASON: I am.

REED: — by people —

JASON: So that's it.

REED: — who feel differently. It's as I said in my letter.

JASON: Fine, fine —

REED: No — !

JASON: — should we get some appetizers?

REED: No. We have hummus.

JASON: (*Beat.*) No, fine, I'm sorry! You got the brunt of it. You got it — go ahead! Those two years, all that, the binges, vent, you're allowed — the lies, that night, I know. I know you have to see those people all the time and how it must be and I'm sorry.

REED: Please understand.

JASON: No, I do, the money —

REED: Please understand.

JASON: I know you think it's impossible, I know you think because — I know you think —

REED: This has happened to so many other people.

JASON: No, I know you think —

REED: So many others.

JASON: There comes a time when you say what happened when I was a child no longer matters. I'm not the first or only person to have a wicked father drink himself to death. (*Beat.*) You make a decision. You make a decision. To be done. A few broken bones. To be done. Twenty years ago! I'm sorry. You got the brunt of it. I don't want us to be constantly saying look here, look what you've done and me having to say "I'm sorry," I'm sick of it. I don't want to keep setting that up.

REED: I'm not asking for you to keep saying "I'm sorry."

JASON: You are.

REED: I'm sick of it too!

JASON: You are, you don't know it.

REED: I'm sick of thinking that's what you'll say! That I'm invested in this dynamic whereby I'm oppressing you and you're poor-little-wronged-little-whoever-you-are whose apologies are never heard. They're heard!

JASON: Fine.

REED: But that's it?

JASON: If they're heard, fine, what else?

REED: Change!

JASON: Change from what?

REED: Some hope —

JASON: Change from what?

REED: Ambivalence, you tell me, conflictedness, I don't know! You tell me you're doing well, you're doing well and so I think —

(Jason stands as if he will leave.)

JASON: This is so stupid.

REED: I think there might be hope! If you want it.

(Jason starts to go.)

JASON: This is —

REED: Do you think about us?

(Jason stops.)

JASON: *(Beat.)* I think, I think there is some, there is something or — always inside me — or — something you should know, something that inside me will always be maybe something — be maybe be always ambivalent, I think, about being — being — being — loved. *(Beat.)* And I think that's OK. It's OK.

(They are silent a moment.)

REED: How's the new apartment?

JASON: Fine, good, you know, great. Up six flights, I keep walking and walking. And once you're up, you're up, forget it. Ice cream? Forget it.

REED: I still don't have the number.

JASON: Work's best anyway, the voice mail. That's where I always am anyway. *(Beat.)* I just don't want to be the crazy one. I can't. *(Beat.)* Are you seeing anyone?

REED: No. *(Beat.)* Are you?

JASON: Yeah.

REED: Oh. *(Beat.)* And what's that like?

JASON: Good. It's good. It's very adult.

REED: Good.

JASON: Yeah. *(Beat.)* We're talking about New Year's Eve and there's all this jabber about where to go, different ideas and — what are you doing for New Year's?

REED: Crawling under my bed. *(Beat.)* You didn't see me at that bar the other night, did you?

JASON: When'?

REED: Uh —

JASON: No, when?

REED: Saturday.

JASON: No, where were you?

REED: Sitting by the bar. You came in, the both of you. Your hair was wet. You must've just showered. You kissed each other.

JASON: I'm sorry.

REED: That was him?

JASON: William. *(Beat.)* He's an architect. *(Beat.)* I'm sorry.

REED: You looked so happy.

JASON: I didn't see you.

REED: I ran out.

JASON: I didn't.

REED: I kept saying, "He didn't see me, he's too nearsighted."

JASON: I'm sorry. I don't —

REED: I was just there.

JASON: — know what I'd do if I saw —

REED: We live in the same city. It's going to happen. And it will keep happening. It will always happen, always, always. *(Beat.)* Would it be impossible for us to not talk? To not talk. Don't you think it's too upsetting sometimes?

JASON: I don't want to not talk.

REED: I don't either. *(Reed looks at his watch, as Jason pours the rest from the martini shaker.)* I have to meet the girls soon.

JASON: How are they?

REED: Still kickin'.

JASON: Dykes rule. How's Georgie?

REED: This high — *(Indicates kid's height.)* They're finishing up their duplex. It has a turret.

JASON: A turret, wow.

REED: I don't envy it, anymore, that.

JASON: You don't have to.

REED: What do you mean?

JASON: You have a country place.

REED: I do.

JASON: Things are going well.

REED: They are.

JASON: I think you're tremendous. *(Beat.)* I think you are. *(Beat.)*
I should go.

REED: I always want us to have more time, we just get through the anecdotal —
(Jason stands again.)

REED: — and then — are you happy with him? You smiled at him like you
were happy.

JASON: I didn't know you were there.

REED: Like you would smile at me.

JASON: It's very adult.

REED: Your hair was wet.

JASON: It was raining.

REED: I think you always thought I was impervious.

JASON: I never thought you —

REED: How could you be ambivalent about *me?*

JASON: I didn't know this —
(Jason starts off; Reed stands.)

REED: I was the one supposed to cure you of that. Right? When you used to
pick me up —

JASON: I didn't —

REED: — you lifted me —

JASON: I didn't know any of this.

REED: I'm sorry —

JASON: I have to go.

REED: What we could have again. With some work. Everything! A child? *(Beat.)*
What we always talked about? Someone to raise, better than we were. For
our, um, extra love. All of it that was left over. That was too much. And
I'll work too — I'm not saying you're the only one. I'll work too!

JASON: I — have to go.
*(They smile and nod. Jason goes off, and Reed heads for Bev and Shelly's duplex.
When he arrives there, Bev greets him while sipping a glass of wine, and Shelly
shows off the renovation.)*

REED: I can't believe what you've done . . .

SHELLY: Pretty good.

BEV: It's been hell.

REED: Six months . . . !

SHELLY: The contractors!

BEV: One tried to commit suicide. Not here. He went home one day after work. And then we got a call from his wife at the hospital saying he couldn't finish the kitchen 'cause he'd OD'd.

SHELLY: Unbelievable.

BEV: Well, we were trying to cut corners.

SHELLY: He came recommended, but you never know.

BEV: You never know.

SHELLY: If there's —

BEV: If there's suicidal depression in those you hire. But he was a few rungs down costwise, with the estimate.

REED: I guess you get what you pay for.

SHELLY: That's what we're learning.

(They laugh.)

SHELLY: I have to go over some work in the other room, then I'll come back to visit. And there's drinks, whatever, in the fridge, help yourself. And there's cheese. And we bought olives — did you get the garlic ones?

BEV: I think —

SHELLY: And there's Stilton.

BEV: Stilton.

SHELLY: And pears.

BEV: Pears.

SHELLY: From the island.

BEV: Incredible.

SHELLY: They're juicy and they're just ripe so they have to go. There's a baguette somewhere too, check the baskets over the cutting board.

REED: I'm fine.

SHELLY: And I think there's a beer in the back of the fridge.

(Shelly goes into another room.)

BEV: She's bringing work home. We're set up so she can.

REED: Things are going well.

BEV: Oh —

REED: It's incredible.

BEV: You wouldn't believe. I mean you wouldn't believe.

REED: This place.

BEV: This place, the dinners.

REED: Six months!

BEV: We're going to Deruda next week. We need a china service.

REED: I never know where you are.

BEV: We're everywhere. I don't know where we are. It's certainly different.

REED: You made it.

BEV: I did.

REED: Your fortitude.

BEV: With help, I did.

REED: Deruda?

BEV: Right? I mean where the fuck is Deruda?

REED: I always knew because of your, whatever, fortitude, or something.

BEV: No.

REED: You always had rich ones.

BEV: But this one I was sure. And we have to keep that in mind. This one I loved. And then the money came. In buckets.

REED: I think Deruda is in Umbria.

BEV: Gobs and gobs. *(Beat.)* You'll make it too. You will. *(Beat.)* I want you to see our new faucets.

REED: I hope so.

BEV: Sure you will. Oh, and there's a sconce I wanted to show you I'm not sure goes. Get your opinion. Before we go out.

REED: We're not here? I brought wine.

BEV: We were gonna be here.

REED: I thought we were here.

SHELLY: *(Off.)* We have reservations at Ferris!

BEV: Big time.

REED: Ferris?!

(Shelly re-enters wearing glasses, holding some papers.)

SHELLY: It's nothing. And you're dressed fine.

BEV: How bout it?

REED: I am not dressed fine —

BEV: You're fine —

REED: I thought you were going to toss some pasta?

BEV: It's your birthday!

SHELLY: A little celebration. And we called Costanza and she's coming over for Georgie —

BEV: We've got things to celebrate — your birthday, all these years. The things we've been through. And look at all of us. Not bad.

SHELLY: I've been —

BEV: No, sir.

SHELLY: I've been jealous of your friendship. I have.

BEV: *(Beat.)* Come on.

SHELLY: But now I'm glad.

BEV: She is.

SHELLY: We're like friends now. That's something to celebrate.

REED: Of course —

SHELLY: We don't know each other as well —

BEV: Not as much history.

SHELLY: But the stories. Sunday nights with the recipes — those summers stumbling home over each other. Almost dawn. The sun just —

BEV: That big bouncer trailing after us — we'd forgot something. Scarves, my wallet. You left your keys at the piano with that fat chick singing "Memories." The phone numbers we threw away. We could throw off a trail. A pretty good team.

SHELLY: She always said. And I hear them and I wish I'd — known her sooner.

REED: That was forever ago.

BEV: Not so long.

SHELLY: It seems ancient.

BEV: That time with those bar stools and you toppled off and took me with you. They shouldn't put drunks on high bar stools! I hardly drink at all anymore.

SHELLY: Cause I'd kill her.

BEV: She would. We grow up.

REED: We do.

SHELLY: We do. I'll kill you though.

REED: *(Beat.)* Where's the little one?

BEV: Down the hall. He's got his own bathroom.

SHELLY: He gets to choose the color.

BEV: He's campaigning for polka dot. I keep telling him it's not a color.

SHELLY: OK. I just have another to go over, one more thing and then we're at 9:30. Have some food, though — or that beer. I think it's Belgian. And did he see that book? We want to show you this book from Charlotte's imprint.

(Shelly returns to her office.)

BEV: God, we were children. We were drinking way too much, I put on all that weight.

REED: You look great.

BEV: I'm down twenty.

REED: So am I.

BEV: Lean and mean.

REED: We were kids.

BEV: She's not jealous.

REED: There's something —

BEV: No —

REED: Not on my end. On hers.

BEV: It's history, no —

REED: A feeling.

BEV: It's natural. And it's over. That's when we met and she was wondering — you and I spent all this time together and everyone had to adjust, struggle. There's a little brutality there when love comes into the picture. She's very fond of you, that's the point. Very. She loves who I love. Now she's secure enough to love who I love. There was a little bloodletting there, but that's — of all our friends — the friends we have everywhere — *YOU* stand in a class, a different class. A class apart. We, you know, cherish you. The struggle's over and we're all a little punch drunk, but still standing.

REED: It upsets her that you and I screwed.

BEV: Just twice. Well, what can you do? Do you want to see the sconce now?

REED: I really haven't been drinking that much anymore.

BEV: She knows that.

REED: Those stories get around.

BEV: She knows.

REED: With all the work it's impossible —

BEV: She's just against anything she perceives as a fault. A character fault, a flaw. She's clean and good and she makes me sturdy. I'm not some kid wandering around at dusk with a six pack anymore. Peeing on sofas. Sleeping with boys. I haven't peed on anyone's sofa in ten years!

REED: Sure, I'll see the sconce. *(He moves to go; Bev doesn't follow.)* What?

BEV: We want you to live with us.

(A moment passes in silence.)

REED: What?

BEV: He needs a father.

REED: Who?

(Another silence.)

REED: Is he asleep?

BEV: He's asleep now, yeah. He usually goes down around nine. We're trying to make it earlier and tonight he fell for it. He's got this little doll, this monkey, if you dangle it long enough it has a hypnotic effect. *(Beat.)* He's four — he knows everything. He knows the whole setup, so it's not an illusion, to *create* one — a father or a male — he's asking about men. What they're like when they're around. Not for sports or jockey things — but how they're different. He's got all these women and he's great and they love him but there's something else. He knows it.

REED: We've been through this way back.

BEV: No, that was different, that was sperm!

REED: Yes, and it's not mine!

BEV: *(Beat.)* Shell thinks we have to do something. And I'm in agreement. All around. You look in his eyes and you want to answer that. *(Looks into her wine glass.)* I'm having more, how are you?

REED: Fine.

BEV: You don't want that beer?

REED: No.

BEV: *(She pours herself more wine.)* You want to, um, satisfy whatever you see. In his eyes, whatever that is. Where's Daddy is too complicated to get into. Who ever knows really? But men — that's an easier question to answer. They're everywhere! We just need one to come over the house every now and then.

REED: And what am I doing?

BEV: During daylight hours.

REED: I come over in the day! And the rest — the official — the title or formal title — there's no room for that. *(Beat.)* I don't know how to say this without —

BEV: Say it.

REED: — sounding meager —

BEV: No —

REED: — mean or —

BEV: *(Simultaneous with Reed's next line.)* — no — no — no — no — no — say it.

REED: — and I know we're supposed to be creating — I know all that, what you're trying to do here, everything you're building, and you two are great and totally sufficient, I'm sure —

BEV: Say it!

REED: I am! I'm saying the whole thing sounds like a minefield.

BEV: Break it down.

REED: It's a minefield!

BEV: We need sturdiness, that's all I'm saying. And you're single now after Jason, and we have these empty rooms — rent-free by-the-by — and he's asking me where the men are. Rent-free and "where are the men, Mommy?" and *rent-free.*

REED: Everything doesn't have to be a list.

BEV: It's not a list.

REED: Checking off things —

BEV: It's not a fucking list —

REED: — sconce, faucet, daddy! *(Beat.)* No, but I'm sorry.

BEV: I got it.

REED: No, I am, I'm sorry — some people don't get everything.

BEV: OK, drop it.

REED: *(Beat.)* I just don't want it to come up again. Like I'm somehow lacking. Like I'm some freak because I don't want children.

BEV: I thought you did — ?

REED: People who want children are the only people who should have them.

BEV: But you always said —

REED: I hated it, being young. I hated it. So what am I supposed to convey to a kid? And what about when do I get to be carefree? My mother — being the oldest, all that — when am I allowed to be — have my carefree time? I'm not gonna turn around just when I have some semblance of —

BEV: Fine.

REED: — freedom —

BEV: Fine.

REED: I'm not, I'm sorry — I am. It would work out well. It would.

BEV: It would.

REED: I know. But I don't want it. He's lovely, he's great. I have a crush, with his pictures, and I quote all his little things to people, his little things he says about poop and monsters, go around like some suburban mom saying, Georgie said blah blah —

BEV: He's verbal.

REED: He's very verbal.

BEV: He is.

REED: I know, he talks. I'm saying he is. And I like that in a kid. I know what he's thinking. The ones who don't talk, they spook the fuck out of me! Staring there with their eyes, judging me or something, feeling superior, knowing I don't know shit, little devil children. Fuck them, they give me shivers. Hester Prynne's kid. The power they have. The power they have over you. *(Beat.)* Which can be . . . fun. Sometimes. A kid can be a lot of . . . It's just I — I wanted one with Jason.

BEV: OK.

(Shelly comes in carrying a coffee-table book.)

REED: *(To Shelly.)* I'm sorry.

SHELLY: Just think about it. We don't need a yes today. We're celebrating today. All we need to focus on is all the good that's happened. Everything in our lives. Going up. Getting what we've ever wanted. You are our best male friend. *(Offers the book she's holding.)* Here's the book. It's about the Nubians. Did you open a bottle?

BEV: *(Regarding the bottle she's been pouring.)* It's from the holidays. It was already.

SHELLY: That's old stuff. Let's open a new one. We have a split somewhere. Verve — *(She looks for it.)* — somewhere — Cliquot —

BEV: It was half-full still —

SHELLY: No, fine, we're celebrating, why not? *(To Reed.)* Take some time with it, tonight's a party.

REED: *(Beat.)* Do you mind if we have dinner another night?

(They don't. Reed smiles and goes. He returns home and to his bed, which he lies on only a moment before shutting his eyes. Jason then appears in the room. Reed sits up, not knowing what to say. Jason paces before beginning.)

JASON: You can't do that. You can't anymore. Calling me. And some set place. Some agreement we come to and showing up at a certain time only to — to — you can't. That's it. I don't want the keys anymore. *(He throws keys on the floor.)* It's too easy. It's this thing that we should be sure we're thinking. I don't want to be in intimate situations and not have thought behind them. Not be conscious, not consciously know what we're doing. And fuck you! Fuck me? Fuck you! I am fine. I'm fine. I'm sitting there fine at my desk and you call and make plans?! Fuck you. Like nothing's happened. Six months now! Something's happened and fuck you. Everyone knows. My friends say this is *nothing*. No reason at all. You overreacted and then, what, I have to come meet you in some place you've found in what, Zagats? And sit there and eat hummus? I don't like hummus, it dries me out! And I'm meeting you places like we're still together when we are not. And getting into this whole thing that you start — and I'm just getting clear in my head — you know — and every time I start to get clear you call me up. And I don't call you — you call me. I'm sitting there fine, at my desk doing well. Everyone there says my work is excellent. That's what they say and you call me. You call me . . .

REED: *(Beat.)* I didn't mean to. *(Beat.)* I just wanted to see you.

JASON: You shit. What about me? Those shirts, that closet full of shirts for who? No one else likes them. You're the only one who likes me in blues and purples!

REED: I'm sorry.

JASON: Shut up.

REED: You can say that.

JASON: Shut up, shut up.

(Jason reaches for Reed's hand. Eventually he sits on the bed.)

JASON: I don't want any of those pictures. Don't make copies for me. Vieques — I picked out the ones I like. That time in Atlanta, or upstate. Anything. Any of that. You know I don't collect things. I've left boxes everywhere and I forget what's in them and I never need them again. So don't track me down with souvenirs. Sentimental little kitschy little maudlin little things. That stuffed thing with the key chain, I don't need that. I've taken everything I need to take. If you, in the next months, a book, something turns up — I don't care. Salvation Army. Poor people can have those things. Give anything you find that's mine to someone who wants it. I don't. Things don't matter to me. *(He stands.)* Monday I'm going to Litchfield. One of our clients. This campaign we're presenting.

REED: OK.

JASON: *(Beat.)* You don't know what you've done. Do you?

REED: No. Yes, I do. No.

JASON: *(Beat.)* I'm sorry. You have the keys back. I'm sorry. I miss — everything.

REED: So do I. I'm sorry.

JASON: Yeah. Yeah. *(Beat.)* If I — if I — if I do come back — *(Beat.)* If I come back. If I come back and we — are — here — I'm here — back here — there are, um —

REED: OK.

JASON: Things.

REED: OK.

JASON: That.

REED: Some — some — I know.

JASON: Things. Not — not — not —

REED: No.

JASON: Not just like on a, you know, the ways and means —

REED: No, yes, absolutely. No.

JASON: If I get my act together, see someone — *therapy* — whatever —

REED: Of course.

JASON: — and you — you — you have to do things! It's not just me. You think it's easy for me with you, all over creation? Sometimes for days —

REED: I know —

JASON: How flirty you are!

REED: What?

JASON: You know.

REED: You're flirty too!

JASON: You mean it, though, you mean it! Those assistants, those notes. "Thank you for this opportunity, I want to someday be who you are. I emptied the trash, too, even though you didn't ask me to — think more of me!" That little sprite from Chicago, are you serious?

REED: I —

JASON: Little post-its with stylized writing, calligraphy — that is inappropriate. It's unnecessary. Assistants should assist and get out. Help and get out. Don't help and flirt and leave little notes — you're twice his age.

REED: Oh, for God's sake —

JASON: No, no, you listen.

REED: I encouraged none of that.

JASON: No, no.

REED: He's ten years younger!

JASON: Oh, he's ten years —

REED: He's not *two times* —

JASON: That's an improvement.

REED: — you know, one half my age, for God's sake —

JASON: He's younger.

REED: They're all younger! They're *assistants* — that's why they're younger. And they'll always be younger because people keep making more of them. They'll never be older — only we will be!

JASON: That's just it!

REED: Because they're making less of us!

JASON: That's just it!

REED: *(Beat.)* You are the most beautiful — the most beautiful. Those notes — ? Some kid — ? You. Do you know who you are? Do you know when I think of you? What I think? You can't possibly think as much as me.

(Jason returns to the bed, lies in Reed's lap, and wraps Reed's arms around himself.)

What about this new guy? This adult relationship you've been having. The one where you're all adultish . . .

JASON: Come on.

REED: OK.

JASON: What if we did have a child?

REED: What?

JASON: I want to have to be responsible. I'm ready.

REED: You do?

JASON: Everything we always talked about. I don't want to leave. Can we —
can we talk and — and think — and try? A kid, Reed? Someone to raise.
Better than we were. For our extra love? *(Beat.)* What? What is it?

REED: Yes.

JASON: Yes what?

*(Reed looks toward Bev and Shelly's apartment, where Shelly finds Bev fin-
ishing a phone call.)*

SHELLY: OK, let's not get excited.

BEV: I'm fine.

SHELLY: Don't get all excited.

BEV: You're the one who's up.

SHELLY: What did he say?

BEV: He said —

SHELLY: No, verbatim, the words.

BEV: Yes.

SHELLY: What exactly did he say? You were on the phone. Where was he?

BEV: On the phone.

SHELLY: No, calling from.

BEV: I don't know.

SHELLY: You don't know where he was calling from?

BEV: He was —

SHELLY: Come on! OK, he was home probably and he said what?

BEV: He said yes.

SHELLY: Verbatim — yes, a firm yes?

BEV: A yes to —

SHELLY: And this was what time?

BEV: — to proceeding. He had questions. This was just before you came in.

SHELLY: And that's when? That's when?

BEV: You came in right in the middle. What?

SHELLY: When was that?

BEV: You came in! It was ten minutes ago.

SHELLY: Bev! Exactly?

BEV: I guess!

SHELLY: Good, so he must've been home. Good.

BEV: Yes.

SHELLY: He was in a place where decisions — surrounded by things, books, his things that remind him — pictures, family photos of his life. Friends, vacations, in a good place, so this doesn't sound —

BEV: He was fine.

SHELLY: — capricious —

BEV: He was having a drink.

SHELLY: — or jumped-to. A drink of what?

BEV: Lemonade.

SHELLY: He said that?

BEV: Strychnine, I don't know. He said he'd taken the phone to the roof and it was hot —

SHELLY: On the roof?

BEV: — so he'd brought up something —

SHELLY: On the roof?

BEV: He's got that little deck thing.

SHELLY: I've never been there.

BEV: I could hear ice — and he said it was hot there.

SHELLY: What, a cocktail?

BEV: Oh, for Christ —

SHELLY: On the fucking roof?

BEV: I'm not going to have this conversation.

SHELLY: You heard ice in a glass on the roof?

BEV: Please, it was lemonade! It wasn't a drink.

SHELLY: People put booze in lemonade.

BEV: He'd squeezed some —

SHELLY: They put vodka in, it's allowed!

BEV: It was a fucking power drink or something! He's working out — some fruit drink! There wasn't booze in it! It's 9 AM for Chrissake!

SHELLY: That hasn't stopped him in the past!

BEV: Please.

SHELLY: Or you.

BEV: Here we go.

SHELLY: Him or you. In the past. If it was the morning — why not? The sun never stopped either of you! The sun in the morning never got in the way of anyone's cocktails in that group!

BEV: I'm not going to proceed if you're going to be all cunty. Do me the courtesy, please, of not being totally cunty. Please. You just turn into this raving, paranoid, twelve-foot cunt.

SHELLY: Forget the whole thing.

BEV: And two isn't a group.

SHELLY: What, please?

BEV: You called us a group.

SHELLY: Whatever.

BEV: Two isn't a group.

SHELLY: Well, it's something.

BEV: It certainly is.

SHELLY: Forget the whole thing.

BEV: He's coming over.

SHELLY: When? To talk to me?

BEV: You're half the battle.

SHELLY: That's good.

BEV: Tonight.

SHELLY: That's good.

BEV: OK.

SHELLY: I'll smell his breath, for one. *(Beat.)* But good. Shows he's serious.

BEV: You're not going to smell his breath.

SHELLY: Shows he understands the seriousness. He wouldn't dare come over drunk. *(Beat.)* I know it was the past and I'm sorry.

BEV: He's changed for fuck's sake.

SHELLY: I know.

BEV: I've changed. I had to. And I did. Less — less — less — you know — more — more adult. I had to! I would have sooner or later. But I was impelled. Our relationship. What was being offered —

SHELLY: You know I'm grateful.

BEV: — what could be exponentially —

SHELLY: I am —

BEV: — more.

SHELLY: and you don't know.

BEV: More all around.

SHELLY: You don't know. How grateful. I get up every morning and look at you asleep and think! You don't know I know. The faith you've had.

BEV: Thank you.

SHELLY: And I know.

BEV: *(Beat.)* He was good to me. Before you. Before you there was someone who was good to me, in his way. That should — and we shouldn't be

threatened by those who loved our lovers before US. We should be —
please — grateful.

SHELLY: When did you say he was coming?

BEV: He just said tonight.

SHELLY: Do we have anything in the fridge?

BEV: I said we'd go out for dinner.

SHELLY: Did we finish the pears?

BEV: No, we bought too many.

SHELLY: They're just going to rot if we don't eat them.

BEV: Let 'em rot!

SHELLY: *(Beat.)* And he said dinner?

BEV: I said we would pick a place and call so he could dress appropriately.

SHELLY: And where's Georgie?

BEV: On his play date.

SHELLY: Good. And when does the play date end?

BEV: It's open ended until they get cranky.

(They reach for each other's hands.)

SHELLY: Good.

BEV: Thank you.

SHELLY: Can we make love? It's been weeks.

BEV: Shell, everything we're doing —

SHELLY: I miss you.

BEV: I'm right here. I'm tired.

SHELLY: You sure? *(Beat.)* OK.

BEV: We will.

SHELLY: Call him and tell him eight.

BEV: Can I call him in a bit? I need to take a walk.

(Bev goes out and Shelly follows as, across town, Jason comes into Reed's apartment and puts down a box.)

JASON: That's the last of it. For now.

REED: We can put them somewhere.

JASON: It's just clothes and necessary things.

REED: Right.

JASON: I mean, we can put them somewhere and hang a few things out of the
way and —

REED: Great.

JASON: — and so then most of the stuff is still at my apartment, which is
important.

REED: Yes!

JASON: I think it's important I keep it, right?

REED: Yes, absolutely!

JASON: I mean, I think that was part of the problem, that I didn't have anywhere to go — that was *mine!* I didn't have a place.

REED: No, I absolutely think so too! And that will be good for me.

JASON: Good.

REED: If I'm doing work at home and I'm spread out, we won't be underfoot like we were — you're right.

JASON: Good.

REED: And I think that caused things to —

JASON: It wasn't good!

REED: Tensions.

JASON: I needed my own place. To have it, for once. And I like it. I've never had that. I'll probably never sleep there again, but —
(They laugh.)

JASON: But it's there.

REED: I'm glad. I'm so — glad.
(Reed smooths Jason's hair.)

JASON: Let's do something tonight.

REED: I've got the girls tonight.

JASON: Oh.

REED: Not all night.

JASON: Can I come?

REED: Uh —

JASON: Can you cancel?

REED: Not all night, there's just this thing we're working on, they want to discuss and I said I would and that should be early. And then I'll come back and we'll go somewhere. Try that new place. Ox tail cerviche! Is this weird?

JASON: A little.

REED: I'm glad though.

JASON: *(Suddenly hugging Reed.)* Don't do that again. Please don't do that. Don't throw me out. You can't.

REED: Sweetie, I didn't —

JASON: No, I know, shhhh.

REED: OK.

JASON: Shhh. Say you won't, even though that's what you didn't do.

REED: I won't.

JASON: OK. *(Beat.)* And I'll put my stuff away, out of the way! I'll hang what I need to hang, and I'll only take a couple drawers.

REED: We should maybe get another dresser.

JASON: Really?

REED: I think, yeah!

JASON: Great, 'cause there was never enough room! And I won't put my papers everywhere, or anything on the floor — which I know you hate.

REED: It's just things on the floor gather dust bunnies.

JASON: I know!

REED: This ancient place!

JASON: I know and I'll put everything up. Up high. On surfaces! No books or papers on the floor. And I'll return my library books, I swear, on time so they're not everywhere.

REED: It's just such a small —

JASON: You're right.

REED: — space.

JASON: And if something needs to go, it goes. And if something needs to stay it does — or hang or something, then it will! And I want to meet your friends up at the house. Maybe not all at once, but — and I called that woman. That referral I got. She's a lot, she's not cheap, but my insurance covers twenty sessions at eighty percent, so I should be sane by then. *(They laugh.)*

REED: I could go with you! We could go together. To that one — or another one if you decide.

JASON: Um.

REED: If you decide you don't like her, you might not click right away, not everyone does.

JASON: I think —

REED: The last one — you were always distracted during the sessions by her white stockings — that's real. That happened. There's something that bugs you and the whole therapy is for nothing.

JASON: I think I'd like to try her alone.

REED: OK.

JASON: For me. So I can tell her things.

REED: Sure.

JASON: If I need to. Things I might not feel—

REED: No, gotcha.

JASON: OK?

REED: Absolutely.

JASON: Great.

REED: But what "things?"

JASON: Um.

REED: No, just please tell me, it's OK, of course, but for instance do you mean is everything new? Do we have to negotiate everything again or are we OK?

JASON: I don't —

REED: Or maybe should we maybe should see someone who could see the both of us? You with yours, your own, by yourself, and the both of us with someone else entirely. Because if this is suddenly a whole new deal maybe we need to clean slate and start right.

JASON: No —

REED: Some guidance —

JASON: Wait, can we just go slow! Slower?

REED: OK.

JASON: I need to wait — and go slow. *(Beat.)* Can we take a nap? Do you have time to take a nap? I can unpack when you're gone.

REED: Really?

(They lie down together.)

JASON: When we have a kid we won't be able to do this.

REED: And you're sure you want that?

JASON: Think of all the children who need fathers. Good ones. Wouldn't we be good ones? Yes.

REED: And what about William?

JASON: Shhhh . . .

(Jason falls asleep and Reed gets out of bed. He heads across town to Shelly and Bev's. Once over their threshold, he is greeted with big smiles.)

SHELLY: Well. Hello.

REED: Hi.

BEV: *(Beat.)* I told her what you said. The gist.

REED: Hi.

SHELLY: Hello.

BEV: Can I get anything?

REED: No, no.

BEV: A pear?

SHELLY: We have cider. We bought too much when we had everyone over once the floors were done.

REED: They look great.

BEV: They were a bitch. So we had people over to dance on them.

SHELLY: You were out of town — which won't be a problem —

REED: Where was I?

SHELLY: We know that's part of your life. We travel too, so we know.

BEV: *(To Reed.)* Boston.

SHELLY: We only travel for vacation. Sometimes business. Rarely, but it happens. Mostly to get away and see things. Galapagos, the turtles. And Georgie loves it. Someday we'd like to do that with all of us.

REED: *(Correcting.)* Cambridge.

BEV: Cambridge, Boston, who cares, it's all just clean.

(They laugh.)

REED: I had some questions.

SHELLY: Sure.

BEV: Before he says yes through and through.

SHELLY: We can say — right off the bat, OK —?

REED: Uh — no, sure.

SHELLY: Right off the bat we know —

BEV: Maybe let him ask his first —

REED: No, no.

BEV: — and then you can respond.

SHELLY: Sure.

REED: It's OK if you know things off the bat, say it.

BEV: Can I say something?

SHELLY: Yes.

BEV: *(To Reed.)* Just because you know so much of this has been mulled over extensively. His life. In the future. What it should be, blah, blah, our hopes, blah, blah, plans for all of us — savings, schooling, the money in trust, blah blah — and so there are some things we feel strongly about. And if there's —

SHELLY: Good.

BEV: Will you let me finish, please? And if there's to be any parent, guardian, big brother whatever-we-call-it situation here, the rights — your rights will have to be very carefully —

SHELLY: Exactly.

BEV: — thought out.

SHELLY: Good. Right. I thought you were finished.

BEV: I am, but how did you know that?

REED: Look.

SHELLY: You want anything?

REED: Cider would be great.

(Bev goes for it.)

REED: Should I keep talking?

SHELLY: Sure.

REED: She's out of the room.

SHELLY: She catches up.

REED: I know there's a whole setup here, in place, and I don't want to disturb that. Of course I don't.

(Bev comes back with a glass of cider, which she hands to Reed.)

REED: I was saying I don't want to disturb, or I wouldn't, anything that's already in place.

SHELLY: But you couldn't. You couldn't.

REED: What I mean —

SHELLY: You wouldn't be able to.

BEV: OK. Please.

REED: I mean, I respect what's in place.

BEV: We know.

REED: But I am another person, added to the mix. And my life could change too.

SHELLY: *(Beat.)* Something's changed.

BEV: Will you let him —

SHELLY: You've gone back to Jason.

(Reed does not respond.)

BEV: Reed?

REED: He's changed.

SHELLY: Oh, Christ.

BEV: Are you serious?

REED: He's been quite thoughtful, and we've been having dinners.

(The women look at each other.)

REED: And he's seen, I think, the error — not just of his, not just his — our ways. I've seen, too. It's a two-way street —

BEV: Yeah, but —

REED: Although he caused most of it.

SHELLY: Are you kidding?

BEV: Reed —

REED: I allowed for it to happen — no, no — and you took my side because we're friends. That's why he's the baddy. He's not a real baddy! I allowed and created situations repeatedly. Not being diligent, last year, all that — I wasn't watchful! My father, the money, the work back to back. I melted. I just fucking melted.

SHELLY: He destroyed your life.

REED: And I let something go when I didn't know I was!

SHELLY: He's totally unreliable.

REED: I wasn't cognizant.

SHELLY: Worse!

REED: And I lost something. Something I've wanted back.

SHELLY: This changes things.

BEV: Wait.

SHELLY: Those nights —

BEV: Wait.

SHELLY: No, everything.

BEV: OK.

SHELLY: Bev?

BEV: OK, peace, everybody, one second. Let's not let our —

REED: He's changed.

BEV: — or run with —

SHELLY: It changes everything.

REED: That's why I wanted to come over.

BEV: *(After a beat, to Reed.)* Really? Are you really?

REED: He wants a child. To be responsible. To be less selfish.

SHELLY: Oh, shit.

REED: You've seen him with kids —

SHELLY: I knew this didn't make sense.

REED: — they love him. They fall asleep, like he's an angel. Georgie, that time, his first New Years? Uptown after that day — his little head, Jason's shoulder. So soundly. He'd be a better father than I'd ever be. Two for one. This is a two for one sale.

SHELLY: No, it's not.

BEV: Reed.

SHELLY: I'm sorry. I'm sorry.

REED: *(Beat.)* OK. *(Beat.)* No, OK, I figured.

SHELLY: We're sorry.

REED: I know.

SHELLY: But it still stands. Our offer.

REED: How? How can it?

BEV: Shell —

SHELLY: He's asking. *(To Reed.)* If — if things don't work out with Jason. Our offer stands.

REED: I love him.

SHELLY: It's about Georgie.

REED: I do. *(He starts to go. He stops before he's out.)* He makes me happy.

BEV: I know.

SHELLY: We know.

REED: I know he's — he makes me — I know — but happier than anyone.

SHELLY: He struggles, Reed.

BEV: OK —

SHELLY: Right?

BEV: OK!

SHELLY: No, there's a reason!

REED: I know.

SHELLY: — his drinking, his depressions —

BEV: OK, Shell —

SHELLY: — no, there's a reason!

REED: I know.

SHELLY: — no —

BEV: — OK, Shell —

SHELLY: — no, this revisionist —

REED: OK.

SHELLY: — this idea that —

REED: No, no, no —

BEV: SHELL!

REED: No, she's RIGHT!

SHELLY: — that things — thank you — can change! Sometimes they cannot. They can't. Sometimes they are bad and they stay that way. And then you cut your losses. You cut them. He's been proven time and time again. To be unreliable. To someone we love. And so he should be involved in raising a child?

BEV: *(To Shelly.)* But maybe things can. *(To Reed.)* Maybe he has. Shell? What if he has? And then all of us — there was a time when all of us —

SHELLY: I know.

BEV: — a brief time —

SHELLY: I know.

BEV: — we were happy. We were good.

SHELLY: That was then. And now there's — *(She points to Georgie's room.)* We have to think of him. He's who we're thinking of. All of us. No chances. A child. Us. Strength. Which will make everything clear. Wait. *(She listens.)* Shh, he's up.

BEV: *(Listens.)* He's up all right.

SHELLY: *(To Reed.)* Go into him.

BEV: *(Beat.)* Yeah, go in.

(Reed doesn't know what to do.)

REED: We were happy.

SHELLY: You'll find someone.

BEV: *(Beat.)* You will, Reed.

SHELLY: Someone who is your equal. Who can give you a home.

BEV: He couldn't. Really. Which I want for you. And could he now? I don't know . . . But if you want to — to hold out — to hold out hope — we wouldn't — *(She looks to Georgie's room.)*

REED: You want me to go in?

SHELLY: Yes.

BEV: *(Beat.)* Go in and tell him polka dot isn't a color. *(Off Shelly.)* What? It's not. He should know. Polka dot is . . . two colors at the very least.

SHELLY: We think so much of you.

BEV: I always wanted to take you with me.

REED: Thank you.

SHELLY: You look like your father, when I met him.

REED: Thank you.

SHELLY: You had a good father. Everyone deserves that.

(Reed looks to his apartment. He can see Jason there and goes to him, leaving the women without an answer.)

JASON: You're early. I thought — are we having dinner?

(Reed realizes Jason is drunk.)

JASON: I had a little, but I'm OK. William called. *(Beat.)* I gave him this number. Is that OK? He's been good to me and I had to explain. But didn't know how. How do we explain all this back and forth? *(Beat.)* When do we land? Where we're safe? When are we where we never have to move from again?

REED: *(Beat.)* What?

JASON: *(Beat.)* Yeah.

REED: I can't do this again.

JASON: Sure. Sure. The minute things get tough.

(Reed starts to leave.)

REED: I have to —

JASON: Fine, the minute things get tough. You want me to change, but this is it! This is who I am and you *love me!* I am a drunk and *that's who you love.* You love a drunk.

(Reed goes.)

JASON: Everything's unpacked! And I am not a child! I AM NOT! *(Beat.)* Reed . . . ? AND YOU SAID YOU WOULDN'T! YOU SAID YOU

WOULDN'T DO EXACTLY WHAT YOU'RE DOING NOW! *(Beat.)*
You said! *(Beat.)* I'm sorry. I'm so sorry.

(Reed returns to Shelly and Bev's apartment, where they have been waiting. When they see him they realize what's happened.)

BEV: I'm sorry.

SHELLY: *(Beat.)* Do you want anything?

(Reed looks down the hall to Georgie's room.)

SHELLY: Go into him. He's still awake. Make sure his light is on. It's just as you go in. His doll is on the table. It's Curious George.

BEV: His favorite.

SHELLY: You'll need to know these things.

(After a moment Reed moves towards the child's room.)

END OF ACT I

ACT II

June, the following summer. A beach. Bev and Reed, in bathing suits, occupy beach chairs. Bev is half reading a book.

BEV: And then we'll get salt-water taffies.

REED: Excellent.

BEV: *(Beat.)* What's up your ass?

REED: Nothing.

BEV: It's just you're not so much fun.

REED: *(Beat.)* Nothing. *(Beat.)* I don't like the beach anymore. *(Beat.)* I've got jelly on my hands from Georgie's sandwich, and it's caked in my nails and includes salt now from the water. And I scratched myself somewhere that shall go unmentioned, and in the scratch now is salt with sugar from the jelly caked over where I itched, forming a kind of irritating poultice.

BEV: *(Beat.)* Fine.

REED: A little inadvertent, some kind of Band-Aid made from only irritating things.

BEV: Go back to the place.

REED: No.

BEV: Take a shower, have the place to yourself.

REED: No, then I will get a big lecture from Shelly and I'm not in the mood.

BEV: What lecture?

REED: Some diatribe about, you know, the need to be together at the beach.

BEV: Do you want to take a walk?

REED: My shoulders are burnt.

BEV: Keep your T-shirt on.

REED: The sun still comes through! I'm wearing 45 and a reflective white T-shirt which should bounce the sun away in big beams but it doesn't. And that's because of that totally inefficient car you bought. *(Beat.)* Yes. *(Beat.)* Yes, destroying the environment, yes. *(Beat.)* There's a reason the polar caps are melting and it's your fucking car! *(Beat.)* And every time we go for a walk we run into somebody. The last thing I want to do is run into somebody. "Hi!" And I always forget everyone's name. *(Beat.)* Maybe I'll make another sand castle.

BEV: *(Pointing to a sand castle out of view.)* This one is pretty good.

REED: It sucks. I didn't have enough water.

BEV: I'm gonna read my book. *(She does.)*

REED: *(Beat.)* Should we move the blanket because of the surf?

BEV: *(She looks at the surf.)* We've got another hour before we need to. *(She looks down the beach.)* Do you think he's OK down there?

REED: He's made some friends.

BEV: What kind of friends? Big friends?

REED: They look about average.

BEV: I mean are there bigger kids?

REED: Juergen is with him.

BEV: Good. I didn't see Juergen.

REED: He's there — *(He points to Juergen.)*

BEV: I see him. Good. *(Beat.)* You two seem to be getting along. You and Juergen.

REED: We have to.

BEV: I mean getting along more so. I'm not trying to make you self-conscious. I've just got my eye peeled. And I notice things. You two like each other or something. Which is OK.

REED: He smells like birdseed.

BEV: What?

REED: I don't like him, he smells like birdseed. So don't get all excited that we hooked up. It was only twice, so don't go sending —

BEV: I'm just —

REED: — engraving —

BEV: — you two seemed —

REED: — engraved things —

BEV: — a few laughs —

REED: — wedding announcements —

BEV: — and time together —

REED: No one wants a lover who smells like birdseed! *(Beat.)* And he's all interested in my feet. And I know that's very chic or something, feet are in, but get the fuck off my feet and come up to my torso once in a while. God forbid I should get kissed every now and then. I mean whatever happened to tonguing? It's like I'm at this especially ardent podiatrist's.

BEV: No one's saying anything. If you like him, great. If you don't, fine.

REED: I have to like him.

BEV: No you don't.

REED: He's across the hall, we're sharing the same bathroom! I have to. *(Beat.)* I don't know what you even need him for.

BEV: You've been travelling a lot.

REED: I don't know why you need him. I've always travelled and suddenly Georgie needs something — a what? A nanny or —

BEV: Not a nanny.

REED: — something, whatever this guy —

BEV: A live-in.

REED: — this helper. When who am I?

BEV: We know who you are. Georgie knows. You're the guy who's always in Boston.

REED: *(Beat.)* Cambridge, please. You just do that to bug me.

BEV: Go down and play with them.

REED: No, my scrape hurts me.

BEV: Wash it off with the water.

REED: I just said —

BEV: The water in the cooler, you fag, the spring water. Wash the damn scrape off and go down and get in the game if you're feeling so out of it —

REED: I don't want to be "in the game." I am just commenting on the unnecessary need for the nanny.

BEV: You spend two nights letting him suck your toes, you'd think you'd have a friendlier take on things.

REED: *(Beat.)* I hope he doesn't expect that will continue. Is he expecting some big relationship or something?

BEV: He's a nice guy.

REED: Did he say something to you?

BEV: No.

REED: What — he has a fucking crush on me or something?

BEV: Just shut up and rinse your scrape.

REED: Oh, man, that's it. This is too weird. *(Beat.)* I can't rinse my scrape until I get home.

BEV: I'm reading my book now.

REED: I need iodine. *(Beat.)* I'm hungry. *(Beat.)* Where's Shelly with the burgers? I'm hungry. *(Beat.)* I'm sorry.

BEV: Then shut up.

REED: I'm . . . unhappy.

BEV: *(Beat.)* There was probably a long line for the burgers.

REED: I'm sorry.

BEV: You don't have to keep saying that. *(Beat.)* Do you want to read my book?

REED: *(Beat.)* Yes, please.

(As Bev is about to hand over her book, Shelly approaches with a takeout container full of burgers, fries, drinks, etc . . .)

SHELLY: The kids they hire for the registers are idiots. These inbred — these local townies on god-knows-what. They just have to ring up fast food, but no. They have to talk to their *little friends,* they have to be *slow* — *(Looks for Georgie.)* Where are they?

BEV: *(Pointing to Georgie and Juergen.)* There.

SHELLY: There they are. Who are those kids? Those other kids? Those boys?

BEV: They're —

REED: Big, threatening older boys.

SHELLY: Who?

REED: Full of burgeoning testosterone.

BEV: They're those kids from across the patio, I think. Juergen's been with him.

SHELLY: Oh, fine.

REED: That should make it OK.

BEV: *(About Reed.)* He's cranky cause he's hungry.

(Shelly passes out the food.)

REED: And my scrape has salt and jelly in it.

SHELLY: Wash it off.

BEV: He wants iodine.

SHELLY: I think Juergen's got some iodine in his things. *(She finds iodine in Juergen's things.)* Look at all this, my God. There's three different kinds of Band-Aids in here, sunblock, lotion, Skintastic. This guy is unbelievably prepared.

REED: He's a boy scout.

SHELLY: What'?

REED: It's their motto. "Prepare for the worst."

SHELLY: Juergen was a boy scout?

BEV: No —

SHELLY: That's not their motto.

REED: It should be.

SHELLY: *(Beat.)* Are you in a mood, Reed?

BEV: OK —

REED: You were gone for two hours getting burgers!

SHELLY: Yeah, well, 'cause if you're in a mood —

REED: I just don't want Juergen up in my face. If you want a nanny or a helper or a boy scout with a foot fetish because I had to go to Cambridge in twice as many months for something you know — both of you — was crucial business for that deal that Shelly knows she encouraged, if you need to then, I guess, want to somehow perversely punish me for something you totally understand because who knows why, by hiring this guy that, yes, granted, I fucked twice, but mainly because he was in the bath-room when I wanted some water at 2 AM, then fine. I will not complain. It's your life it's your child it's your money it's your home I am just some fag in a room.

(After a beat, Shelly throws her soda on him.)

SHELLY: Don't talk to me like that.

(A moment passes. Reed is speechless.)

SHELLY: *(To Bev.)* I'm sick of him.

BEV: Oh fuck.

(Another moment passes.)

REED: You twat.

(After a beat, Shelly is on top of Reed. They grapple in the sand as Bev looks on, too stunned to intervene. Finally, Bev steps in and pulls Shelly from Reed. At this point, Jason comes from further down the beach. Seeing him, Shelly runs off. After a moment, Bev follows. It is only then that Reed sees Jason.)

JASON: What happened?

REED: I got sand on me.

(They laugh. Jason points to Georgie.)

JASON: He got big.

REED: He's almost five.

JASON: He's gonna be a bruiser. You look good.

REED: Thanks.

JASON: I'm fat.

REED: No.

JASON: It's OK.

REED: I always liked when you had a belly.

JASON: Well. Fading beauty.

REED: No, you have the bones. You'll always be good looking. Your coloring.

JASON: You're all covered in sand!

REED: I think my foundation is shifting. *(Beat.)* How are — is things? How's everything?

JASON: Good. Yeah. We're up there — *(He points up the beach.)* About a hundred yards.

REED: Did you see us or were you just walking?

JASON: Come on, the whole beach was like, "Who's that dyke beating up that fag?"

(They laugh.)

REED: Are you with people?

JASON: Yeah. William and some friends. We have a house. We got this summer.

William got. He's been getting a lot of work and we wanted a place to come. You?

REED: Nobody.

JASON: I mean a place. Where you're staying.

REED: Right. With the girls. They still have their place. And they bought the lot next to it. They put in a court and, so, I can do that, for exercise. Bat a ball around.

JASON: So you're beach now? No more country?

REED: There were a few problems.

JASON: I'm sorry.

REED: Yeah. We all started sleeping with each other. It was pretty bloody there, at the end. So many people were sneaking into so many bedrooms that people lost track and actual couples kept crawling into bed with each other by mistake. Doors slamming, the wrong underwear, incriminating notes — very French farce. We're letting a court decide how the property splits. It's a mess. We can laugh about it sometimes. I can't believe I haven't run into you.

JASON: What's it been?

REED: Nine months. *(Beat.)* Are you happy?

JASON: *(Beat.)* Yes. *(Beat.)* You?

REED: *(Beat.)* No!

JASON: There's no one?

REED: A male nanny who smells like birdseed.

JASON: I've been seeing your picture.

REED: Yeah, well.

JASON: I cut it out when I see it.

REED: You do?

JASON: I cut it out.

REED: *(Beat.)* What do you do with it? When you cut it out?

JASON: I save it. In a book you gave me.

REED: Which one?

JASON: Just one of them.

REED: Does William know?

JASON: Yes, yeah, he respects the, uh — I've always set out parameters with him, and he's always been, um, very respectful. We've been able to have our own lives and not meld into each other. And it's all more or less even.

REED: I think about you a lot.

JASON: Yeah?

REED: Uhuh.

JASON: Why?

REED: Because I do. Because I miss you. And because I'm always . . . startled by how life can be so — *awful*. That things haven't — found a way to work this out. I'm always, I'm always — amazed when life becomes so — awful! And I feel like I've been somewhere or in a dream this year — a hold — um — a dream or fog since —

(Shelly runs back on and stops when she sees the two men.)

SHELLY: *(To Reed.)* It's over. I want you out. Go back to your crazy ex — no one wants you in our house —

(Bev runs on, in tears.)

BEV: Don't listen to her!

SHELLY: No, listen to me! You listen to me. You are out as of now.

(Reed stands, stunned. After a moment, he gathers his things and goes off.)

BEV: *(To Shelly.)* Don't do this.

SHELLY: *(To Jason.)* And you too. I'm sick of all of you. The only one who's worth anything is Juergen.

(Jason goes off, in the direction of Reed. Shelly looks out at the water.)

SHELLY: Where is he? I can't see them.

BEV: *(Pointing.)* They're there.

SHELLY: Where is my son!

BEV: THERE!

SHELLY: GOOD! Good.

(Reed arrives at a motel room, followed by Jason. Reed hasn't yet showered and is still a mess from the beach. He puts his things down and sits on the bed. Jason stands in the doorway, keeping the door open to the gallery outside.)

JASON: There's cable.

REED: Great.

JASON: *(Beat.)* There's probably a Bible. We could read Leviticus.

REED: You don't have to stay.

JASON: Just till you get settled.

REED: I don't think I should. I think I should think where I go.

JASON: Didn't you keep your apartment?

REED: They found out I'd been subletting it.

JASON: Oh, no, I loved that place.

REED: You did not. You were always on about —

JASON: What? I was —

REED: — the light, the lack thereof, the roaches.

JASON: We took care of that.

REED: I know. But we were only roach-free a month when we broke up. So you didn't get to appreciate the roach-free environment.

JASON: My loss.

REED: It is!

(They laugh, and Jason comes into the room a bit — but still he does not close the door.)

JASON: I liked the fireplace, and the ivy on the wall, that wall. And the rooftops, out the window you could see.

REED: Yeah, well it's gone.

JASON: Do you want a soda?

REED: Nah.

JASON: We passed a machine.

REED: No, thanks.

JASON: There must be somewhere.

REED: Someone has a room somewhere. But recently I've been alienating people. People can suddenly only take so much of me. I always thought I was charming. Now I'm difficult.

JASON: This'll blow over.

REED: It's never really worked out. Georgie stares at me and I don't know what to say and everyone pretends I'm some sorta male figure when, really, I'm just a kind of very interesting boarder. Won't William be worried?

JASON: I called when you were checking in.

REED: Good. Sit or something.

(Jason sits on the other end of the bed.)

JASON: He's out with friends tonight. They're going to this show I don't want to go to. Stand-up comics, telling anecdotes. Sketch comedy or improvisation or something. And I just hate it when people have to be funny. Some kid, you know, someone who was told he was funny in high school, selling out his family on stage with cute little stories, or something, his bathroom habits — any of that humor I hate. Bathroom stuff, body stuff, anything that has to do with the body or scabs or leakage. Once I saw this comedian do a whole riff about ear wax and I was like, that's it, forget it. Pay all that to be mushed in with a bunch of assholes yukking it up with a two-drink minimum for, basically, liquor-flavored water?

REED: You don't like comics.

JASON: I don't. I like TV though.

(They laugh.)

JASON: Do you want to turn it on?

REED: Now?

JASON: I like TV. We could watch something.

REED: *(Beat.)* Is this weird?

JASON: What is?

REED: This —

JASON: Oh.

REED: You here.

JASON: Yeah, no, I just —

REED: — me covered in sand and —

JASON: Just a little—

REED: — is it bad?

JASON: No.

REED: I don't think I want to watch TV though.

JASON: Do you mind if I sit here a bit?

(Reed shakes his head and Jason sits.)

REED: *(Beat.)* Tell me — tell me about him. You can tell me now. About him, please. William. All about him. It's OK. I think — I want to imagine — I'd like to hear your days.

JASON: No.

REED: I would.

(Jason collects his thoughts before proceeding.)

JASON: He's — he's — he likes his work. He's a consultant on parks. How they should be arranged. Where the fountains go.

REED: Oh.

JASON: How they look at night with the lights, the shrubs, are there enough benches. Or too many. What style. We have all these models at home, little benches like in a doll house. He carves them. I move them around when he's late and I'm mad. And, you know, I didn't know people like him existed. I guess I thought there were just parks! But there are consultants on them and it's very precise and everybody comes in and dickers over everything for months and months, sometimes years. A lot of times years. There's one just got finished he took me to the week we met. And we had a picnic. *(Beat.)* I shouldn't —

REED: No. Please.

JASON: *(Beat.)* He's um — he's um —. I need water. *(He goes into the bathroom and continues from there.)* He's close to his family. And they're OK, they're Southerners. So they eat and say "y'all." I mean they're not hicks. They're not with pick-up trucks on cement blocks in the yard or anything. They're respectful and treat me like, um, when we've gone down, like some kind of dignitary. *(He returns with a glass of water.)* Some exotic person from a far away place, you know, that they've been told they should treat well. And they do. And they do.

REED: Good.

JASON: Which is where he gets it. I don't want to do this if you're going to be sad.

REED: Why not?

JASON: I don't want to make you sad.

REED: It's a favor I need. How is the — the — the — when — the love-making?

JASON: Uh, no.

REED: No, please.

JASON: Forget it.

REED: Jason. Is he better than I was?

JASON: This is not fair.

REED: Is that why? No, please. How is this successful? How has it gone on? Why do you live in a house with someone who loves you and I'm in a room with a kid who stares? No one believes I'm a "role model." I don't have an apartment. Where will I go? I'm in fights with everyone, business is complicated — I daydream. I'm too old to daydream. And I hate Cambridge, all that colonial crap! I was the first one of everyone to want a home and someone and then everyone got that and now I'm the last. Like musical chairs. Is he beautiful to you in bed?

JASON: *(Beat.)* Yes.

REED: And wasn't I?

JASON: You were.

REED: Wh — wh — are *you* still in therapy?

JASON: No.

REED: Do you still drink too much?

JASON: I —

REED: Do me this favor!

JASON: Yeah, I do! I do. Every now and then it's a mess. Every few months there's a night when he has to pick me up from somewhere, some stranger's, some bar I found I wouldn't be caught dead in, but there I am, puke on my shoes — we don't talk about it. That's the deal. That's what's implicit.

REED: Was I wrong?

JASON: No. About what?

REED: To want more?

JASON: I couldn't — I couldn't bear — I couldn't — please — I always — no, you weren't. I was just used to myself by then. And you asked me to change. And there's been —

REED: I know —

JASON: — too much —

REED: Believe me.

JASON: — change! *(He tries not to cry.)* So I couldn't elect to have more. I've only been able to keep up with —

REED: I know.

JASON: — William doesn't make me change. He lets me be. He doesn't need much. He takes care of himself. And I take care of me. *(Beat.)* I should go and you should wash that sand off.

REED: I have a scratch. I think it's infected.

JASON: Where'?

REED: In a not-so-great place. There's no name for where it is.

JASON: Let me see.

(After a moment, Reed pulls open his bathing suit and indicates where the scratch is. Jason looks at it.)

JASON: You have to clean it.

REED: It hurts. No, it really hurts. Maybe we should go to a hospital. My eyes water every time I move the slightest bit.

JASON: I'll clean it. But you'll have to be still. I'll do it.

REED: *(Beat.)* You will?

JASON: Can you be still while I do that?

REED: I think so.

(Jason moves toward him.)

REED: We can't have sex, I have an open wound.

(Jason continues to move toward Reed. Back in the city, morning begins and Shelly is found at her office, talking on the phone.)

SHELLY: Hi, Mom, it's me. I wanted to go over the plans for your trip. I have the itinerary here. Because I paid for the tickets. I can send you a copy. It's just how they do it. It's just how it's done and there won't be confusion at the airport, no. I'll send you everything in advance. You'll have it *on your person.* So you're flying into Rome. No, it's just outside the city, it's — mmm — *(She looks.)* — it's called da Vinci, it's near the beach and then you — no, you're staying in the city in Trastevere. If Daddy wants to bring his bathing suit, fine, but Rome doesn't have a beach and the hotel doesn't have a pool. Should I be relaying all this to him, instead? Fine. You're welcome. You're welcome. You don't have to keep thanking me. Really, Mom, stop or we'll have to talk later. You sent me that jelly as a thank you and I don't have time for all this gratitude. And I think — you know what I think? Forget it. No — you know what I think? It's some fucked up way of making me feel guilty somehow for being able to treat you and Dad so well. Just accept it and be grateful, tell your friends and don't keep feeling the need to express this forced gratitude. *(She listens.)* She's fine. He's fine, he has the sniffles. Well, it's his birthday soon and then you can come over. No, he's on a business trip in Vancouver. He's been overextending a bit lately and he's been gone a lot and — no. We've hired someone. A nice guy who has training. He's Swiss so he keeps everything running. I know you like Reed, everyone likes Reed, but we need this professional who's more consistent. That is what is important for a child. *(She listens.)* Good, so everything's working out and you fly into Rome and from there a bus to Umbria. Which is beautiful. It's where Bev and I — when we first met and we couldn't afford Tuscany. I was still downtown and Bev was waitressing and we thought, OK, so not Tuscany, but someday! And then Umbria. So beautiful. How could Tuscany be better? And we thought maybe we found a, uh, new place. A new way. To do things. Based on disappointment. Which sets you off to some-place . . . unimagined . . . and — and — and — she's left me, Mom. She took Georgie. We were at the beach. I don't know what I've done. I yelled at Reed, but I don't — I don't think that's it. It's been . . . I don't know what to do — we haven't been sleeping together and — what do I do? Mom? Mommy? *(She listens.)* Uhuh. Uhuh. Uhuh. OK. No, OK. OK, sure. Then — have a good trip. No, we don't need to talk before you go. I'll have Sonia send you all the info. She's my new assistant. She puts up with me, but I think it's 'cause I pay her. I just wanted everything you had with Daddy. That's all. OK. Send him my love. And — and — to you too. *(She hangs up the phone, puts some papers in a leather satchel, and makes a call to the outer office.)* Sonia? I'll be taking work home. I'd just rather be there today. Thank you. And Sonia? I just want to say you've been working out very well. Thank you for that.

(She hangs up and goes home. She finds Bev there, packing things.)
BEV: There were some things I needed.
SHELLY: Of course.
BEV: Why aren't you at work?
SHELLY: I couldn't concentrate. This new assistant is always hovering.
BEV: Georgie's been asking for you.
SHELLY: Tell him I was asking for him. Tell him, please, I said I love him.
BEV: I do.

SHELLY: Good. How are you?

BEV: I'm OK. I'll just be a few minutes.

SHELLY: No, of course.

BEV: And Reed will be coming up in a minute. He's parking the car. To help me with some things.

SHELLY: Who's got Georgie?

BEV: He's at my mother's. Probably on some sugar high.

(They smile.)

SHELLY: She spoils him.

BEV: Everyone does. He's beautiful. He misses you.

SHELLY: I'm having my attorney arrange a temporary schedule, I didn't want you to be surprised by it — visiting — just so it's down on paper.

BEV: Of course. Absolutely. I expected. And we need to be comfortable with things.

SHELLY: I might have to let Juergen go. I didn't know what to tell him or how long this might be, or if ever — if it would be ever resolved. He has a list of people who wanted him if he was ever free. Imagine — to be so in demand. I said I'd be happy to keep paying him, but that wasn't the point. He wants to be doing his job, not sitting around reading magazines. He's one of those people who loves his work, which is children. And that's nice.

(Reed comes in. He nods at Shelly when he sees her.)

REED: The car's by the curb.

SHELLY: Hi.

REED: Hi.

(Jason enters. Shelly looks at Bev.)

REED: I thought we could use some help lifting.

SHELLY: Are you taking *the fridge?*

REED: No —

BEV: No, boxes —

JASON: I'll wait on the —

BEV: No. Come in.

SHELLY: Please.

(Jason comes in. A moment passes when no one knows what to say.)

SHELLY: I'll be in the office. *(She goes to her office. Another moment passes in silence, and then Shelly returns.)* I need to do some reading so if you could keep the noise to a minimum.

BEV: Sure — ?

SHELLY: And does anyone want anything?

REED: No —

BEV: No.

SHELLY: There's a fridge full of things that have gone uneaten. So you might as well pack up as much as you want.

BEV: I can buy groceries.

SHELLY: What?

BEV: *(Beat.)* It's just I don't need to take your groceries.

SHELLY: *(Beat.)* They were things we bought last week.

BEV: I know.

SHELLY: *(After a beat, about Jason.)* Why is he here?

BEV: Jason is putting us up.

SHELLY: Oh.

BEV: Which is sweet.

SHELLY: *(Beat.)* I'm just surprised.

BEV: Why?

REED: He lives in a big house.

(Without replying, Shelly returns to her office.)

BEV: I just need to get some things.

(Bev puts down what she's doing and goes into Shelly's office. The men listen in silence to the women's conversation.)

SHELLY: *(Off.)* I can't believe —

BEV: *(Off.)* Is there somewhere you can go — ?

SHELLY: *(Off.)* — traipsing in —

BEV: *(Off.)* — until I'm done —

SHELLY: *(Off.)* — those two —

BEV: *(Off.)* — the deli —

SHELLY: *(Off.)* — who are they — ?

BEV: *(Off.)* — or a cafe or a deli — ?

SHELLY: *(Off.)* I want them out.

BEV: *(Off.)* Then call your attorney.

SHELLY: *(Off.)* Right, Jason has a big house!

BEV: *(Off.)* You heard me, call your fucking attorney.

(Bev returns to the room and immediately resumes packing; Shelly is on her heels.)

SHELLY: Can the boys go so we can talk?

BEV: They're helping me.

SHELLY: I don't want us to yell. Please.

BEV: We can talk tonight on the phone if you want, after Georgie's off.

SHELLY: OK. OK. *(Turns to Jason.)* I'm sorry. *(Beat.)* Where do you live now, Jason?

(Jason looks to Bev to see if it's OK; Bev nods.)

JASON: We have a house in town and one on the island.

SHELLY: Who's "we"?

JASON: William. He's —

REED: His boyfriend.

BEV: That's where we're staying, so we have to go all the way out there, so we have to get on the road before the rush.

SHELLY: And — you're all — staying there?

BEV: Yes.

SHELLY: Everyone and you and the new lover and the old one?

JASON: William is out of town.

SHELLY: What does Georgie make of all this?

REED: What?

SHELLY: This little group, this hodgepodge.

BEV: It's hardly —

SHELLY: This upheaval. It's just pretty unconventional. *(After a beat, to Reed.)* You, your ex, his present —

REED: He's not —

SHELLY: — no Juergen, no me — or what do you make of all this? Very convenient isn't it? Almost perfect, almost pre-me, when it was just the three of you on one big party, waking up at noon, figuring out who'd pick up the bill later — those were the days! Except — you can't go back.

BEV: That's it.

SHELLY: That's right, Reed. You can't go back.

REED: What — ?

BEV: Forget this.

SHELLY: Yeah!

BEV: Come on!

SHELLY: No, you can't because his "present" who — his whoever-his-name — who's probably footing the bill too, right?

JASON: He's generous.

SHELLY: Sure!

BEV: We're not —

SHELLY: No, you're not! Why should you? Health insurance? Fuck that! If you're dead in a ditch — who cares! Let someone else get the bills! Broken glass! Picking it out of your hands — out of your hands! As my friends watched! Mortified for me — a dinner honoring me and you have glass imbedded in your palm and these two completely helpless, drunk themselves, and everyone around me — everyone! — saying who is this investment, Shelly? Who is this child you are marrying? My defenses on your behalf! Defending this and I'm glad we're here and you're with the boys, which is where you wanted! And go be with them, but I will take our son. He will not become like them, you will not make him that. Do you hear me? I will do everything in my power to keep him from that.

BEV: *(Beat.)* I gave birth to him.

SHELLY: *(Beat.)* Go, take your things which I paid for. Eat your own groceries, wake up on Tenth Avenue where I found you — all of you.

(She leaves the apartment. A moment passes.)

REED: We'll go to Jason's. We can stay there as long as we want. We'll light a fire. Georgie likes that. Lawyers will be later. She'll cool down. This is the worst for someone like her. And she's wrong. We've all changed. She's not fair to — the past? She's always been jealous —

BEV: I know.

REED: OK? Get your things and we'll do here.

BEV: OK.

(She goes into the bedroom.)

REED: When does William get back?

JASON: Not for a bit.

REED: So it's just us.

JASON: Yeah, for a bit.

REED: And Georgie.

JASON: For a month about.

REED: A whole month! I thought we could go tubing. And there's a couple of house tours I thought you might know about. And some friends, too, out there I never get to see who always ask about you. Is it weird again?

JASON: Yes. Isn't it?

REED: But not bad.

JASON: No!

REED: Like a reprieve. Who gets that?

JASON: No one. But here's the thing.

REED: Uhuh?

JASON: Which is something I've been meaning to bring up.

REED: We're sharing costs, she's wrong. We'll pool everything and no one will be out of pocket.

JASON: No, it's when the month's up William will be back from Europe a few days.

REED: We'll go someplace else then. We've got time to look, that's how this is helpful —

JASON: Yes, but then I go back with him. We're moving there. He's got a job near Bordeaux, there's a park that dates back centuries and it's very prestigious, a contest actually he's won, people competing from all over. It was such a remote chance he'd get as far as he got, but it was his model that put him over. They all looked at it and just said, "Wow." He'd done the whole thing himself, he was pulling all-nighters molding this fountain — I had to keep bringing him tea. And a French garden is a real coup and something he has only a little of on his résumé. It's a special, you need a special ability to respond to a paradigm that's so cultivated, so precise. And it really appeals to him. And he speaks French, I don't know if I mentioned.

REED: You brought him tea.

JASON: And it's always been a dream of mine, France. I've been reading up on everything about it now that I'm in this groove at work, so I have time. To read.

REED: I know that makes you happy.

JASON: It does. And there's a child that we'll be adopting. We didn't know and we'd been waiting and he — he's a boy — finally came through. He finally came through.

REED: My God.

JASON: I know.

REED: I've wanted that for you.

JASON: So this — this has been in the works for some time now.

REED: So we have a month.

JASON: Uhuh.

REED: It'll be July then.

JASON: We have till July.

REED: I was looking forward to July.

JASON: You still can. Right? *(Beat.)* Are you back on biographies yet?

REED: No.

JASON: I'm reading one on de Gaulle.

(After a moment, Bev returns with some bags.)

BEV: We should get going.

JASON: Yeah, if we wait another minute the drive will be terrible.

(Reed picks up a bag and goes off. Jason picks up another bag and goes off in another direction. Bev looks around a moment, then catches up with Reed.

They continue into a small apartment which has only a sofa for furniture.
They put down their bags.)

REED: That should be it.

BEV: Well.

REED: Yup.

(They look around.)

BEV: This is a shit hole.

REED: It's where businessmen stay. It rents by the week, so we can camp out till we find a place.

BEV: For businessmen and those who love them.

REED: All work and obviously no play.

BEV: Nope. *(Beat.)* It needs a woman's touch. So you should get busy —

REED: Then I should get busy. It's all I could find with a separate room.

BEV: No, we're fine. You think he's asleep?

REED: I checked him ten minutes ago. He felt a little warm, but I think it's from the day.

BEV: I'll check him.

REED: You might check him in a bit. And we need to get his cereal. He was all in a panic about Count Chocula. Or I can run to the market, but I've only got — *(He empties his pockets and produces some bills.)* Is this enough for Count Chocula?

BEV: Wait, I've got — *(She empties her pockets and they pool their money.)* That should do us.

REED: There's got to be an ATM somewhere.

BEV: And get some coffee for the morning.

REED: Good thinking.

BEV: We'll need it.

REED: And the paper.

BEV: Anything in the fridge?

(Reed goes off to see.)

REED: *(Off.)* Half a bottle of Blush.

BEV: Eww.

REED: *(Off.)* Want a glass?

BEV: Why not?

(Reed returns with the blush and two glasses. He pours a glass for Bev.)

BEV: Not that much.

(They sit and toast and drink.)

REED: What is blush anyway?

BEV: White wine that feels ashamed. *(Beat.)* What are you thinking about?

REED: What are you thinking about?

BEV: Georgie. He seemed a little girly on the playground today. He wanted to play outfield but he kept running away from the ball.

REED: So he'll cut hair. *(Beat.)* Wait.

BEV: What?

REED: We're sleeping on the couch?

BEV: You said it pulls out.

REED: You aren't going to pee in your sleep?

BEV: On a half a glass of wine?

REED: OK!

BEV: That happened once and you keep bringing it up like I'm ready for diapers!

REED: I like that it makes you cranky.

BEV: Well it does! *(Beat.)* I like it actually, too. I only peed that once though. And you've spun it into this decades long loose bladder story. And I was sleeping when it happened. It's not like I elected to whiz on the furniture. It was not premeditated pee. And to this day everyone I know starts shaking when they pour me wine! I saw Marci pat the sofa once after I got up. It's not fair. I don't have a pee story for you.
(They laugh.)

REED: Let's come up with one!

BEV: And it's not like I ever drank all that much.

REED: Please, you drank like it was your job. *(Beat.)* Whatever happened to her?

BEV: Who?

REED: That girl whose sofa you relieved yourself on?

BEV: It was a chaise, actually. See, always embellishing.

REED: She was funny. I liked her.

BEV: She's in the Northwest somewhere. Probably with plastic all over the upholstery. She left me when I met you.

REED: She was threatened. Were you threatened when I met Jason?

BEV: Sure. At first. Then I found Shelly. And then were you threatened?

REED: Still am.

BEV: Me too.

REED: No. I was glad. 'Cause things evened out. We went from a two-legged beast to a three-legged one, so we needed a fourth.

BEV: So we didn't really break up, I guess.

REED: Who?

BEV: Us.

REED: One night is hardly a relationship. I mean, that's how I do the math.

BEV: Yeah, but two times though. It wasn't a bad night.

REED: I was feeling sexual. In a way that, you know, that could've been directed at anything.

BEV: Thanks.

REED: Aim and fire.

BEV: Thanks a lot.

REED: You know I don't mean that.

BEV: *(Raising her glass.)* You weren't inept.

REED: *(Raising his.)* You weren't grossed out.

BEV: You kidding? I liked guys till I was twenty-four. Then I just got pussy crazy.

REED: I never got that. But it didn't seem — it seemed we were comfortable, and it seemed like we were, um, doing each other a favor.

BEV: We were curious.

REED: The sweetest favor.

BEV: We were drunk.

REED: Curious like kids. We'd had a lot, it's true.

BEV: *(Looks off to Georgie's room.)* He'll be there someday. *(Yawns and looks at her glass.)* See? I can't do it anymore.

REED: I'm about ready myself — *(He looks at the sofa.)* I wonder how this thing pulls out.

(They both unfold the bed.)

BEV: There —

(They undress. They look at each other. They look at the bed.)

REED: Should we check on him?

BEV: He's flushed from the sun is all.

REED: Should we go to bed?

BEV: Yes. You first.

REED: OK.

BEV: Shouldn't you go to the market though?

REED: We can do that in the morning. We'll go together.

BEV: Thank you.

(He steps into the bed. She follows. He turns out the light. They lie face up in bed, silent for a long, long moment.)

BEV: What's gonna happen?

REED: When it comes to things like this . . . I'm not sure.

(They begin to move toward each other as the lights go out.)

END OF PLAY

THE WEST END HORROR

by Anthony Dodge and Marcia Milgrom Dodge
Adapted from the novel by Nicholas Meyer

*We began work on this play shortly after
returning from Russia as new parents,
venturing from adoption to adaptation, and
happily linking forever both joyous events.
This is dedicated to our sweet Natasha,
who makes the impossible attainable.*

PLAYWRIGHTS' BIOGRAPHIES

Marcia Milgrom Dodge's work as a director and choreographer has been seen throughout the United States and in Canada, Great Britain, and South Korea. Off Broadway she staged *Radio Gals* (John Houseman Theater); Maltby and Shire's award-winning *Closer Than Ever* (Cherry Lane); *The Music Man* (New York City Opera); William Finn's *Romance in Hard Times* (New York Shakespeare Festival) and the musical-within-the-play for Donald Margulies's *The Loman Family Picnic* (Manhattan Theater Club).

World premieres include *The West End Horror* (Bay Street Theater), which was nominated for an Edgar Award; Rupert Holmes's *Thumbs* starring Kathie Lee Gifford and Diana Canova (Helen Hayes Theater Company and Cape Playhouse); *Cookin'* (South Korea and International Tour); *One Foot on the Floor* by Jeffrey Hatcher (Denver Center Theater Company); *Off-Key* (George Street Playhouse); and *Casino Paradise* by William Bolcom and Arnold Weinstein (American Music Theater Festival).

On Broadway she served as associate choreographer of *High Society* at the St. James Theater. For the 92nd Street Y, she directed Aaron Copland's *The Second Hurricane*, an opera for young people. For The Cape Playhouse, she directed *Crimes of the Heart* starring Sandy Duncan, *Accomplice* with Richard Kind and Stephanie Zimbalist, and *Angel Street* starring David McCallum. Favorite projects include *Olympus on My Mind* (Florida Studio Theater); *Kismet, Forum,* and *The Unsinkable Molly Brown* (Sacramento Music Circus); *Hair* (Bay Street Theater); *Goosebumps Live on Stage* (Wintergardens Opera House, Blackpool, England); Ken Ludwig's *Sullivan & Gilbert* starring George Grizzard (Phoenix Theater Co. at SUNY Purchase); *On the Town, Merrily We Roll Along,* and *Of Thee I Sing,* which was nominated for a Helen Hayes Award for Outstanding Choreography (Arena Stage); and *Pacific Overtures* for NYU's Tisch School of the Arts.

Her extensive regional credits include exciting collaborations with Rupert Holmes, Stephen Sondheim, Robert Falls, Des McAnuff, Richard Adler and Bill C. Davis, Douglas C. Wager, Gregory Boyd, Michael Cristofer, and Joanne Woodward. Ms. Dodge's Goodspeed Opera House production of *On the Town* won critical raves, and her Virginia Stage production of *Ain't Misbehavin'* played five more regional theaters and received two Barrymore Award nominations.

Devoted to the training of young performers, Ms. Dodge is a frequent guest director at New York City universities and conservatories. For CAP21/NYU, she directed *Divorce Me Darling*, David Krane's *Times Square, The Mystery of Edwin Drood,* and *Merrily We Roll Along*. At Fordham College, she directed and choreographed *Of Thee I Sing* and *Guys and Dolls*. For television, she choreographs *Sesame Street* (Emmy Award–winning episode "The Tango Festival") and "Remember WENN" for American Movie Classics. Also for *Sesame Street* she choreographed an Elmo's World video, *Wild Wild West*, featuring Bill Irwin, Michael Jeter, and Kristin Chenoweth (Sony Wonder). Ms. Dodge is currently on the faculty of the American Musical and Dramatic Academy.

Anthony Dodge appeared as Dr. Watson in the world premiere production of *The West End Horror* at Bay Street Theater. He was a featured actor with The Phoenix Theater Company at SUNY Purchase, New York, for three seasons playing Charles in *High Spirits*, Pontagnac in *There's One in Every Marriage*, Dr. Watson in *The Crucifer of Blood,* and Duke Alfred in Ken Ludwig's *Sullivan & Gilbert* starring George Grizzard. Mr. Dodge is a longtime member of Actor's Equity Association, the Screen Actor's Guild, and the American Federation of Television and Radio Artists. Regionally, he created the Gable-esque role of Rod LaRue in *One Foot on the Floor* by Jeffrey Hatcher (Denver Center Theater Co./world premiere).

Favorite roles include Doc in *Crimes of the Heart* opposite Sandy Duncan and Havalind Morris at The Cape Playhouse, Mr. McLenahan in *The Second Hurricane* for the 92nd Street Y, Derek/Hal in Rupert Holmes' *Accomplice* at the American Stage Festival, Preacher Hugh in *The Merry Wives of Windsor, Texas* with The Red Clay Ramblers for the Cincinnati Playhouse in the Park, Lord Evelyn in *Anything Goes* at The Birmingham Theater, Murray in *The Odd Couple* for StageWest, and Mayor Shinn in *The Music Man* at New York City Opera. On television, Mr. Dodge has appeared in that requisite show for most every New York actor, *Law and Order*, as well as in several roles on *The Guiding Light*. When not working with his wife, Marcia, Mr. Dodge is happily chasing their active five-year-old daughter, Natasha. He is a member of The Dramatist Guild of America.

ACKNOWLEDGMENTS

We would like to acknowledge the support of The Director's Company, New York City, in the inception of the play. We also thank the following people for their help: Jack Tantleff, John Santoianni, Charmaine Ferenczi, Maura Teitelbaum and Elsa Neuwald at Abrams Artists; Andrew Schultz, Jeffrey Hatcher, Rupert Holmes, Mark Shanahan, Matt Kovich, Beau Bernarda, Polly Dodge, Carole Jo Lasser, and Matt Loney. To all the actors who did readings, we send our enormous gratitude.

INTRODUCTION

The West End Horror joyously takes the tradition and excitement of *Sherlock Holmes*, the world's foremost consulting detective, into mysterious doings involving the most famous theatrical luminaries of Victorian London's West End. We chose this particular story, adapted from the Nicholas Meyer novel, because of our love for mysteries. But *The West End Horror*, with its murder of a drama critic to set the plot in motion, if not best described as a dream come true, is at the very least perfect fodder for a theatrical adaptation. Which created a problem.

We were seemingly charted for *big* waters — dozens of actors, lavish costumes, and enough scenery to keep two shops operating fulltime. Which is, of course, not feasible. So, we determined to write a producible play, maintaining the episodic nature of the novel while keeping the large number of colorful characters, always with an eye toward economy.

Our production concept requires seven actors and one musician in an intimate setting. This small troupe of players also creates the environment, helps with props and produces sound effects — using a minimum of scenery and a maximum of imagination.

We were undaunted in our passion to do this play. Rather than feeling constrained by budgetary economics, we felt liberated by unbudgeted imagination. Sweet indeed are the uses of adversity, because it helped us write stronger and braver while allowing us an insight to inform our characters with a self-awareness only possible from a twenty-first century perspective.

ORIGINAL PRODUCTION

The world premiere production was presented by Bay Street Theater, Sag Harbor, New York from June 18 to July 7, 2002. Sets by Troy Hourie, costumes by Christianne Myers, lighting by Brian Nason. Directed by Marcia Milgrom Dodge. The cast included Terrence Mann, Anthony Dodge, Wynn Harmon, Mark Shanahan, Martin Hillier, Dennis Ryan, Jennifer Waldman, Matt Kovich, and Matt Loney.

CHARACTERS

A PIANIST

PROLOGUE MAN ONE

PROLOGUE WOMAN

PROLOGUE MAN TWO

MR. SHERLOCK HOLMES: a detective.

DR. JOHN H. WATSON: a writer.

MR. GEORGE BERNARD SHAW: a music critic.

MRS. HUDSON: a Scottish landlady.

A CABBIE

MR. STANLEY HOPKINS: a constable.

MR. G. LESTRADE: an inspector at Scotland Yard.

DR. BROWNLOW: a police surgeon.

A FLOWER SELLER

A KNIFE GRINDER

A *STRAND MAGAZINE* SANDWICH-BOARD MAN

BOSIE: a singularly deep young man.

MR. OSCAR WILDE: an earnest playwright.

HERBERT: a doorman at the Savoy.

MR. RICHARD D'OYLY CARTE: a producer.

MR. W. S. GILBERT: a lyricist.

MR. GEORGE GROSSMITH: a Savoyard.

MR. FRANCOIS CELLIER: a musical director.

MISS JESSE RUTLAND: an ingenue at the Savoy.

DR. BENJAMIN ECCLES: a theater physician.

SHROPSHIRE: a rat catcher.

A COUPLE OF THEATERGOERS

MR. BRAM STOKER: a stage manager.

MISS ELLEN TERRY: a famous actress.

MR. HENRY IRVING: an actor manager.

SIR ARTHUR SULLIVAN: a composer.

MR. ACHMED SINGH: a Hindu shopkeeper.

A LITERARY FIGURE

A SECOND LITERARY FIGURE

A THIRD LITERARY FIGURE

MR. JONATHAN MCCARTHY: a theater critic.

The Company also takes the roles of Policemen, Covent Garden Street-Sellers, Wilde's Hangers-on, Savoyards, Carpenters, and London Citizenry.

TIME
March 1895.

PLACE
London.

SETTING
In and around London's West End.

ACT I
Prologue

A pianist walks to the piano, flips his tails, sits, and begins playing the overture Danse Macabre. *It segues into music dissonant and delirious. Man One staggers into a pool of light. Well-fed and fierce, dressed in a silk waistcoat and lounging jacket, he is clearly in agony. In another pool of light is Man Two, filled with still fury. In a third pool of light is Woman, a lovely young woman with dark russet hair, who cannot be more than twenty-five.*

MAN ONE: *(Holding his left side, somewhat below the heart.)* A plague o' both your houses! Go, villain, fetch a surgeon.

MAN TWO: Why the devil came you between us?

WOMAN: My reputation stained with slander.

MAN ONE: 'Tis not so deep as a well, nor so wide as a church door; but 'tis enough, 'twill serve.

MAN TWO: Thou wretched one, that didst consort him here,
Shalt with him hence.

WOMAN: This shall determine that.

(Woman points her finger like a gun at Man Two. Blackout. A Player says "Bang!" into a megaphone.)

Scene One

In the black, the Player repeats "Bang!" several times, as lights come up on the interior of 221B Baker Street. It is March 1895. Sherlock Holmes is reclining on his divan. His pistol propped on his knee, he fires off round after round at the wall, spelling out the pattern "V R." Dr. Watson enters carrying the latest edition of the Strand Magazine *behind his back.*

WATSON: Holmes? Holmes! You are menacing the neighborhood! Mrs. Hudson has had complaints from the elderly invalid next door who claims your pistol practice is having a deleterious effect on her unstable condition. Do you imagine shooting "V R" in bullet holes to be a proper tribute to Queen Victoria?

(Watson snatches the gun away from Holmes.)

HOLMES: Her Majesty is no more interested in my bullet-riddled wall than she is in the latest edition of the *Strand Magazine* secreted behind your back.

WATSON: May I remind you that my writings fund this consulting detective agency?

HOLMES: That is the familiar reprise of a too-familiar tune. I managed quite sufficiently on my own when you were otherwise engaged and will gladly return to that arrangement posthaste.

WATSON: I must protest! The *Strand Magazine* —

HOLMES: I am not finished. About your writings, there is no need to remind me, for I am beset upon by an adoring and equally unwanted public wherever I go. Because of your overwrought prose people treat me as if they were long-lost relations, or presume that I am some circus refugee performing tricks for tuppence. And all the while having lurid expectations of my being a seven-foot-tall cocaine fiend, clad in a cape and deerstalker cap, shrouded in a constant swirl of pipe smoke!

WATSON: Look at you, Holmes. Papers of all variety strewn hither and yon, scientific experiments left half finished, books opened and discarded with equal dispatch. You have not taken a case for these past several months, choosing instead to skulk about Baker Street —

HOLMES: *(Interrupting.)* There is nothing new under the sun! It's all been done —

WATSON: *(Interrupting.)* I am not finished — You annoy and bully poor Mrs. Hudson — and me, I might add — and now you see fit to endanger the local citizenry with gunshots.

HOLMES: *(Walking about the room.)* Don't you see, man? Since Professor Moriarty's death plunge down Reichenbach Falls the criminal mastermind is no more. He was the last of his kind and I fear that his demise is also the end of me, for Moriarty's evil genius engaged me like a conflagration. Some unseen piece of me must have gone over with him, invisible yet as real as any corporeal part. Was it a Pyrrhic victory? I wonder, Watson, I wonder. I drift vaguely from day to day, inured to sorrow, ignorant to delight. Books have lost their luster and work is flavorless and gray. Of course I have taken no new cases. What, pray tell, would you have me do? Am I now to use my faculties to divine clandestine details in unhappy matrimonial cases? Should I employ deductive reasoning in order to solve drunken disputes at some nearby gin palace? Or perhaps you'd prefer that I follow behind Scotland Yard with broom and dustpan like a roustabout trailing a circus elephant and clean up the mess they chronically create?

(Holmes slumps into his divan.)

WATSON: *(Imploring.)* Come, come, Holmes, you'd think a grown man like yourself would be able to occupy his time in some sensible fashion!

HOLMES: *(After a very long pause.)* Very well, Watson. So be it. You leave me no recourse but to surrender to Taboo.

(Holmes crosses to a table, looks hard at Watson, then deliberately pushes up his left sleeve. He turns out of view.)

WATSON: Holmes! Not that!

HOLMES: I'm afraid so. I feel compelling urges.

(Turning around, Holmes is holding a violin and begins playing. Music: Danse Macabre.*)*

WATSON: Candidly, Holmes, I'm not entirely certain that the sound of your fiddle playing is preferable to the sound of your infernal gunshots.

HOLMES: No use, Watson. My bow is undaunted.

WATSON: Really, Holmes, I had hoped you would put your mind to something a bit more useful.

(Holmes stops playing.)

HOLMES: The mind is like a large field, Watson. It is available for cultivation only if the land is used sensibly and portions of it are permitted to lie fallow periodically. Part of my mind — my professional mind — is on holiday at the moment. During its leave of absence I am exercising another quarter of it.

(Holmes begins playing again. Watson gazes out the window.)

WATSON: It's a pity your professional mind is out of town.

HOLMES: What do you see?

WATSON: I believe we are about to have a visitor, someone interested in that portion of your intellect that is currently lying fallow. And from the look of him, he certainly appears a likely candidate for 221B.

HOLMES: *(Petulantly.)* I am not in the mood for visitors. *(He abruptly stops playing.)* What does he look like?

WATSON: For one thing, he has an insubordinate beard, slightly reddish, in desperate need of a barber.

HOLMES: Clothes?

WATSON: Norfolk jacket and knickerbockers. They look well worn, even at this distance. He keeps adjusting his shirt cuffs.

HOLMES: Probably false. Height?

WATSON: Above medium height.

HOLMES: Age?

WATSON: Roughly forty, with an incessant grin that suggests he might be mad.

HOLMES: Gait?

WATSON: The man walks like a gigantic leprechaun.

HOLMES: And does he carry a silver-handled walking stick?

WATSON: He does not.

HOLMES: What? Strange, but that sounds like Shaw. Hello, it *is* Shaw. I've never seen him sans the company of his prized cane. And whatever has made him change his mind and decide to pay me a visit.

WATSON: Who is he?

HOLMES: I met him at a concert of Wagner some years ago. We got into a rather heated disagreement about the Tannhäuser tenor that lasted several hours and have been friendly ever since. Shaw has got hold of some of the oddest notions, not the least of which is his connection with the Fabian Society —

WATSON: What, those socialists?

HOLMES: Indeed. Shaw is a zealous advocate of their mission and the absent walking stick was presented to him on his tenth anniversary with the Fabians — red mahogany with a silver filigreed handle, it has the initials GBS on a silver plate and the staff is entwined with the engraved motto: "Educate! Agitate! Organize!" I have never seen him without it. But, apart from all that, I am told he is a very brilliant Irishman.

WATSON: Who told you that?

HOLMES: He did!

WATSON: Good Lord!

HOLMES: Like most Irishmen, he has a ready tongue equally comfortable advertising his political beliefs as well as himself. And, of course, poor as a church mouse.

WATSON: A *brilliant* church mouse.

HOLMES: Oh, you want to be careful of him, Watson. You want to watch him and give him a wide berth.

WATSON: Why, what does he do?

(There is an energetic knock on the door.)

HOLMES: He's a critic!

(Holmes flings wide the door and admits his friend. On his heels is Mrs. Hudson, carrying a broom.)

MRS. HUDSON He burst right in, Mr. Holmes!

HOLMES: That's all right, Mrs. Hudson, thank you.

(Mrs. Hudson swats Shaw with the broom and leaves.)

HOLMES: Shaw, my dear fellow, Welcome! Welcome! I know you have heard me speak of Dr. Watson, who shares these lodgings with me? Ah, good.

Watson, allow me to present "Corno di Bassetto" of the *Saturday Review,* known to his intimates as Mr. George Bernard Shaw.

SHAW: By god, I believe your rooms are more untidy than my own. However, they are somewhat larger than my hovel, which allows you to be creative with your sloppiness.

WATSON: Now see here, my good man —

(Shaw flashes Watson an impish grin.)

HOLMES: You've no idea what a pleasant surprise this is. I'd quite given up hope of ever persuading you to set foot in these digs. I trust, in any event, that you have not come all this way merely to visit us with your Philosophy of Socialism.

(Shaw warms his hands at the fireplace. Two Players provide the sound effects.)

SHAW: It wouldn't hurt you if I had. My eloquence on the subject has been declared alarming by those in a position to know.

HOLMES: Even so. I can't offer you any breakfast — that's long since been cleared away — but in any case, I perceive by your right sleeve that you have already dined on eggs.

SHAW: Ah, you are fallible, how comforting. That's yesterday's breakfast.

WATSON: What would you say to some brandy?

SHAW: I'd say it would destroy me as surely as it did my father and countless other drunkards. I'd say I'd remain a teetotaler. I'd say no thank you!

WATSON: Certainly a snifter of brandy won't ruin you.

SHAW: What's certain is I'll outlive the pair of you. With all the drink, meat, and tobacco you consume you're digging yourselves early graves.

WATSON: Yes, Holmes has cautioned me of your Fabian views to educate. Which reminds me, where is your walking stick?

SHAW: *(Sheepishly.)* Ah, yes, I was obliged to pawn it yesterday, a temporary expedient until my next week's wages. A ludicrous state of affairs for a middle-aged man, don't you find? Critics are not revered — as they should be.

WATSON: With critics you have me at a disadvantage — as a writer, I am forced to actually work for a living.

SHAW: Could you manage on two guineas a week, Doctor? Your writing brings you a deal more, I daresay.

WATSON: Why don't you attempt something in a more lucrative vein?

SHAW: No, I shall continue as a critic, occasionally turning out a play of my own on the side. I shall keep at it. After all — all the great English playwrights are Irish. Look at Sheridan! Goldsmith! Look in our own time at Mr. Oscar Wilde! All Irish! One day Shaw will be included in that glorious pantheon.

WATSON: Shakespeare was English.

SHAW: *(Leaping to his feet.)* Shakespeare?

HOLMES: *(Laughing mischievously.)* Now you've done it, Watson.

SHAW: *(With scornful relish.)* Shakespeare? A mountebank who had not the wit to invent his own plots, much less embellish them! Tolstoy was right — a conspiracy of nineteenth-century academia that's what Shakespeare is. Ask Queen Victoria, do rulers really "kiss away kingdoms," or don't they rather hold on to power just as long and as tenaciously as they can? *Antony and Cleopatra* — what ineffable romantic twaddle! They were as cynical a pair of politicians as you could conjure, the both of 'em!

WATSON: *(Protesting.)* But, the poetry — the poetry!

SHAW: *(Overlapping.)* Poetry — rubbish! People don't talk poetry, Doctor! Only in books and bad plays! Oh, the man had a brilliant mind but he should never have wasted his intellect on plays. What he should have been was an essayist. He had not the gifts of a playwright.

(Watson gapes at Shaw with incredulity.)

HOLMES: *(Placing himself between the two men.)* Surely you didn't come here this morning to take on Shakespeare any more than Capitalism — though I would like to point out the discrepancy of your views on the redistribution of wealth and your own desire for an increase in salary.

SHAW: *(Peevishly.)* You've swayed me from the point with all this talk of Shakespeare. I have come to you this morning on quite a different errand, for I believe I have a case for you!

(Holmes and Watson snicker.)

HOLMES: Some fascinating literary mystery, no doubt. Tell me, has some blackguard purloined a monograph of yours?

WATSON: No, Holmes, it's The Case of the Dangling Participle!

SHAW: There has been a murder done.

(An ominous chord. Watson watches Holmes intently as Shaw awaits a response.)

HOLMES: *(Finally.)* Who has been murdered?

SHAW: A critic. Jonathan McCarthy. Writes for the *Morning Courant.* — Or wrote, I should say, since he will write no more.

HOLMES: I confine my attentions as a rule to the agony columns, but I can't have missed such a story as —

SHAW: *(Interrupting.)* You won't find it in the papers — yet. Word of the deed was just circulating at the *Review* offices this morning. Instead of finishing my article due today, I came here directly to tell you of it.

HOLMES: Why me?

SHAW: Surely this is obvious, I wish you to investigate the matter.

HOLMES: *(Plopping into his divan.)* I'm on vacation!

SHAW: I too share your feelings for the dubious abilities of Scotland Yard. Wasn't it you that said, "When the police are out of their depths — which, by the way, is their normal state — the matter is —

HOLMES: — Laid before me."

WATSON: *The Sign of Four.*

HOLMES: Yes, and?

SHAW: And I lay it before you: are you up to the challenge? *(Adding as incentive.)* The man was stabbed.

HOLMES: Had this critic any enemies?

(Shaw laughs long and heartily. Watson joins him laughing.)

SHAW: You ask that question about a critic? In any case, it must surely be obvious that he possessed at least one. For McCarthy I should postulate a score. He was even less agreeable than I.

(Holmes rises abruptly and throws off his dressing gown.)

HOLMES: Come; let us have a look. *(Opening the front door.)* Mrs. Hudson!

MRS. HUDSON: It's no use, Mr. Holmes! I'll nay go out to get you more of your cursed bullets!

HOLMES: Perhaps just a cab, then?

MRS. HUDSON: *(As she goes out.)* Straightaway.

WATSON: Have you the unfortunate man's address?

SHAW: One moment.

(Holmes and Watson turn and regard him.)

SHAW: I have two points of concern. First, I have that blasted deadline but will join you presently.

HOLMES: At?

SHAW: Number Twenty-four Regent Street.

WATSON: *(Wistfully.)* Near the Langham Hotel.

HOLMES: *(Pressing on.)* And your second point?

SHAW: The matter of a fee.

HOLMES: I haven't yet said that I will take the case.

SHAW: Nevertheless, I must tell you I am not capable of paying a brass farthing for your services.

HOLMES: I have worked for less on occasion if the matter interested me —

WATSON: Hah!

HOLMES: — And Watson is eager for me to resume my professional investigations.

WATSON: Well, there are cobwebs on your magnifying glass.

HOLMES: What is your real reason for wishing me to look into this business? *(Shaw opens his mouth to speak; Holmes cautions him from embellishing.)*

SHAW: All right, fair enough. You've asked an honest question and force me into the unsavory situation of replying in kind. The late Jonathan McCarthy was not much of a critic, and even less of a human being if such a thing is possible. However, in a heretofore unseen display of insight, McCarthy was the first person to recognize my multitudinous talents and singular writing ability and used his position to help me secure my first job as a critic. Consequently, I am beholden to the bastard.

HOLMES: Let an Irishman talk long enough and eventually the truth will emerge.

(Shaw holds up Watson's copy of the Strand Magazine.)

SHAW: Also, as long as I'm being forthright, I was thinking that if Dr. Watson pays his share of the rent with prose accounts of your work, perhaps I could do the same by putting Sherlock Holmes on the stage.

HOLMES: *(Holding the door open.)* Pray do not or, like the late Professor Moriarty, you'll find it's a long drop off the Reichenbach Falls. *(He goes.)* *(Watson grabs the Strand Magazine from Shaw and they follow Holmes out. Traveling music in.)*

Scene Two

Holmes and Watson are sharing a hansom cab driven by the Cabbie. A Player provides the sound of horse hooves. Music out.

HOLMES: Well, Watson, what do you make of him?

WATSON: Make of him? I must say I find him insufferable. Holmes, how can you tolerate the conversation of that know-all?

HOLMES: He amuses me. Don't you find him stimulating?

WATSON: Stimulating? *(The "carriage" swerves.)* Gibberish about Shakespeare writing essays?

HOLMES: Well, admit I warned you that he held some queer ideas. With Shakespeare, unfortunately, you tumbled on to his bête noire. *(The "carriage" slows.)* There, I confess, his views appear radically unsound, but then, his prejudices can be explained. He reads plays not as we do, Watson, but rather to take the measure of himself against the minds of other men — *(The "horse" whinnies and snorts, the "carriage" stops.)* "Such men as he be never at heart's ease whilst they behold a greater than themselves."

WATSON: Ah, but you haven't finished Caesar's speech: "And therefore are they very dangerous."

HOLMES: Just so my dear Watson. Just so.

(Watson pays the Cabbie.)

CABBIE: Beware the Ides of March, Guv'nuh.

(The "carriage" hurries away. A musical flourish.)

Scene Three

24 Regent Street.

HOLMES: Here we are!

(They approach the front door where young Constable Hopkins is posted.)

HOPKINS: Oh, morning, Mr. Holmes, Dr. Watson. *(Calling off.)* Inspector! *(Back to Holmes and Watson.)* Is he expecting you, then?

HOLMES: Constable, let us just say he won't be surprised to see me.

LESTRADE: *(Entering.)* Mr. Holmes, why am I not surprised to see you?

HOLMES: May we survey the damage, Lestrade?

LESTRADE: May I ask — how did you come to know there was any?

(Holmes smiles elusively at Lestrade.)

LESTRADE: I don't mind if you do but you best be quick. The Police Surgeon will be here any minute now for the body.

HOLMES: Brownlow?

LESTRADE: Aye.

HOLMES: We shall try to stay out of the way.

LESTRADE: *(Watching Holmes narrowly.)* The fact is I was thinking of coming by your Baker Street lodgings a bit later on in the day.

WATSON: *(Going in behind Holmes.)* Haven't the foggiest, have you?

LESTRADE: *(Calling after Watson.)* For a cup of tea!

(Music: Schuman's Important Event. They go in to —.)

Scene Four

McCarthy's apartment. The music plays a sour chord and then stops abruptly.

HOLMES: Will they never learn?

WATSON: Good heavens! What an unnerving sight.

(Holmes steps into the room, shaking his head over the mess Lestrade and his men have made of the carpet. During the next speech, Holmes proceeds to give the room a thorough inspection of the kind only he could manage. Crawling about on all fours, peering through his glass, examining the walls, the shelves, the desk, the table, the day bed, the most minute inspection of the corpse itself. He keeps a running commentary of whistles, exclamations and mutterings. Watson takes out his journal and a pencil. Music: Chopin's Nocturne, Opus 9.)

WATSON: The flat of Jonathan McCarthy combines the features of a library and sitting room. Lavishly equipped with books, it boasts a small tea table, which supports one glass containing what looks like brandy. A second glass has found its way to the floor and been broken, either fallen or thrown.

HOLMES: Aha!

WATSON: Next to the first glass, a cigar sits unmolested in a marble ashtray, where it has been allowed to go out of its own volition. On the opposite wall there is a fireplace, recently ablazed. The poker has been removed from its holder and lies upon the hearth in a considerable amount of ash. Across is a day bed and behind it the writing table of the dead man. This is covered with papers, all related to his calling — programs, theater tickets, notices of cast substitutions, the latest edition of the *Strand Magazine* —

HOLMES: *(Groans.)* Ohh . . .

WATSON: — As well as cuttings from his own reviews, neatly arranged for easy reference. Beside these papers is an engraved invitation —

HOLMES: Aaaah!

WATSON: — To the premiere of something called *The Grand Duke,* at the Savoy two days hence. Those walls devoid of bookshelves are literally papered with portraits of members of the theatrical profession. Some are photographs, others are executed in pen and ink, but all bear the signatures of the notables who had sat for them. One is assailed by the testimonials of affection from all quarters and awed by the likenesses of —

HOLMES: — Forbes-Robertson, Miss Ellen Terry, Beerbohm-Tree, and Henry Irving —

WATSON: — Who stare or scowl dramatically down at the visitor. All these, however — the books, the desk, the pictures, the table, and the fireplace — were but as set decorations for the main attraction —

HOLMES: The corpse —

WATSON: — which lay on its back, the eyes fixed and staring, the jaw dropped, and the mouth open wide in some terrible, silent scream.

HOLMES: Watson, your medical observations.

WATSON: The man has been stabbed in the left side, somewhat below the heart, and bled profusely. The instrument of his death is nowhere apparent. Blood has dried on the silken waistcoat and on the oriental carpet beside it. The body is cold, and parts of it are already quite hard. Time of death roughly two hours ago.

HOLMES: And yet, what else? Something seems to puzzle you.

WATSON: I must confess I am a bit perplexed by the manner in which rigor mortis has set in. One does not expect to find it so pronounced in the neck and abdomen and so conspicuously absent in the fingers and joints.

HOLMES: Hmmm. Thank you, Watson. Perplexing indeed. Lestrade, the other rooms are undisturbed, I take it?

LESTRADE: Yes, this room's where the business took place, all right.

HOLMES: What then are the facts?

LESTRADE: *(Referring to his notebook.)* He was found like this some two and *one half* hours ago. The girl came up with his breakfast, knocked on the door, and receiving no answer, made so bold as to enter. He's overslept before it seems. As to what happened — He was entertaining here last night. They sat down to a brandy and cigars here at the table when an altercation began. Whoever it was reached behind him to the writing desk and grabbed this.

(Ominous chord. Lestrade hands Holmes a folded handkerchief, which he unfolds to reveal an ivory letter opener, its yellowish blade tinged a tawny red. Holmes examines it with his magnifying glass.)

HOLMES: Javanese. *(Pause.)* It came from the desk, you say? Ah, yes, here is the sheath, which matches it. Go on, pray.

LESTRADE: *(Routinely.)* Whoever it was seized the letter opener and stabbed his host, knocking over his brandy glass as he thrust home. McCarthy crumpled in a heap at the foot of the table whilst the other departed, leaving his cigar burning where he had left it. McCarthy stayed beneath the table for some time — you can see quite a pool of blood — and then with his last reserves of strength, he crawled to those bookshelves —

HOLMES: So much, as you say, is obvious. *(Holmes steps forward and carefully picks up a cigar, holding it gently in the middle.)* This cigar is less so. I cannot recall having ever seen one like it. Can you, Lestrade?

LESTRADE: *(Scoffing.)* You're going to tell me about all those tobacco ashes you can recognize.

WATSON: Holmes, if I —

HOLMES: One moment. On the contrary, I am trying to tell you about one I cannot.

(Holmes holds up the cigar, smells it, turns it back and forth between his thumb and forefinger, holds it to his ear and listens to the crackle, then sights along its length like a rifle.)

WATSON: Holmes, if you'd just —

HOLMES: Not now! Lestrade, I can identify twenty-three kinds of tobacco from the ash alone. If you could tell me what this is, I shall have incorporated a twenty-fourth into my repertoire.

LESTRADE: Well, it's foreign.

HOLMES: So much I had already deduced.

WATSON: Holmes, please!

HOLMES: What is it, Watson?

WATSON: It's an Indian cheroot. Haven't smelled one of those since I served in Afghanistan. Beastly things.

HOLMES: *(Clearly surprised.)* Well done, Watson. Now don't make a habit out of it. India, you say. That nicely explains the square cut end and the heavy proportion of Latakia.

WATSON: They are a great favorite with the boys serving in India, but then those lads will smoke anything.

HOLMES: And undoubtedly unavailable for purchase in England.

WATSON: That's right, Holmes. Do you think it figures in the case?

HOLMES: Why don't you tell me?

(Lestrade grabs the cigar from Holmes as a noise is heard offstage. Shaw arrives, breathless but triumphant.)

SHAW: Well, where's the carcass?

LESTRADE: And who might this gentleman be?

HOLMES: He's a colleague of the deceased, Inspector Lestrade. May I present Mr. George Bernard Shaw of the *Saturday Review.*

(The two men bow slightly.)

HOPKINS: *(Entering.)* Inspector, the police wagon's arrived downstairs with a stretcher in it.

LESTRADE: Yes, yes. Well, gentlemen, as you can see —

HOLMES: Ah, Constable, do you, by chance, have the book poor McCarthy had used his last ounce of energy to retrieve.

LESTRADE: Stop a bit. Here, how did you come to know he was after a book before he died?

HOLMES: What other reason for him to have struggled so valiantly towards the bookshelves. I perceive one is missing. A volume of Shakespeare, is it not?

(Shaw snorts loudly near the tea table.)

HOLMES: Shaw, will you kindly refrain from trampling the clues!

SHAW: *(Chastened.)* Beggin' your pardon.

HOLMES: May we see the book?

(Lestrade nods to Hopkins, who brings him the book, wrapped in a second handkerchief. Holmes raises his glass again and conducts a careful examination of the volume, pursing his lips in concentration.)

HOLMES: *Romeo and Juliet.* Well, Watson, since you are so well versed in foreign-made cigars, why not — see how you do with books. You're our Shakespeare aficionado, you know my methods, care to elucidate us with your deductions?

WATSON: Oh, I see, this is where I make a series of conclusions and you then concisely and publicly show everyone how wrong I am on every point. Thank you, no.

HOPKINS: Ahem. With your permission, sir.

HOLMES: *(A trifle miffed.)* Yes?

HOPKINS: When we found it, it was opened.

HOLMES: Indeed? *(Holmes shoots a keen glance at Lestrade, who shifts his weight uncomfortably.)* And where was that?

LESTRADE: *(Defensively.)* The book wasn't in his hands. He let go of it when he died.

HOLMES: But it was open.

LESTRADE: Aye.

HOLMES: To what page?

LESTRADE: *(Grumbling.)* Somewhere in the middle. *(Testily.)* It's a perfectly ordinary book. No secret messages stuck in the binding, if you're thinking along those lines.

HOLMES: I am not thinking at all. I am observing, as you, evidently, have failed to do.

HOPKINS: *(Volunteering.)* It was page forty-two.

(Holmes favors him with an interested look, then begins carefully turning the bloodstained pages.)

HOLMES: You're very keen. How long have you been down from Leeds? Five years?

HOPKINS: Six, sir, after my father —

(He stops and regards the detective with amazement.)

LESTRADE: Here, Holmes, if you know the lad, why not say so?

HOLMES: It is no great matter to infer his birthplace, Lestrade. Surely you can't have failed to remark on his distinctive A's and his peculiar manner of handling diphthongs? I would hazard Leeds or possibly Hull, but then, he has acquired a local overlay, which makes it difficult to be precise. You live in Stepney now, don't you, Constable?

HOPKINS: Aye, sir.

SHAW: Wait one moment! Are you trying to tell me that you can place a man geographically by his speech?

WATSON: George, I think you've got it.

HOLMES: If it's English, within twenty miles. I'd know your Dublin origins despite your attempts to conceal them. Ah, here we are, page forty-two. It concludes Act Three, Scene One —

SHAW AND WATSON: The duel between Tybalt and Mercutio.

HOLMES: Yes. Thank you. Hmm, a curious reference.

LESTRADE: *If* he made it. Hopkins, go wait for Dr. Brownlow.

(Hopkins exits.)

LESTRADE: The book wasn't in his hand, as I've said, and the pages might have fallen over in the interim.

HOLMES: *(Agreeing.)* They might. But since there is no message in the book, we must infer that he meant to tell us something with the volume. It could hardly have been the man's whim to pass the time with a little Shakespeare while he bled to death.

SHAW: Even McCarthy would not have been capable of such a gesture.

LESTRADE: *(Suspiciously.)* You don't seem very disturbed by what's happened to the deceased.

SHAW: I'm not disturbed except by his browsing Shakespeare at the last. The man was a charlatan and a viper and merited his end.

LESTRADE: *(Totally perplexed.)* Shakespeare?

SHAW: McCarthy. *(Shaw points at the photographs and sketches.)* You see those signatures on the walls? Lies, every one of 'em, I'll swear to it. Proffered in fear.

LESTRADE: Fear of what?

SHAW: Bad notices, malicious gossip, scandal in print or out of it.

(Hopkins returns.)

HOPKINS: Inspector, Dr. Brownlow is here.

LESTRADE: Oh, yes. Right.

(Lestrade exits.)

HOLMES: What is your name?

HOPKINS: Stanley Hopkins, sir.

HOLMES: Well, Hopkins, in my opinion, you'll go far but you oughtn't to have touched the book. It might have made all the difference in the world had I been able to see the relation between the man's fingertips and the volume. Do you understand?

HOPKINS: I shall see that such a thing never happens again, sir.

LESTRADE: This way, Dr. Brownlow.

(Lestrade returns with Brownlow, who carries a black medical bag, and two policemen.)

SHAW: *(Seeing the corpse for the first time.)* Good God!

WATSON: *(Bracing Shaw.)* Steady.

BROWNLOW: *(Cackling.)* What's the matter, laddie? Have y'ne'er before seen a stiff one?

SHAW: Not one that was stabbed to death!

BROWNLOW: Well faint not, one way or t'other all we're guaranteed is a feet-first exit and ha'pence for our eyes. If ye feel ye might pass out, as a doctor I prescribe that y'smoke a cigarette.

SHAW: I never partake of tobacco!

BROWNLOW: *(Chewing his nails.)* Sadly, neither do I, owing to the strict intolerances of "She-in-Charge."

SHAW: Queen Victoria?

BROWNLOW: Mrs. Brownlow. *(Regarding the corpse.)* Aye, there shall be no return passage for this one. He felt the knife and he felt the pain and wherever he may be — the pain and the knife are inseparable.

(Hopkins, Brownlow, and the Policemen exit with the corpse. Holmes is discreetly occupied behind the writing table.)

LESTRADE: Well, Mr. Holmes, the deceased has been removed and our work here is done. I hesitate to ask, but ask I must — what have you uncovered?

HOLMES: Nothing very much, I grant you. The murderer is a man. He is right-handed, has a working knowledge of anatomy, and is very powerful, I should say six feet in height — as calculated by the length of his stride. He smoked what is definitely a foreign-made cigar purchased abroad, nervously chews his fingernails, and he wore new boots, expensive, oxblood in color, and purchased at Harrods. Inspector.

(Holmes starts out, then stops.)

HOLMES: Oh, and before he left, he tore out the page dated twenty-eight February in McCarthy's engagement diary with his name on it. Watson! Shaw! Close your mouths and follow me — we're on the case!

(Holmes exits. Music: A tension chord. Watson, Shaw, and Lestrade remain frozen in awe. Beat. Watson and Shaw exit, calling after Holmes. Music in. Lestrade takes off his hat, scratches his head. Puzzled, he points around the room, vainly attempting to recreate Holmes' deductions. Finally, he winds up at the engagement diary, and, opening it makes his own discovery.)

LESTRADE: *(Chuckling quietly.)* Well, Mr. Sherlock Holmes, I believe I have you this time! For there are not one but *two* missing pages!

(Lights change to —)

Scene Five

A street near Covent Garden. There are several Street Sellers peddling their wares.

HOLMES: *(Holding up the second torn diary page.)* BUNTHORNE!

WATSON: What's that?

HOLMES: A page from McCarthy's engagement diary.

WATSON: I thought you said his murderer had pinched the page for twenty-eight February.

HOLMES: So he did. This, as you can see, is for the twenty-seventh, and I pinched it.

SHAW: Larceny! Now I'm convinced I should depict you on stage.

(Watson takes the page. Flower Girl approaches him.)

FLOWER GIRL: Buy a flower off a poor girl, Captain?

(Watson, Holmes, and Shaw move away from her.)

WATSON: It contains but one entry for six-thirty at the Cafe Royal.

HOLMES: Precisely. With someone named Bunthorne.

(The Tinker approaches the three men.)

TINKER: Now then, for your shillings!

SHAW: *(Pulling Holmes, and Watson away.)* I can tell you who Bunthorne is — and so could anyone else in the West End, I fancy, but as you don't frequent anything but Covent Garden and the Albert Hall, I doubt very much if you'd know.

(The Strand Magazine *Sandwich-Board Man moves to the three men.)*

STRAND SELLER: Buy the latest edition of the *Strand Magazine?*

(Holmes, Watson, and Shaw move away as the Street Sellers recognize the celebrities and begin eavesdropping.)

HOLMES: Is he famous, then, this Bunthorne?

SHAW: One might even say infamous — but not under that name. My late colleague appears to have noted his engagements in a sort of code. Bunthorne is Oscar Wilde!

STREET SELLERS: Oscar Wilde?

(Holmes shoos the Street Sellers away.)

WATSON: *(Laughing.)* BUNTHORNE! For *that* one must be familiar with the comic operas of Messrs. Gilbert and Sullivan.

HOLMES: Who?

SHAW: On what planet do you spend your time?

HOLMES: Aside from my own particular musical interests, which lean toward violin concerts and the grand opera, nothing is less likely than knowing anything of London's fads and rages.

SHAW: Then you are missing the greatest combination of words and music since Aristophanes. Wagner excepted. Bunthorne is to be found in *Patience.*

WATSON: Of course! You know Mr. Wilde personally?

SHAW: I know him, though not well. We are too awed by one another's gifts, with the result that we intimidate ourselves.

HOLMES: I am trying to understand the dramatis personae in this business. You didn't think much of Jonathan McCarthy. I should like your estimate of Oscar Wilde.

SHAW: Very well. His plays will be remembered as among the most scintillating in the language — and they are the least of his creations. Brilliant — but he is courting ruin.

HOLMES: Why?

SHAW: *(With great difficulty.)* I am not at liberty to be specific.

HOLMES: Very well, tell me about *Patience.*

SHAW: The opera parodies Wilde in the person of Reginald Bunthorne —

(Bell Tone. Shaw breaks into song, his tenor voice proving to be surprisingly musical. Music: "If You're Anxious for to Shine" from Patience.*)*

SHAW: If you're anxious for to shine

In the high aesthetic line

As a man of culture rare

You must get up all the germs
Of the transcendental terms,
And plant them everywhere.
You must lie upon the daisies
And discourse in novel phrases
Of your complicated state of mind
(Watson joins in — a hearty baritone.)

SHAW AND WATSON: The meaning doesn't matter
If it's only idle chatter
Of a transcendental kind.
And every one will say,
As you walk your mystic way,
"If this young man expresses himself in terms too deep for me,
Why what a very singular deep young man this deep young man
    must be!"
(Watson and Shaw harmonize.)
Why what a very singular deep young man this deep young man
    must be! —

HOLMES: Keep your day jobs.

SHAW AND WATSON: *(Shaw and Watson end with a big finish.)* MUST BE!"

HOLMES: *(Pounding his walking stick to get their attention.)* Shaw, you said you were not at liberty to be specific about Wilde. What *can* you tell me?

SHAW: *(With great concentration.)* Oscar antagonizes. He delights in antagonizing and treats everything as if it were some competition; a challenge for his own amusement. He doesn't take much seriously, except for winning. That he prizes most highly. And people are not inclined to forgive him for it. Also, there are sacred rites and conventions, which will not be flouted. Everyone is waiting for Wilde to get his comeuppance.

WATSON: Mr. Gilbert has flouted them for years, hasn't he? Are people howling for his blood, as well? I don't believe so.

SHAW: Mr. Gilbert's private life is beyond reproach. Or if not, Mr. Gilbert is discreet. The same cannot be said of Oscar Wilde.

HOLMES: Still, he must answer my questions.

SHAW: Well, don't just expect to be invited in and given his every secret. Especially you. Crossing swords with Sherlock Holmes will prove too irresistible for him. *(Sound of clock chimes.)* Heavens, I must be off. *(Shaw starts to leave.)*

HOLMES: Shaw, where can I find Wilde?

SHAW: These days I believe he puts up at the Avondale Gentlemen's Club — in Piccadilly!

HOLMES: Then, unless you have an encore in your repertoire, Watson, the Avondale is our next port-of-call.

(Music in. They're off — Shaw one way, Holmes and Watson the other, to —.)

Scene Six

The Avondale Gentlemen's Club in Piccadilly. Holmes and Watson enter the lounge where several young men are singing, reciting poetry and drinking each other's health, elegantly dressed, — albeit some of it rather askew, surrounding the leviathan Oscar Wilde. His odd long hair is wreathed with a laurel and he is standing with his arm draped over the shoulders of a slender young man, Bosie, whose blond curls frame the face of an angel. Subdued whispers of "Policemen" circulate. A halt in the merriment causes Bosie to turn and face Holmes and Watson. Music out.

BOSIE: Have the rules of this club drooped so low as to allow in policemen?

WILDE: Policemen? No, I think not, Bosie, by no means. There's nothing so unattractive on the planet as a policeman.

HOLMES: I am inclined to agree.

WILDE: Whenever people agree with me, I feel I must be wrong.

HOLMES: You must be Mr. Oscar Wilde. Allow me to introduce myself.

(Holmes hands Wilde his card.)

WILDE: *(Reading.)* "Mr. Sherlock Holmes, The World's Foremost Consulting Detective." And this must be Dr. Watson. Yes, it must; it positively must. Everyone in the Avondale Gentlemen's Club is hopelessly enthralled with the latest edition of the *Strand Magazine* and the chronicles of London's most — adventurous couple. Well, what is it you gentlemen wish?

HOLMES: To speak about Jonathan McCarthy.

WILDE: McCarthy? Has he dared, after all . . . ?

HOLMES: He has dared nothing, Mr. Wilde. Jonathan McCarthy lies dead in his flat this day, some hours after his rendezvous with you at the Cafe Royal.

WATSON: I think this interview might be better conducted in private.

WILDE: Yes, perhaps you're right. For murder we best go to the Derby room.

BOSIE: Will you be all right, Oscar?

WILDE: It's not me you have to worry about, Bosie. You lads carry on without me. "Once more unto the breach, dear friends."

(Wilde leads them into the adjacent room. As Holmes and Watson take seats, Wilde sits opposite and asks with mock seriousness.)

WILDE: I take it I am under suspicion in the matter? *(Wilde sniggers.)*

HOLMES: Dr. Watson and I do not represent the police. I follow my own methods and tell as much or as little as I choose. May we proceed?

WILDE: I never put off till tomorrow what I can possibly do — the day after.

HOLMES: Can you account for your whereabouts after your meeting with Jonathan McCarthy?

WILDE: Account for them?

HOLMES: For the purpose of an alibi.

WILDE: An alibi, I see. Yes, that's all right. I was with my solicitor, Mr. Humphreys. Tell me, how was it managed?

WATSON: Managed?

WILDE: The murder, my dear fellow, the murder! Was there incense burning? Did you find the footprints of a naked woman who had danced in his blood?

HOLMES: As you dance away from my questions, Mr. Wilde. What was the nature of your appointment with McCarthy yesterday?

(What follows is a kind of duel, as Wilde rises . . .)

WILDE: It is an old maxim of mine that some cause happiness wherever they go; others, like McCarthy, whenever they go.

HOLMES: It is an old maxim of *mine* that there is no practical joke here, we are investigating a serious crime.

WILDE: Quote: "Murder is always a mistake. One should never do anything that one cannot talk about after dinner."

HOLMES: Quote: "There is the scarlet thread of murder running through the colorless skein of life."

WILDE: "Society often forgives the criminal, it never forgives the dreamer!"

HOLMES: "Like most criminals, he is too confident in his own cleverness and imagines that he has completely deceived us."

WILDE: "True friends stab you in the front."

HOLMES: "Danger is part of my trade."

WILDE: "Work is the curse of the drinking class."

HOLMES: "It is cocaine, a seven-percent solution, care to try it?"

WILDE: "The truth is rarely pure and never simple."

HOLMES: "Any truth is better than indefinite doubt."

WILDE: "To live is the rarest thing in the world. Most people exist, that is all."

HOLMES: "I abhor the dull routine of existence. That is why I have created my own particular profession."

WILDE: "Man can believe the impossible but never the improbable."

HOLMES: "When you have eliminated the impossible, whatever remains —"

WILDE: "However improbable!"

HOLMES AND WILDE: "Must be the truth!"

WATSON: *(Jumping in.)* Gentlemen, I declare a draw. You may sheathe your fingers.

(Holmes and Wilde retreat to their corners.)

HOLMES: Mr. Wilde.

WILDE: Mr. Holmes. You asked about the nature of my appointment with McCarthy. You did not know him, did you? How can I explain to you what the man was? Were you acquainted with Charles Augustus Milverton?

WATSON: *(Looks sharply at Holmes.)* The "King of the Blackmailers"?

HOLMES: Our paths crossed before his mysterious demise.

WILDE: That look must be one of a multitude of secrets shared between you roommates. Let's just say Jonathan McCarthy pursued a similar line of country.

WATSON: He was engaged in blackmail?

WILDE: Up to the neck, my dear John. It is John, isn't it? Up to the very neck. He did not prey upon society but rather upon us denizens of the theater.

HOLMES: Was McCarthy threatening you with a letter?

WILDE: With several. He heard about the business at my club.

(There is a pause.)

HOLMES: You will have to speak more plainly, I'm afraid.

WILDE: But you've heard! Surely you've heard! It must be across all of London by now!

HOLMES: Everywhere but Baker Street.

WILDE: February the fourteenth, St. Valentine's Day, was the opening night of a new play by our greatest living playwright.

WATSON: You?

WILDE: Guilty. At that opening night the Marquess of Queensbury, the father of the divine Bosie, was frustrated in his attempt to leave me the dubious gift of a bouquet of rotten fruit, undoubtedly spoilt by his own peculiar Midas touch. However, yesterday the Marquess was successful in leaving a card for me at my club. I do not propose to tell you the words the barbarian wrote on that card — beside the fact that he misspelled them — only that having read them, I swore out a complaint against him for criminal libel.

HOLMES: Mr. Wilde, your candor is admirable. What else can you reveal?

WILDE: I am the repository of a great many secrets myself, concerning affairs and excursions in the West End. Theater people are so colorful, don't you find? I know, for example, that George Grossmith, who does the patter songs for Gilbert and Sullivan — he played me, you know! — has been taking drugs. I know that Bram Stoker keeps a flat in Soho, the existence of which neither his wife nor Henry Irving is aware. My intuition tells me it isn't to play chess.

(Wilde begins chewing his fingernails.)

HOLMES: But what of McCarthy's secrets? It's an easy deduction that you had parity with the blackmailer. What did you have on him?

WILDE: He was keeping a mistress. Her name is Jessie Rutland and she is an ingenue at the Savoy. For McCarthy, a prig who paraded himself as a man of high moral virtue, disclosure of this tawdry affair would mean instant ruin. After I informed him I was aware of this liaison, we very shortly discovered that we had nothing more to say to one another. A sordid story, I fear, but mine own.

WATSON: You are a font of information.

WILDE: A little flattery is a dangerous thing, and a great deal of it is absolutely fatal.

WATSON: Is that yours?

WILDE: Not yet, John, but it will be.

HOLMES: Thank you for your time, Mr. Oscar Wilde. Since you have been so forthcoming, I have a small divulgence of my own. You are eliminated as a suspect. The only violent act you are capable of is a cutting remark.

WILDE: Touché.

(Wilde shows the two men out.)

Scene Seven

Outside the Savoy Theatre. Shaw rushes toward the two men.

SHAW: Holmes! There you are! Tell me what has happened. Did you speak to Wilde?

HOLMES: He regaled us with exhaustive theatrical gossip.

WATSON: And considerable talk of his favorite subject.

SHAW: Yes, Oscar Wilde! Geniuses are always talking about themselves. Was my name mentioned?

HOLMES: It was not.

WATSON: Strangest by far was a story of the Marquess of Queensberry and some rotten fruit.

SHAW: *(Nervously chewing his fingernails.)* The Marquess? Quickly — what did he say?

WATSON: That Wilde had sworn out a complaint against the Marquess for criminal libel.

SHAW: *(Abruptly starting to leave.)* The fool! This shall be his undoing!

WATSON: Shaw?

SHAW: *(Running away.)* His eternal curse!

WATSON: Shaw? Where are you bound? What in the world is going on?

HOLMES: Watson, our adventures have been far ranging and various, covering a vast spectrum of man's misdeeds. We have investigated supernatural happenings on the moors, we have traipsed through Limehouse opium dens in pursuit of nefarious riffraff, we have engaged the seedy underworld of London's worst criminals, but nothing, *nothing* in our adventures has prepared us for the bizarre world into which we have descended — show business! Let us go inside the Savoy Theatre and endeavor to find out. *(Holmes and Watson enter the stage door and approach the Doorman who is reading the latest edition of the* Strand Magazine *and wears a deerstalker cap and Inverness cape.)*

WATSON: Good afternoon. We are —

DOORMAN: Oh, no need to say your names. You're Sherlock Holmes and you're Dr. Watson!

WATSON: Quite so.

DOORMAN: *(To Watson.)* You probably don't remember me — Herbert? We met outside of Simpson's last November? I told you that I was your biggest fan, said that I am something of a writer myself, and mentioned that you were much taller in person.

HOLMES: The moment is indelibly etched.

HERBERT: Really! Well, what brings you gentlemen to the Savoy?

WATSON: We are here, Herbert, to see Gilbert and Sullivan.

HERBERT: *(Chewing his fingernails.)* Sir Arthur's not here and Mr. G is leading the rehearsal. You'd best speak to their manager, Mr. Richard D'Oyly Carte. *(He goes off, calling —.)* MR. CARTE!

HOLMES: Before your grin grows any wider, Watson, you would do well to note how short a trip it is from "fan" to "fanatic."

CARTE: *(Entering with Herbert.)* Herbert, you know the press is not permitted here before opening night. There's a rehearsal in progress: I must ask you to leave.

HERBERT: *(Excited.)* Ha-ha! They're not newspaper writers! Well, he's a writer, of course, though for no mere newspaper. Look at my hat! This is Mr. Sherlock Holmes.

CARTE: *(Recognizing the two men.)* Sherlock Holmes! And you must be Dr. Watson!

(Watson nods. Holmes rolls his eyes.)

CARTE: But this is capital. Capital! I have in my office the latest edition of the *Strand Magazine. (Conspiratorially.)* Is the *game afoot?*

HOLMES: It has led us to the Savoy.

CARTE AND HERBERT: The Savoy is honored.

CARTE: Ehm, Herbert, would you be so kind as to excuse us? These gentlemen have a few questions that are, I believe the proper phrase is "for my ears alone."

(Carte shows Herbert the door.)

HERBERT: Righto, sir. Say, Mr. H., Dr. W., I have a story idea you might find engaging about a time-traveling detective. I'll stop by!

CARTE: *(Closing the door.)* He's a "temp."

HOLMES AND WATSON: Ahh.

CARTE: Now then, Mr. Gilbert has been at the actors all day rehearsing and spirits may be a trifle under just now, but you are welcome, nonetheless.

WATSON: What is the name of the piece?

CARTE: *(After a beat, gloomily.)* The Grand Duke.

HOLMES: I believe there is a young woman attached to the company by the name of Jessie Rutland?

CARTE: *(Chewing his nails.)* Why d'ye want to know? Is she in any difficulty?

HOLMES: The difficulty is none of hers, but she must respond to some questions.

CARTE: Must?

HOLMES: Either to me or the police, quite possibly to both.

CARTE: I could ask for nothing more — a scandal! There has never been a breath of scandal at the Savoy. Sir Arthur hand picks the singers and their conduct is beyond reproach. Mr. Gilbert sees to that.

WATSON: Would you consider the use of drugs by George Grossmith to be conduct beyond reproach?

CARTE: Wherever did you hear such a thing?

HOLMES: No matter where, the story will go no further than it has. May we speak with Miss Rutland now?

CARTE: Let's see if we can find her on the stage.

(They go. From the stage voices are being raised. George Grossmith sings "A Pattern to Professors of Monarchical Autonomy" from The Grand Duke accompanied by Francois Cellier. W. S. Gilbert is watching from the house.)

GILBERT: Once more, Mr. Grossmith. Cellier!

GROSSMITH: A pattern to professors of monarchical autonomy,

> I don't indulge in levity or compromising bonhomie,
>
> But dignified formality, consistent with economy,
>
> Above all other virtues I par-ticularly prize.
>
> I never join in merriment —

GILBERT: *(Cutting Grossmith and Cellier off.)* No, no, no, Mr. Grossmith! It is still too fast, *too* fast!

GROSSMITH: *(Chewing his nails.)* This is the tempo we set in rehearsal.

GILBERT: Cellier!

CELLIER: I must insist, Mr. Gilbert. This is the proper tempo.

GILBERT: If the words cannot be distinguished then the tempo is incorrect.

CELLIER: I am a man, not a metronome!

GILBERT: Sadly, I can only admonish the former and regret the latter.

CELLIER: I'll not be talked to in this manner. Sir Arthur —

GILBERT: — *Sir* Arthur is not here at the moment, as you have quite possibly divined. Sir Arthur is either at cards with some of his titled friends or else at the Lyceum wasting his talents on incidental music for Irving's revival of *Macbeth.*

(Grossmith gasps.)

GILBERT: I suppose it would be too much to ask *Sir* Arthur for the overture to our piece, or even to coach the singers once or twice before opening night!

CARTE: *(Appearing in a theater box with Holmes and Watson, shouting to Gilbert on the stage.)* Gilbert, my dear, let's halt for supper. *(Adopting a cheerful timbre.)* Ladies and gentlemen, let us forbear and renew our energies over supper. We open within thirty-six hours, and we must all sustain our strength. *(Muttering.)* Played out.

HOLMES: Which is Miss Rutland?

CARTE: Strange, I don't see her, she must be —

(An unearthly wail permeates the air.)

HOLMES: Miss Rutland! Come on, Watson! *(Music in. Holmes rushes down the aisle.)* The dressing rooms are downstairs?

CARTE: *(Following behind Holmes and Watson.)* Women, stage left, men, stage right. *(This sequence is created choreographically. Music: Danse Macabre. Holmes dashes across the footlights and into the wings as Watson and Carte follow.*

Backstage, they plunge into a labyrinthine mass of theatrical apparatus that obstructs their path to the dressing rooms below. Behind them they can hear the pounding feet of the Savoyards, hurrying in their wake. A series of doors lead to the ladies' dressing quarters. Holmes flings them open in rapid succession, stopping abruptly at the fifth door.)

HOLMES: Keep them out, Watson.

(Holmes closes the door behind him. Savoyards are babbling questions. Suddenly into their midst strides Gilbert.)

GILBERT: What is happening here?

WATSON: Sherlock Holmes is endeavoring to find out, Mr. Gilbert.

GILBERT: Sherlock Holmes? The detective? And are you —?

WATSON: Correct. I am Dr. Watson. The woman who screamed, I take it, was Miss Rutland.

GILBERT: Miss Rutland was not at my rehearsal — something about a sore throat.

WATSON: Do you know Miss Rutland well, sir?

GILBERT: *(Automatically, preoccupied.)* Know her? Not really. She is in the chorus, and I do not engage the chorus.

(He turns to speak to the Savoyards.)

Here everybody! Go and have your supper. We shall continue after supper with Act One from the sausage-roll number. Go on and eat my dears; there's nothing of consequence that need detain you here, and you must keep up your strength!

(Savoyards disperse on cue. Carte enters hurriedly with another man who carries a black medical bag.)

CARTE: *(Rushing towards Watson.)* Dr. Watson, this is Dr. Benjamin Eccles, the doctor who is on call at the Savoy.

ECCLES: I make the rounds of several theaters in the district when on call and I'd just stepped into the stalls to see how the rehearsal was getting on. Mr. Carte saw me and summoned me downstairs. He seemed to think I might be needed.

(Behind them, the door opens, Holmes appears.)

WATSON: Holmes, this is Dr. Eccles, the house physician.

HOLMES: *(Nods curtly.)* Miss Rutland is dead. Mr. Gilbert and Mr. D'Oyly Carte, I must ask that you remain beyond the threshold. Watson, you and Dr. Eccles may come in. It isn't a pretty sight.

(Eccles coughs once and sets about his examination. Gilbert and Carte stay in the hallway.)

ECCLES: Her throat has been severed quite cleanly and her blood is still — is still —

(Holmes whispers something to Watson.)

WATSON: Is there pronounced rigidity in her neck and abdomen?

ECCLES: Yes. Can rigor have set in so quickly?

GILBERT: *(Chewing his fingernails.)* Death, scandal, ruin!

CARTE: But why, her? Who would do such a thing?

ECCLES: *(Looking about the small room.)* I don't see a weapon.

HOLMES: That is because it is not here.

CARTE: We should cancel the performance.

GILBERT: We can't. You know we can't.

CARTE: It wouldn't be the first time the playhouses were closed.

HOLMES: There is nothing further for us here, Watson

> *(Holmes resumes his jacket and ulster and goes into the hallway, followed by Watson and Eccles.)*

HOLMES: Gentleman, there has been a murder done and all must remain as it is until viewed by the authorities.

> *(Carte rushes forward.)*

CARTE: You can't go! You mustn't! You know what this is about! I insist that you tell me. What questions were you going to put to the girl?

HOLMES: You may refer the police to our lodgings at 221B Baker Street. Come, Watson. *(He goes.)*

WATSON: *(Stopping Eccles.)* You look a little shaken, Doctor. Are you all right?

ECCLES: Yes, I think so . . .

> *(They depart.)*

WATSON: Poor man. He must be more accustomed to sore throats than to cut ones.

> *(As they approach the stage door, a Man appears out of the backstage gloom.)*

MAN: 'Ere, what's all the bloody screaming, then? One of them actress women spot one a' me lovelies?

HOLMES: One of your what?

MAN: *Me rats, guv'nuh. (He holds up his prize — a squirming, teeming burlap bag filled with very much alive rats.)* I be Shropshire, the rat catcher.

WATSON: Filthy, disease-ridden things!

SHROPSHIRE: *(Chewing his nails.)* Hang on here, say, I think I know who you are. You're Sir 'igh 'n Mighty and you're Lord Toffee-Nose. Let me tell you, ain't a fing wrong with these rats, and I takes umbrage at your casting aspersions. So there's the door and quicks your steppin'. Be off, the *pair* of you, before I put my boot to your bums!

> *(They exit through the stage door, into —.)*

Scene Eight

An alley, outside the Savoy, near a kiosk.

WATSON: What an odious little man.

HOLMES: The case begins to assume a familiar shape.

WATSON: Which shape is that? I am utterly at a loss, I confess.

(Two Theatergoers approach from the opposite direction.)

HOLMES: A triangle, if I am not mistaken.

(The frigid wind hits Watson and he stumbles. The Two Theatergoers are amused.)

MALE THEATERGOER: He's well behind the cork!

HOLMES: *(Noticing Watson.)* Watson?

MALE THEATERGOER: "Celebrities."

FEMALE THEATERGOER: Come along.

(The Theatergoers exit.)

HOLMES: Are you unwell?

WATSON: No — a bit queasy. Must be all this talk of rats. A triangle, you say?

HOLMES: Yes, I shall be greatly astonished if it does not prove to be the old story of a jealous lover, discarded by his mistress in favor of another; possibly a more powerful one.

WATSON: It must be a very peculiar triangle if it includes so depraved an angle as McCarthy. Are you asking me to believe that sweet-faced young woman took up with a man of his stamp? My mind rejects the whole idea.

HOLMES: I ask your mind to remain open a little longer, Watson, for she did take up with him. At least the evidence points in that direction.

WATSON: What evidence?

(Watson sways a bit.)

HOLMES: Why not fan yourself with your beloved *Strand Magazine,* perhaps it will prove useful after all.

(Watson does so.)

HOLMES: I confess to feeling slightly hazy myself. To answer your question, Oscar Wilde's evidence. If his information about Grossmith's recourse to drugs elicited the response it did from D'Oyly Carte, we may, I think, grant its accuracy. And what, Watson, have you to offer in rebuttal for your Miss Rutland — her sweet-faced appearance? Really, Watson, what romantic nonsense when her very actions belie any supposed propriety. No, indications are that she lit both ends of the candle to enjoy a fiercer heat and to her lasting surprise got burned. That she was McCarthy's mistress, I will credit on the basis of the evidence so far; what her motives were for being, I will learn.

WATSON: From whom?

HOLMES: That will depend on Arthur Sullivan. He hired her; it is to him I shall turn for a better portrait. *(Holmes notices Watson's interest is elsewhere.)* What is it, man?

WATSON: You've written in my *Strand Magazine*. Really, Holmes, this is most irritating —

HOLMES: I've done no such thing, Watson. What are you on about?

WATSON: Stop a moment, this isn't my magazine. I must have picked up the wrong one at McCarthy's.

HOLMES: *(Grabbing the magazine, he reads —.)* "Jack Point, Regent Street?" Who is Jack Point?

WATSON: *(Excitedly.)* Another Gilbert and Sullivan character, a jester who loses his love to a highborn lord in *Yeoman of the Guard*.

HOLMES: Ah. Jack Point is our man, no doubt. You see, Watson? We are dealing with that geometrical configuration I postulated some minutes ago. *(Watson slumps.)*

HOLMES: My dear fellow, you're not truly ill? You do feel quite warm, but then so do I. It appears we've both caught something.

WATSON: I'll be myself in a little.

HOLMES: You're quite sure?

WATSON: Quite so.

(Watson collapses. Music in. Holmes tries to call for help, loses his balance, and slumps onto the kiosk. Out of the shadows, Holmes is seized from behind by a powerful pair of arms. One of the gloved hands reaches around and holds his nose while the other brings a vial of liquid to his lips and forces them open. He drinks. As the lights dim on Holmes, four Players appear, swirled in dry ice. They move in towards Watson and circle around him as he stirs.)

PLAYER/SHAW: There has been a murder done.

PLAYER/CARTE: McCarthy's mistress is Jessie Rutland.

PLAYER/GILBERT: Jessie Rutland? Is she in some scandal again?

PLAYER/WILDE: My Jessie was not at rehearsal.

PLAYER/CARTE: She lit both ends of the candle.

PLAYER/WILDE: That sweet-faced young woman is seeking a fiercer heat.

PLAYER/GILBERT: Do you *know* Miss Rutland well?

PLAYER/SHAW: Not one, but *two* men!

ALL FOUR PLAYERS: *(Overlapping as they disappear.)* Miss Rutland — Miss Jessie Rutland — Miss Rutland — Jessie Rutland —

(A Woman appears across the stage. it is Jessie Rutland. She sings "Love Is a Plaintive Song" from Patience.*)*

JESSIE: Love is a plaintive song, sung by a suffering maid,

    Telling a tale of wrong, telling of hope betrayed;

    Tuned to each changing note, sorry when he is sad,

    Blind to his every mote, merry when he is glad!

    Merry when he is glad!

    Love that no wrong can cure,

    Love that is always new,

    That is the love that's pure,

    That is the love that's true!

    (During the song, Watson moves toward Jessie. She turns and moves seductively towards him. He responds, reaching his arms to her.)

WATSON: Miss Rutland. Jessie. O! My dearest!

    (They embrace. Music swells. Blackout.)

END OF ACT I

ACT II
Scene One

In the blackness we hear Jessie singing "Love is a Plaintive Song."

JESSIE: Rendering good for ill, smiling at every frown,
    Yielding your own self will, laughing your teardrops down,
    Never a selfish whim, trouble, or pain to stir;
    Everything for him, nothing at all for her!
    Nothing at all for her!
    Love that no wrong can cure . . .

WATSON: O! My dearest!

HOLMES: Watson!

(The lights abruptly come up. Watson is grabbing Holmes in a passionate embrace. They are at 221B Baker Street and Watson is evidently coming out of a feverish dream. The music stops just as abruptly.)

WATSON: Holmes!

HOLMES: It is safe assume that your fever has finally broken?

WATSON: Holmes, I, uh . . . yes!

HOLMES: Don't worry, old friend, I'll not speak of this. But, I would suggest that for the time being you avoid Oscar Wilde and the Avondale Gentlemen's Club.

WATSON: I'm bewildered by the evening's events. The last thing I recall we were discussing Jack Point outside the Savoy Theatre. What happened next?

HOLMES: Well, after you collapsed, gloved hands reached 'round and held my nose —

WATSON: *(Remembering.)* — So that I could not breathe save through my mouth —

HOLMES: — And brought a vial of liquid to my lips.

WATSON: It was either drink or suffocate.

HOLMES: And I drank. It tasted bitter and —

WATSON: — Was faintly charged with alcohol.

HOLMES: I have known parents who cozened reluctant children into swallowing medicine in that fashion. Eventually, two constables on their rounds spied us, and ascertaining that I could not describe our attacker, put us in a cab bound for Baker Street. At any rate, It doesn't seem to have caused us any real harm.

WATSON: Rather the reverse. But why were we attacked? Are we getting too close?

HOLMES: Ah, but too close to whom, Watson, that's the question. McCarthy led us to Bunthorne who in turn led to Gilbert and the Savoy and that led to another corpse and finally, Jack Point. We must find the other side of our triangle.

WATSON: And does this lead us to Arthur Sullivan?

HOLMES: Indeed it does, I'm — Hullo. Whom have we here? Come in, Shaw.

(Shaw opens the door revealing a letter stabbed into the door by a dagger.)

SHAW: *(Sheepishly.)* I believe this is for you.

(Holmes grabs the letter, walks over to the window, and holds it up to the sunlight.)

HOLMES: Hmm. No postmark, of course — hand-delivered. Shaw, you didn't see anyone? No, of course you didn't. Address — typewritten on a Remington in need of a new ribbon. Paper . . . hmm. Paper is Indian — yes, definite watermark — no visible fingerprints —

WATSON: Holmes, for once would you just read it?

HOLMES: Very well. *(Handing the dagger to Watson, Holmes opens the letter.)* Liverpool Daily Mail, Morning Courant, London Times and The Saturday Review if I am not mistaken.

WATSON: Mistaken about what?

HOLMES: The different sources for the cuttings. Here.

(Holmes passes the paper to Watson who reads the page.)

WATSON: "As you value your lives stay out of the West End."

HOLMES: Still game, Watson?

SHAW: Perhaps I best be going.

HOLMES: Hush, Shaw.

WATSON: 'Til the very last, Holmes. No anonymous coward will dissuade us from our course.

HOLMES: Capital. Then let us press on to Sir Arthur Sullivan and the Lyceum Theatre, a place I know you have avoided these past several years but which I must now implore you to revisit.

WATSON: *(Stiffly.)* If you'll excuse me for a moment.

(Watson goes into his room.)

SHAW: Why does he avoid the Lyceum?

HOLMES: On the case to which you alluded earlier, he met his late wife there, Mary Morstan.

SHAW: I didn't realize. How long has it been since she passed on?

HOLMES: Three years. You need not mention this, as it would serve only to embarrass him.

(Watson returns.)

WATSON: Gentlemen. Shall we go?

SHAW: I'm afraid you must go on without me, for I *am* persona non grata in the eyes of Henry Irving and am barred at present by threat of physical force.

WATSON: Really? What a surprise.

HOLMES: You're welcome to wait here until our return. Come, Watson, to the West End and the Lyceum Theatre.

(Holmes and Watson leave Baker Street. Music: Sullivan's Macbeth.*)*

Scene Two

The shuttered windows of the Lyceum Theatre box office bang open. A dark, bearded Man with a pinched, aquiline nose and expressionless black eyes sits behind a set of bars like a teller's window.

THE MAN: *(In a deep voice.)* May I help you?

HOLMES: We are looking for Sir Arthur Sullivan. Might he be here this morning?

THE MAN: Who wants to know?

HOLMES: Mr. Sherlock Holmes.

THE MAN: Sherlock Holmes? And this must be the writer, Dr. Watson. Sir Arthur is onstage with Sir Henry working on music. *(Without warmth.)* May I help you with something?

HOLMES: You may help me to Sir Arthur.

THE MAN: *(Appraising Holmes.)* Thought you'd be taller.

(The Man bangs the shutters closed and disappears.)

WATSON: What a singular personage. I declare, Holmes, there doesn't seem to be a sane individual connected with this profession.

HOLMES: There was a time when decent hotels wouldn't put them up, and it used to be a commonplace to observe that an actor shot President Lincoln. But wait, did that man say *Sir* Henry? Surely not, no actor has ever been knighted. Perish the thought.

(A Woman dances into the foyer.)

WOMAN: Good morning! Tickets for Shakespeare's Scottish tragedy do not go on sale before noon — though you are quite right to get here early; they've been going like hot cakes all week!

WATSON: Have we the honor of addressing Ellen Terry?

MISS TERRY: *(Offering her hand to Watson.)* Wait a moment. I've seen your likenesses in the *Strand Magazine,* haven't I? Is the game afoot?

WATSON: Yes!

MISS TERRY: How delicious!

HOLMES: There was a dark-haired, bearded gentleman here a moment ago. I believe he has gone upon my errand.

MISS TERRY: Oh, you've met Mama. And may I presume that you're here to see the Crab?

HOLMES: The Crab?

MISS TERRY: You must forgive my penchant for nicknames. The Crab says I'm quite incorrigible.

HOLMES: Irving, I take it, is the Crab?

MISS TERRY: Oh, but you mustn't say I said so. Henry's terribly sensitive about the way he walks.

(Miss Terry mischievously does a bit of the Crab's walk.)

HOLMES: And Mama?

MISS TERRY: Mr. Stoker, our stage manager and general secretary — he's so very protective of us that I call him Mama. May I ask, what is your business with Mama and the Crab?

WATSON: Our business is with Sir Arthur Sullivan, not with Sir Henry.

MISS TERRY: Oh! You mustn't call him Sir Henry yet! It's another two months until Queen Victoria lays sword to shoulder. Oh, think of it! The first from our profession! Of course Mama already calls him "sir" — he's so fond of titles — but it drives Henry quite wild. I know it's ridiculous but *some* thespians are *so* superstitious.

WATSON: And how goes *Macbeth?*

MISS TERRY: *(Screams loudly.)* EEK! Oh no! You said it! Quickly, you must perform the antidote. First, turn round three times . . . one . . . hurry . . . two . . . three! Now say something awful. Say —

(Miss Terry whispers in Watson's ear.)

WATSON: Bollocks?

MISS TERRY: Good. Now, spit!

(Watson spits. Miss Terry is relieved.)

MISS TERRY: Thank you! Dear, dear, Dr. Watson, one must never say . . . that name . . . whilst inside a theater. Or ever, for that matter. It's cursed you know! But yes, we are attempting to recall what we did last time. Revivals are so trying.

(Stoker reappears suddenly, banging the doors open.)

MISS TERRY: Oh!

WATSON: Must he do that?

MISS TERRY: You startled us, Bram!

STOKER: I beg your pardon. *(Coldly, to Holmes.)* Sir Arthur will see you now.

MISS TERRY: Thank you, Bram. I'll take them.

STOKER: They're on stage, Ellen.

(Stoker skulks away.)

MISS TERRY: Dear Mama.

HOLMES: It seems to me I have met Mr. Stoker before. Does he live in Soho?

MISS TERRY: Hush! Oh, please, you mustn't mention anything of the kind in there. It was such a sore point when it happened for the first time! I don't know that Henry's ever forgiven him for it, and that was years ago.

(Miss Terry begins chewing her fingernails.)

WATSON: Whatever do you mean?

MISS TERRY: *(With a finger to Watson's lips.)* Hush, I beg you, Dr. Watson, Mr. Holmes!

(Miss Terry pulls a curtain and gestures for Holmes and Watson to follow her.)

Scene Three

On stage. All around are Carpenters hammering, sawing, and yelling instructions to each other.

IRVING: *(In an odd-sounding, deep nasal voice.)* No, no, no, my dear chap! As music, it may be all very well, but it's not right for our purpose at all. Listen! I *see* the daggers, and I want them *heard* by the audience.

SULLIVAN: *(In a high-pitched voice.)* But, Henry, what do daggers sound like?

IRVING: What do they sound like? They sound like —

(Irving produces the queerest succession of grunts and growls, alternately sounding like squeaks and a beehive.)

SULLIVAN: Oh, yes, yes! I see what you mean! That's much better! Yes, I think I can do that.

IRVING: Good.

(Miss Terry enters with Holmes and Watson.)

MISS TERRY: I'm sorry to disturb you, my dears, but here are the two gentlemen who wish to see Sir Arthur. Mr. Holmes, Dr. Watson, may I present Sir Arthur Sullivan and Sir- ehm — Mr. Henry Irving.

(Irving courteously bows.)

IRVING: Gentleman, we are sorry to have kept you waiting.

HOLMES: This won't take long. I've just a few questions regarding the matter at the Savoy.

SULLIVAN: I have been with the police most of the morning. I don't know what I can say to you that I haven't told them.

(Sullivan suddenly gasps and clutches spasmodically at his side. Irving catches him as he stumbles and lowers him into a chair brought down by a Carpenter.)

IRVING: *(Calling to the Carpenters.)* Tea break! Kindly clear the stage.

SULLIVAN: Thank you. May I ask at whose behest you come to see me?

WATSON: We are here at the behest of justice.

HOLMES: More prosaically, we were asked to look into the matter by Mr. Bernard Shaw.

IRVING: *(Straightening up.)* Shaw? *(He darts a glance at Miss Terry.)* Nellie, is this any of your doing?

MISS TERRY: Dearest, I give you my word I know nothing about it. I met these gentlemen only moments ago in the lobby.

(Irving advances on Miss Terry, thrusting his right shoulder forward, fulfilling Miss Terry's pet name for him.)

IRVING: I give you warning, Nellie — I give you fair warning. I will not have that — that *vegetarian* in this theater —

MISS TERRY: Henry, please —

IRVING: — I will not have him in this theater, and I will not produce his revolting plays. And if he publishes any more drivel about Shakespeare — Or the way we do things here, I will thrash him personally.

(Irving begins chewing his fingernails.)

MISS TERRY: Henry, come along and let's leave these gentlemen to their business.

IRVING: *(Bowing to Holmes and Watson.)* I apologize for my outburst, gentlemen. I know I am sometimes carried away whilst bearing the standard for "the theater" against the vanguard of "the new," championed by the likes of Ibsen and Shaw. *(Irving exits, dramatically.)* Tales told by idiots and signifying nothing, which I shall fight till the last syllable of recorded time. Good day.

(Miss Terry starts off after him, then sweeps back.)

MISS TERRY: Mr. Holmes and dear, dear Dr. Watson, please don't let's say good-bye, for strangers we were, yet are no longer. I hope that from time to time I shall enter your thoughts in a memorable way. And as for me, well, sufficeth to say I eagerly await your next adventure with flushed anticipation. Adieu!

(Miss Terry exits.)

SULLIVAN: Why is Bernard Shaw meddling in this?

HOLMES: He did not engage us specifically in the matter of Miss Rutland but rather in connection with the murder of Jonathan McCarthy.

SULLIVAN: McCarthy was a parasite, preying upon art and artists.

HOLMES: Were you aware, Sir Arthur, that Jessie Rutland was Jonathan McCarthy's mistress?

SULLIVAN: That's impossi —

(Sullivan starts to rise, gives another gasp, and falls back in his chair, doubling over and clutching at his side.)

WATSON: *(Rushing forward.)* You are too ill to continue this interview.

SULLIVAN: *(Sitting up slowly.)* Ill? I am dying. These kidney stones are working their way with me; I work to forget it. Go on.

HOLMES: You violently resist the idea of Jonathan McCarthy as Jessie Rutland's lover. It's not merely because you despise the man. You know better, don't you?

SULLIVAN: *(Chewing his fingernails.)* I am afraid I am not at liberty to say.

HOLMES: *(Emphatically.)* Jessie Rutland is dead; we cannot restore her life. But there is one thing we can do, and that is to bring her murderer to the dock.

SULLIVAN: *(After a long moment.)* Very well. What do you want to know?

HOLMES: Tell us about Jack Point.

SULLIVAN: Pardon me?

HOLMES: McCarthy made a practise of substituting characters from your operas for proper names of people, and had an appointment on the night of his death with "Jack Point." Point is a hapless jester who loses his love, is he not?

SULLIVAN: He is! He is! So you think Jessie had a second lover?

HOLMES: You've as good as told me she had, Sir Arthur.

SULLIVAN: I engaged Jessie Rutland three years ago and never had any cause to regret my decision. She was an orphan who had sung in church choirs. Gaining a position at the Savoy meant everything to her.

(Sullivan gasps — another seeming attack.)

HOLMES: Go on.

SULLIVAN: She was very pretty with a lovely soprano — a little coarse in the middle range, but that would have improved with time and practise. Several weeks ago, Jessie approached me after rehearsal. She was clearly distraught. My first impulse was to refer her to Gilbert —

(Music: "Love is a Plaintive Song." Jessie Rutland appears.)

JESSIE: If I confide in Mr. Gilbert, I am lost! I will lose my place, and he will be harmed as well!

SULLIVAN: Tell me; tell me what has upset you.

JESSIE: Recently I made the acquaintance of a gentleman to whom I have become most attached. He is quite perfect in every way, and his behavior toward myself has never been less than proper. But, oh, Sir Arthur, he is so very perfect that even Mr. Gilbert must approve! I have fallen in love!

(Jessie begins to cry.)

SULLIVAN: But my dear, this is no cause for tears. You are to be congratulated! As for Mr. Gilbert, I give you my word of honor he will dance at your wedding!

(Jessie tries her best to conceal her tears by holding a small cambric handkerchief before her face.)

JESSIE: *(Sobbing.)* There can be no wedding, for he is already married.

(The music changes to a minor key.)

SULLIVAN: *(Outraged.)* If he has deceived you in this fashion, then he is utterly unworthy of your affections and you are well rid of him.

JESSIE: *(Regaining her composure.)* You don't understand. He has not deceived me as you mean. His wife is an invalid, confined to a nursing home in Bombay.

HOLMES: *(Opening his eyes, breaking in.)* One moment. *(Music stops.)* Did she say Bombay?

SULLIVAN: Yes.

HOLMES: Watson, make a note of that. Pray continue.

(Music resumes. Holmes closes his eyes.)

JESSIE: His wife can neither hear nor speak nor walk, as she was the victim of a stroke five years ago. Nevertheless, he is chained to her. He dared not tell me of his plight for fear of losing me. Yet when he saw the direction our affections were taking, he knew he must disclose the truth. And now, Sir Arthur, oh what should I do?

HOLMES: What did you advise?

SULLIVAN: I advised her to follow her heart.

(Jessie disappears. Music out. Sullivan turns to face Holmes.)

HOLMES: Did she say anything at all concerning her young man that would enable us to identify him?

SULLIVAN: She was most careful to avoid doing so.

HOLMES: And how much of all this did you tell the police this morning?

SULLIVAN: None, I fear.

HOLMES: Not a word?

WATSON: The woman cannot now be compromised, surely.

SULLIVAN: But I, I can be compromised. And your visit here clearly underscores that likelihood. I swore to Jessie I would not reveal her secret to Gilbert but warned her that I could not shield her from the consequences should —

HOLMES: Should Gilbert learn of her intrigue from another source.

SULLIVAN: Exactly! And you see, as successful as I may seem, I need Gilbert. Our talents are entangled to the point where I can no longer discern where he begins and I end. However, that is for history to decide, Mr. Holmes. but I hope you won't judge this old fool too harshly.

HOLMES: Don't worry, Sir Arthur, I always leave indiscretions and judgments to others. I thank you for your time.

(Stoker appears.)

STOKER: If you gentlemen will follow me, I'll show you to the door.

(They walk in eerie silence. Holmes opens the door as Stoker exits.)

HOLMES: *(To Watson.)* Did you observe his boots?

(As Holmes closes the door, they are in —.)

Scene Four

221B Baker Street. Shaw is in the room reading one of Watson's manuscripts.

SHAW: *(Looking up — caught red-handed.)* Whose boots?

WATSON: *(Snatching the manuscript away from Shaw.)* Bram Stoker's boots. And I'll thank you not to go snooping about in my manuscript or I'll introduce you to *my* boots.

SHAW: Beggin' your pardon. What did you learn at the Lyceum?

HOLMES: What do you know of Bram Stoker?

SHAW: He's an odd one, all right. His name isn't Bram, of course. It's Abraham.

HOLMES: What else?

SHAW: Born in Dublin, or thereabouts, I believe. He was athletic champion of Dublin University and has an older brother who is a prominent physician.

WATSON: Not Dr. William Stoker?

SHAW: The same.

HOLMES: What was Stoker's occupation before entering Irving's employ?

SHAW: "All roads lead to Rome." He was a drama critic.

WATSON: A critic?

SHAW: And aspiring author of the frustrated variety. Do you think *he* killed McCarthy?

HOLMES: That remains to be seen.

WATSON: Do you think he killed Jessie Rutland?

SHAW: Jessie Rutland?

HOLMES: Yes, there's been a second murder.

(Ominous chord.)

SHAW: Was she . . . was she . . .

(Shaw swallows hard and makes vigorous stabbing motions.)

HOLMES: The same hand committed both crimes.

WATSON: This may prove to be your bloodiest case since the Whitechapel Murders.

SHAW: *(Scoffing.)* What? But, Jack the Ripper was never caught!

HOLMES: Did the murders cease?

SHAW: Yes.

HOLMES: *(With a Cheshire cat grin.)* Ahhh.

SHAW: *(With great trepidation.)* What . . . will . . . you . . . do . . . now?

HOLMES: Smoke. It is quite a three-pipe problem. You're more than welcome to —

SHAW: *(Hurrying out.)* No thank you. I'd sooner risk black-lung disease from a Newcastle coal mine then breathe your noxious fumes.

(Shaw exits as Mrs. Hudson enters.)

SHAW: Mrs. Hudson

MRS. HUDSON Mr. Shaw. Mr. Holmes, Inspector Lestrade is here.

HOLMES: Very well, Mrs. Hudson, send him up.

(She goes.)

HOLMES: Am I to get no respite?

(A very cocksure Lestrade enters.)

LESTRADE: Solved any murders lately, Mr. Holmes?

HOLMES: Not lately.

LESTRADE: *(Crowing.)* Well, I have, a brace of them. I've solved the murders of Jonathan McCarthy and Miss Jessie Rutland.

(A cocky musical flourish.)

HOLMES: Indeed?

LESTRADE: You didn't know these crimes were related, did you? Well, they are. Miss Rutland was the mistress of the critic, they were both dispatched by the same hand, and I have him.

HOLMES: Really? And have you also solved why the murderer should smoke Indian cigars?

LESTRADE: Indian cigars? Still going on about that? Well, I'll explain it to you. He smoked Indian cigars because he's an Indian himself.

WATSON: What?

HOLMES: Amazing.

(Lestrade walks about the room, scarcely able to contain his self-satisfaction and glee.)

LESTRADE: That's right, a Hindu, a bloody wog. His name is Achmed Singh, and he's been in England just under a year, running a used-furniture and curio shop in the Tottenham Court Road.

HOLMES: Where did he meet Miss Rutland?

LESTRADE: His shop is just down the road from her boarding house.

HOLMES: May I ask what he was doing with tobacco if he is a Hindu?

LESTRADE: *(After a long pause, chewing his fingernails.)* What's he doing in England, you might as well ask! But if he came here to mingle with white folk, he'll 'ave taken to some of our ways, no doubt. Why, the fellow is even attending evening classes at the University of London.

HOLMES: Ah. A sure sign of a criminal mind.

LESTRADE: You can jeer. The point is — *(He places a forefinger on Holmes' chest.)* — the point is that the man cannot account for his time during the period when either murder took place. He had the time and he had the motive.

WATSON: What motive?

LESTRADE: Jealousy! Heathen passion! You can see that, surely, Doctor. She dropped him and took up with that critic chap —

HOLMES: Who invited him to his home, where the Hindu drank brandy.

LESTRADE: The glass was broken on the floor. Who knows if he drank a drop? He might have accepted the offer of a glass of brandy as part of his plan to gain admittance to the place.

HOLMES: He went there, of course, knowing a murder weapon of some sort was at the ready.

LESTRADE: I didn't say the plan was murder. He may simply have wanted to plead for the return of his white woman.

HOLMES: You seem quite certain of yourself, Lestrade.

LESTRADE: The Metropolitan Police have our share of solved cases, despite reports to the contrary in the *Strand Magazine.*

HOLMES: Then you would have no objection if I asked him a question or two?

LESTRADE: Suit yourself. Right this way.

(Holmes, Watson, and Lestrade move to outside the jail cell.)

LESTRADE: But before I leave you to your interview I must tell you something, Mr. Holmes.

HOLMES: What is it Lestrade?

LESTRADE: *(Bemused.)* Nothing very much, I grant you. The murderer is a man. He is right-handed and almost the proper height and nervously chews his fingernails. And his shoes, Mr. Holmes — *(Unable to contain his victory no longer.)* — His shoes are expensive new boots, three weeks old, oxblood in color and purchased at Harrods!

(Lestrade exits, beaming. Music in. Satie's Gnossienne, No. 1.)

Scene Five

A cell at Whitehall. Inside is Achmed Singh wearing the thickest spectacles. He reads the latest edition of the Strand Magazine, *held only an inch or so from his nose.*

HOLMES: Achmed Singh?

SINGH: Who is that?

HOLMES: I am Sherlock Holmes. This is Dr. Watson.

SINGH: Crickey! Am I sleeping? Have I drifted off carried on the back of dreams?

HOLMES: To my knowledge, no one has ever confused dreaming with a holding cell at Whitehall. We are here to help you.

(Music fades out.)

SINGH: Oh, there is no help for me. I cannot account for my time and had the impertinence to know Miss Rutland. Worse, my shoes are the right size and purchased in the wrong place. Finally, I am colored. "I am Death, the mighty destroyer of the world."

WATSON: That sounds familiar. Krishna?

SINGH: Yes. Lord Krishna.

WATSON: Ah yes.

SINGH: You're acquainted with the Bhagavad-Gita? The typical Englishman's knowledge of India runs to curry.

WATSON: And curry through him.

HOLMES: Thank you, Watson. Mr. Singh, may I ask what you are studying at University? Cigarette?

SINGH: Thank you, no, my religion denies me the consolations of tobacco and liquor.

HOLMES: *(Scarcely concealing a smirk.)* Pity.

SINGH: I study the law.

HOLMES: I see. I must ask you now to tell me what you know of this business.

SINGH: *(Chewing his fingernails.)* Nothing. I did not kill Jessie — Miss Rutland — and do not know who did.

HOLMES: Let us begin with Miss Rutland. How did you come to know her?

SINGH: I deal in curios from the East and she liked my shop. Slowly we began to converse. We were lonely, Mr. Holmes. Even in Great Britain, I don't believe that is, as yet, a crime.

HOLMES: Indeed, it is not. Go on.

SINGH: We began to go for walks. Only walks. We strolled and continued our discussions.

HOLMES: But in time your feelings altered.

SINGH: She was brave and pretended my color made no difference, and I was cowardly and pretended I was not losing my heart.

HOLMES: And then?

SINGH: And then we began to notice. The looks, the stares, the whispers. And soon after she —

(Singh hesitates.)

HOLMES: She met another man.

SINGH: *(Shaken.)* Yes. A white man. She did not know how to tell me, so I told her. I told her our being seen together was beginning to arouse comment in the neighborhood and I thought it better that such talk be stopped. I could see a great weight had been lifted from her shoulders. It was then that she told me about the man she had met. The white man.

HOLMES: What did she say about him?

SINGH: Only that she had met him and come to love him.

WATSON: What was it that told you she had met another?

SINGH: Her eyes, filled with the very thing that I now see in yours — pity.

WATSON: Not pity, Mr. Singh — kinship. As a medical man I can treat most every injury but that of a broken heart.

HOLMES: "Alas, the love of women! It is known to be a lovely and fearful thing."

(Watson and Singh look at Holmes with something approaching surprise.)

HOLMES: You have Lord Krishna, we, Lord Byron.

(A Policeman enters. Singh rises.)

HOLMES: Mr. Singh, this grievous matter stands against you for the time being, but do not despair. You have my oath that you shall never appear in the dock.

SINGH: I know from reading your chronicled adventures that you're accustomed to far more glamorous and profitable cases. Why should I matter to you?

HOLMES: If you have gleaned anything from those somewhat enthusiastic accounts, then you must know that at all costs, pursuit of the truth is my mantra. The truth of this case is that you are innocent.

(Holmes and Watson exit Whitehall.)

WATSON: I should be remiss, Holmes, if I wasn't to mention that I consider myself fortunate to be both your enthusiastic chronicler as well as your friend. I should also be remiss if I didn't point out that our astigmatic Hindu friend was reading the latest edition of the *Strand* —

HOLMES: And I should be remiss if I didn't state that this case starts to rankle me — a half-blind man who neither smokes nor drinks and hasn't the motive, the temperament, or the physical attributes to commit the crime. And this is what passes for Lestrade's triumph? Ludicrous! Very well, let us see if Mr. Singh's pluck is catching. Might you be up for some mischief, Watson?

WATSON: What do you propose?

(Holmes and Watson find themselves in front of —.)

Scene Six

No. 14 Porkpie Lane, Soho.

HOLMES: Number Fourteen Porkpie Lane, Soho.

WATSON: Bram Stoker's flat?

HOLMES: Yes. Here we are. Second story, in the middle. The window's dark, as you can see. It has a ledge beneath it.

WATSON: Are we to burgle it?

HOLMES: If you've no objection?

WATSON: None. I know all too well your fondness for breaking and entering.

HOLMES: It is always the cause that justifies little felonies such as these. Come along, Watson, I've brought my bulls-eye torch.

WATSON: *(Producing two black silk masks.)* Might these prove useful?

HOLMES: Hah! Our Milverton masks. I've always known that I had the makings of a first-class criminal, but you, Watson, how you do surprise me. *(Music in. They don the masks, enter Stoker's private sanctuary, and survey the small room. Music out.)*

WATSON: Not exactly suffused with romance.

HOLMES: Shabby and spare, although nonetheless neat.

WATSON: Scarcely a trysting place.

HOLMES: *(Going through the desk.)* Ah, Watson. Our Mr. Stoker's secret mistress is the muse of literature. But why all the subterfuge? Have a look at some of this.

WATSON: A series of letters, extracts of diaries, and personal notes.

HOLMES: Some sort of a novel.

WATSON: A novel? Surely not.

HOLMES: Yes, a novel, written in the form of letters and journals. Look at this. *(Watson takes the page and reads.)*

WATSON: "On the bed beside the window lay Jonathan Harker, his face flushed and breathing heavily, as though in a stupor . . ." *(Music: Beethoven's Pathetique Sonata, Opus 3. A Literary Figure appears. It is Jonathan Harker.)*

HARKER: — *Kneeling on the edge of the bed was the white clad figure of my wife; by her side stood the Count. His right hand gripped the back of her neck, forcing her face down on his bosom. Her white nightdress was smeared with blood, and a thin stream trickled down the man's bare chest. The two had a terrible resemblance to a child forcing a kitten's nose into a saucer of milk —*

WATSON: "— To compel it to drink." Great heavens! This is depraved!

HOLMES: *(Handing Watson another passage.)* And this. *(A Second Literary Figure appears. It is Count Dracula followed by a Third Literary Figure. It is Mina.)*

COUNT DRACULA: . . . *And you are now to me, flesh of my flesh, blood of my blood, kin of my kin; my bountiful wine press for a while.*

MINA: *He then pulled open the shirt with his long, sharp nails and opened a vein in his breast. When the blood began to spurt out, he took my hands in one of his, holding them tight, and with the other seized my neck and pressed my mouth to the wound, so that I might either suffocate or swallow some of the — oh, my God, what have I done?*

WATSON: *(Banishing the three apparitions.)* What sort of mad work is this? *(The Three Literary Figures disappear. Music out.)*

HOLMES: No wonder he writes in secrecy. Have you noticed anything else?

WATSON: What do you mean?

HOLMES: Only that our Mr. Stoker knows how to induce swallowing.

> *(Watson looks at the two passages again and they stare at each other, horror written on their faces.)*

WATSON: *(Whispering in awed tones.)* Can we have been forced to drink blood?

> *(We hear the heavy tread of steps on stairs.)*

HOLMES: You can ask him yourself for that's his footstep on the stairs!

WATSON: Great Scot!

HOLMES: *(In hushed tones.)* Quickly, Watson.

> *(Rapidly, Holmes assembles the papers and replaces them in the drawers.)*

HOLMES: Now to the balcony, man! Quick!

WATSON: What?

HOLMES: When you've eliminated the impossible, whatever remains —

WATSON: — However ridiculous!

HOLMES: Go!

> *(Holmes and Watson throw open the window and step out onto the precarious ledge, closing the shutters behind them. There's a stuttering of keys at the front door.)*

HOLMES: *(Sotto voce.)* Don't look down.

> *(Stoker enters, locks the door behind him, lights the gas, proceeds to his desk. Chewing his fingernails, he settles down to work on his ghastly manuscript. Holmes and Watson clutch the window frame for support.)*

HOLMES: Think of England, Watson, and jump!

> *(They land in their chairs at Baker Street! Music: "Rule Brittania.")*

Scene Seven

> *221B Baker Street, Holmes and Watson are drinking tea.*

WATSON: Bram Stoker's secret lair is used for writing, not rendezvous.

HOLMES: Given that his pastime is one of which his family and employer disapprove.

WATSON: I can see why.

HOLMES: No, Watson, we might wish Bram Stoker to be our man, but he is not — no more than Achmed Singh. The only difference between them is that if we cannot find the true murderer, the Hindu will hang. Hullo! Who is here — ?

WATSON: *(Stopping Holmes.)* Let him knock.

> *(There is a knock at the door. Holmes opens the door, addressing Watson in an I-told-you-so way.)*

HOLMES: Constable Hopkins. *(Letting Hopkins in.)* What brings you to Baker Street at an hour when most off-duty policemen are at home resting their feet? I perceive your route here has been a circuitous one and that you have taken great pains to avoid being seen.

HOPKINS: Heavens, sir, how can you tell that?

HOLMES: Look at your trouser leg. There must be seven different splashes there. I recognize some mud from Gloucester Road —

WATSON: *(Cutting him off.)* For the love of God, Holmes, it's late. What brings you here, Constable?

HOPKINS: Our police surgeon, Mr. Brownlow, has disappeared.

HOLMES: When was he last seen?

HOPKINS: In the mortuary today at work on McCarthy. He began acting strangely.

HOLMES: How do you mean strangely?

HOPKINS: He threw the assistants and stretcher bearers out of the mortuary, made all of 'em take off their clothes and scrub down with carbolic and alcohol and shower. And you know what he did while they were showering, Mr. Holmes?

HOLMES: He burned all their clothes.

HOPKINS: *(Astonished.)* Aye, that he did. And then, Miss Rutland's remains were carried in and he —

HOLMES: — repeated the ritual.

HOPKINS: *(Nodding.)* It was almost funny — all them men stark naked. Then, Mr. Brownlow barricaded himself inside the mortuary!

HOLMES: And now?

HOPKINS: Now he is gone.

WATSON: Gone? How? Surely they had sense enough to post a man outside the mortuary door.

HOLMES: But they didn't think to post one outside the back of the mortuary. And where does that door lead?

HOPKINS: To the stables and mews. You're right, Mr. Holmes. It never occurred to any of us that his object was to leave the mortuary. Besides, they could hear him talking to himself in there.

(Holmes closes his eyes and leans back in his chair.)

WATSON: So he left the back way?

HOPKINS: Aye, sir, in a police wagon.

WATSON: Have you checked at his home?

HOPKINS: We've men posted by it, and neither they nor his missus have seen hide nor hair. However —

(Hopkins begins chewing his fingernails.)

HOLMES: *(Leaping out of his chair.)* Brownlow took the bodies with him!

HOPKINS: That is correct, sir.

HOLMES: Have you seen the mortuary since Brownlow abandoned it?

HOPKINS: Yes, sir. I made it my business to have a look.

HOLMES: Capital! Really, Hopkins, you exceed my fondest hopes. Tell me what was left in there.

HOPKINS: Nothing much, rather less than usual.

HOLMES: And the missing police wagon?

HOPKINS: *(On top of it.)* An alarm has been put out, Mr. Holmes. If it's in London, we'll lay hands on it.

HOLMES: That is exactly what none of you must do. *(Ominous chord.)* No one must go near it. Hopkins — *(Putting a hand on his shoulder.)* — The time has come for us to part company. Where we go you must not follow.

HOPKINS: *(Reluctantly.)* If you say so, sir. G'night, then.

(Hopkins exits.)

WATSON: Holmes, I see what you're getting at. There's some matter of contamination or contagion involved.

HOLMES: Precisely. But we have yet to discover what. You conducted a cursory examination of each body. Did their condition suggest anything in the nature of a disease to you?

WATSON: Any number of common ailments begin with a sore throat.

HOLMES: Then there's nothing for it but a visit to the mortuary. We're off!

(They move outside. Music in.)

Scene Eight

Shaw appears.

SHAW: Where're we going?

HOLMES: The mortuary.

WATSON: Someone appears to have made off with our two corpses. Come on.
(They are outside the mortuary. They proceed cautiously. Music out.)

HOLMES: This door should lead to the mortuary. You can see the wheel marks where the wagon was backed up to it. Of course the police have examined it.

WATSON: There are footprints running in every direction all round the place.

SHAW: It looks like they danced a Highland fling.

HOLMES: He went left; that's all we can say. If he departed the mews there's no telling where he was bound. Hullo, what's this? The noose around Achmed Singh's neck begins to loosen!

WATSON: How so?

HOLMES: If the prosecution contends that the Hindu smoked Indian cheroots, they will be hard put to explain the presence of this one outside the mortuary whilst Singh himself is incarcerated at Whitehall.

SHAW: Are you certain it is the same cigar?

(Watson and Holmes shoot Shaw a look.)

SHAW: Beggin' your pardon.

HOLMES: Our man simply threw it aside when the other opened the mortuary door for him.

WATSON: The other? I take it Brownlow did not smoke Indian cheroots?

HOLMES: To my knowledge, he did not smoke at all.

WATSON: Excellent.

HOLMES: There was another man here, and it is that other man who concerns us. Brownlow was talking not to himself but conversing with our quarry. Think — think — think — every minute counts. Watson, what can you tell me about tropical diseases?

SHAW: What have tropical diseases to do with this?

HOLMES: McCarthy and Miss Rutland were not killed to prevent their living but rather to prevent their dying a more horrible and more dangerous death. *(Ominous chord.)*

SHAW: Slain violently in order to prevent their suffering the ravages of some malady.

HOLMES: Just so. A virulent disease that would have made off with them as surely as a knife, given time.

WATSON: Holmes and I, who were most prominently exposed to them, were forced to imbibe some sort of antidote.

SHAW: Antidote?

WATSON: Saved our lives, I shouldn't wonder.

SHAW: What of Brownlow, then?

HOLMES: Brownlow is dead. *(Ominous chord.)* If the murderer's purpose was to contain a spreading epidemic, the police surgeon, by virtue of his occupation, was more exposed to contamination than any of us.

SHAW: And the murderer?

HOLMES: *(Agitated.)* Could be anywhere by now! But I dare not theorize proximity from such threadbare data. It is staring us in the face, I know it, yet I cannot fathom it, cannot for the life of me!

WATSON: Holmes, even as the hour grows late, with us tired and I, for one, in want of a large snifter of brandy, we remain at your service and will persevere until you are no longer plagued by this vexing case.

HOLMES: Plague! *(Music in.)* Watson, invaluable Watson! You held the key in your own hands from the first! *Romeo and Juliet,* Act Three, Scene One —

WATSON: "A plague on both your houses!" He was being literal?

HOLMES: Which explains your mystery of rigor mortis. Shaw, what did they do when the plague came to London?

SHAW: They closed the playhouses.

HOLMES: Precisely. Watson, who is the one person Brownlow would admit to the mortuary while performing an autopsy?

WATSON: Another doctor, of course.

HOLMES: Of course! As well as have the requisite skills to create an antidote to an infectious disease. It was before me all the time, and I was blind to it! Quick, Watson!

(Music swells. Holmes grabs a container and bolts from the mortuary, heading toward the mews with Watson on his heels. Shaw hesitates.)

SHAW: Well, who is it, man? I've never heard such melodrama outside of the Haymarket Theatre!

HOLMES: In a very few minutes you shall hear it from the lips of the man we are seeking — if he is still alive.

SHAW: *(Following after them.)* Still alive?

HOLMES: He cannot have toyed with the disease as much as he has done without succumbing to it, nor can he have gotten very far.

SHAW: But the plague's not been heard of since the Great Fire of London!

HOLMES: On the contrary, it is at present decimating India, as you should know from the papers.

(A sour chord. At once their nostrils are assailed by the most terrible odor.)

SHAW: What is that stench?

WATSON: Carbolic. In enormous concentration. Holmes, the police wagon!

HOLMES: Cover your noses and mouths, gentlemen. Watson, you haven't your revolver with you?

Watson No, Holmes.

HOLMES: What a pity. *(Holmes plucks his handkerchief from his jacket and, pressing it to his face, moves towards the wagon. A sound like the wind wheezing through a pipe organ is heard.)* I hoped we would find you in time, Dr. Benjamin Eccles.

(A shrouded figure, slumped inside, groans. It is dying Eccles.)

Scene Nine

The police wagon on the mews.

DYING ECCLES: *(In a husky whisper.)* Come no closer, Mr. Sherlock Holmes. The disease is transmitted by contact with the flesh.

WATSON: *(Gasping.)* It is indeed the theater doctor who is revealed to us scarcely recognized as human. *(Music in: Fauré's Pavanne.)* His countenance is withered, like a rotten apple, covered with hideous black boils and pustules that split and pour bile like dirty tears. His lips are cracked and parched with bleeding sores. With a chill shock shooting through my bones, I realize that the rasping, pump-like sound we had been listening to is his own labored breath, wheezing like the wind through a pipe organ — and this knowledge told me that Dr. Eccles had not another hour to live. *(Music fades out.)*

DYING ECCLES: You are the one man I feared could find me and yet now I feel relief that you have.

HOLMES: The facts as I see them are these: You have recently returned from Bombay leaving there a wife, most certainly counting her remaining days in some forgotten nursing home. For how else could McCarthy gain footing on your otherwise untarnished life? Your medical career there seems to have been one of research, and from the newspaper accounts from China and India, it is obvious that the plague is the substance of your work. I know from personal experience that you have some success with an antidote. However, there seems to be an extreme time constraint upon its efficacy. This achievement brought you back to England and undoubtedly to St. Bartholomew's, the finest research facility in London. From there you supplemented your days in the laboratory with nights in the theater as the house doctor at the Savoy where you met Miss Jessie Rutland.

DYING ECCLES: That was the beginning.

(As Eccles stops to catch his breath he begins to cough violently.)

WATSON: Is there anything we can do for you, Doctor?

DYING ECCLES: Will you hear my confession?

HOLMES: We will hear it.

(Music: "Love Is a Plaintive Song.")

DYING ECCLES: Jessie was the sweetest creature under a bonnet and we quickly came to love each other. I saw in her love the chance for my soul's salvation. And then a man — an ogre — Jonathan McCarthy told Jessie he knew I was married and extorted from her a twisted ransom paid not in pounds but in flesh. Jessie's! I confronted him with the shameful deed — *(Music becomes dissonant at the mention of "an ogre." Jonathan McCarthy and Dr. Eccles [Eccles from Act One] appear.)*

MCCARTHY: *(Laughing.)* Eccles, you know nothing about the ways of the theater.

ECCLES: *(Pleading.)* No, nor have I ever met such a man in all my travels. I implore you! I beseech you! Return to me my life! My world!

MCCARTHY: *(Still laughing.)* Your world?

ECCLES: I beg of you!

MCCARTHY: *(Laughing.)* You're a good enough fellow, Doctor, but I must warn you, as obviously your mother did not, stay clear of actresses. They go down faster than the curtain at the Savoy.

DYING ECCLES: McCarthy was still laughing as he left the room, leaving me my opportunity to lace his brandy glass with a bacillus of pneumonic plague.

HOLMES: What?!

WATSON: Impossible!

DYING ECCLES: Catastrophic!

(McCarthy drinks the laced brandy.)

DYING ECCLES: As the hours ticked by I came to share your opinion of my deed. In desperation, I found McCarthy enroute to the theater —

ECCLES: Please, it is imperative that you meet me this evening.

MCCARTHY: Off with you, little man.

ECCLES: I warn you, this is of the utmost urgency. It concerns our — mutual friend.

MCCARTHY: Very well. *(Using Eccles' back, McCarthy writes on his* Strand Magazine.*)* Jack Point Regent Street. *(McCarthy leaves.)*

DYING ECCLES: We parted leaving me with the full force of my actions. All England had been threatened by my folly.

HOLMES: And so you returned to McCarthy's apartment to administer the antidote. But something went wrong.

DYING ECCLES: He wasn't at home!

(Music. Tense and repetitive. McCarthy returns. Eccles is already there, holding a glass of brandy, which contains the antidote.)

ECCLES: Where have you been? Your time has ended!

MCCARTHY: Ah, Jack Point, you're early.

ECCLES: I am too late! The twelve hours has elapsed and my antidote may now prove worthless!

DYING ECCLES: I told him what I had done. He didn't believe me and laughed at me *again*.

MCCARTHY: *(Still laughing.)* Infect me with the plague? You're not some scheming Borgia; you're just a jester — a clown — Jack Point! Oh, but if I am dying, Doctor, then you must attend your sweet Miss Rutland, the well-named Miss Rutland, with whom I have been rutting since last night!

DYING ECCLES: My face must have looked absurd, as understanding and I finally became acquainted. And then I astounded myself by committing a deed I would have sworn unimaginable, as I deliberately threw the brandy glass containing the antidote and McCarthy's last chance to the floor— *(Eccles smashes the vial on the floor.)* —And joined him in laughter.

ECCLES: As I had scoured the streets of the West End attempting to find and administer my antidote, this silken brute was savaging my only love. Our actions had doomed all three of us. I seized a letter opener —
(Music abruptly stops.)

HOLMES: — With your *right* hand and stabbed him with it.
(Eccles takes the letter opener and stabs McCarthy in the left side, somewhat below the heart. Music: Dissonant and delirious.)

MCCARTHY: A plague o' both your houses! I am sped.

ECCLES: Why the devil came you between us?
(The following speech and the action in the stage directions that follow it occur simultaneously.)

HOLMES: As McCarthy collapses on the floor, you watch with equal measures of hatred and horror as the bloody, bawdy villain draws his last breaths. Then, you begin to hide all evidence of your visit. First, to the engagement diary, where you tear off the page dated 28 February, wrongly assuming it contains your name. You move to the fireplace, pick up the poker, and stir the embers to get a proper blaze and throw the page in. You stand there watching the paper ignite and burn as you nervously chew on your fingernails and then something happens for which you are not prepared. McCarthy moves. *Crawls. Lurches* toward the bookcase. Startled, you drop the poker on the floor, spreading ash, which you then proceed to step in with your newly acquired boots from Harrods, distinctive for its singular H stamped upon the heels. You ignore the shattered glass as well as your smoldering Indian cheroot and hastily depart in a trail of oxblood leather scuff marks.

(McCarthy falls to the floor. Eccles stands back from McCarthy, shaking for several moments. Eccles then moves hurriedly to the desk, tears out a diary page. Eccles moves to the fireplace, picks up a poker, stirs the embers, and throws

the page in, stands watching, chewing his nails. McCarthy moves. Crawls. Lurches toward the bookcase. Eccles drops the poker and starts for the door. Eccles pauses — looks at his boot bottom — then runs out of the room.)

DYING ECCLES: How can you know . . . ? Yes, my Jessie was now on the wrong side of hope. For several hours I walked the back streets of London knowing that what I must do next was the very thing that I could not do.

HOLMES: Slay your love to prevent her suffering a "more horrible death."

DYING ECCLES: Yes, Jessie was already dead, she just didn't know it.

(Eccles meets Jessie in her dressing room.)

JESSIE: Art thou hurt?

ECCLES: *(Eccles kisses Jessie passionately, for the last time.)* Ay, a scratch; marry, 'tis enough.

JESSIE: I thought it all for the best.

ECCLES: *(Lifting up a scalpel.)* This shall determine that.

(Jessie screams as he slashes her throat then gently lays her down. Eccles talks to Holmes. Music out.)

I did it as tenderly as I could and then I walked 'round to the front of the theater and entered as though on my evening tour. I performed an autopsy on the woman I had just slain, while the bloodstained scalpel nestled in my bag under all your noses.

ECCLES AND DYING ECCLES: *(Overlapping.)* And now, my sweet Jessie —

(McCarthy, Jessie, and Eccles disappear.)

DYING ECCLES: — is but a little way above our heads and I, presently, to the other place.

(Eccles is nearly spent.)

HOLMES: You are acquainted with the Bhagavad-Gita? ? "I am Death, the mighty destroyer of the world . . ."

DYING ECCLES: "I have come here to destroy all these people — " What have I —? Oh God! God have mercy on their souls!

WATSON: And yours too, Benjamin Eccles.

(Eccles sighs with a noise like kettledrums and dies.)

WATSON: He's gone. It's over.

HOLMES: Not quite, he has left us much to do.

WATSON: *(Noticing a badly shaken Shaw.)* Shaw?

SHAW: How disquieting and unsettling has been this gruesome business. A doctor pledged to saving lives who butchers his rival, his true love, and ultimately himself. A learned disciple of Hippocrates on the threshold of scientific breakthrough, who in a fit of jealous rage set loose the plague in Great Britain. The human race saddens me sometimes in a way that confounds my philosophy. I do thank you, Holmes, for you have solved these murders most foul, but now I must beg my leave. I have had enough of bloodshed and treachery and wish to return to my sheltered world of words, where cutthroat is merely a figure of speech and only plays are "murdered."

(Shaw leaves quickly.)

HOLMES: And what of you, my friend? There's grim work ahead.

WATSON: I'll stay.

HOLMES: Then, I must ask you, Watson, have you a match?

(Lights change dramatically. Watson crosses to write in his notebook. Holmes exits.)

Epilogue

WATSON: *(Reading from his notes.)* All theatrical London gossiped about the murder of Jonathan McCarthy, and his killer was never caught. Scotland Yard was also hard put to explain the mysterious death of an actress at the Savoy, as well as the peculiar disappearance of the police surgeon, assorted bodies from the morgue, and one police wagon. *(Writing.)* Equally curious was the fate of the remainder of these unusual suspects. *(Musical fanfare. Singh enters with Lestrade as Holmes returns.)* As for Achmed Singh . . .

SINGH: They tell me I am free. You have done this?

HOLMES: The truth has set you free.

SINGH: You! Sherlock Holmes — breaker of my shackles — from my heart's depths I thank you!

(Lestrade removes Singh's manacles.)

WATSON: And so, Singh was released and Inspector Lestrade took the full brunt of the botched arrest.

(Singh exits.)

WATSON: He was not eager for the full-scale panic that would inevitably and tragically ensue with the arrival of the Black Death —

LESTRADE: — Nor am I particularly proud of my part in the arrest of an innocent man.

HOLMES: Guilty only of being brown-skinned.

LESTRADE: If you do chronicle this matter, you might just have me appear foolish. I'm not certain the fiction of me is that far a journey.

(Lestrade exits.)

WATSON: As for Mr. Oscar Wilde . . .

(Wilde is put into handcuffs by Hopkins.)

HOPKINS: Oscar Wilde, you have been charged under the Criminal Law Amendment Act of 1885 for acts of gross indecency with other male persons.

WILDE: Thank you, Constable Hopkins.

HOLMES: *(Correcting.)* — Sergeant.

WILDE: Sergeant! My, my, my, my. I'm glad to see someone moving up in the world.

HOPKINS: This is not a matter for joking, sir. You've not only broken the law you've committed a sin.

WILDE: There is no sin except stupidity. Please do not, dear Sergeant Hopkins, let mere rank diminish your humanity. And as for sin, I shouldn't let it bother you too much. For if your sins find you out, why worry? It's when they find you *in* that trouble begins!

(Hopkins takes Wilde to jail.)

HOLMES: I very much fear Mr. Wilde does not realize the gravity of his situation. His bravado can only speed his ruin.

WATSON: As for Henry Irving and Miss Ellen Terry — their daring revival of Shakespeare's MACB — *(Several shouts of warning from The Players to Watson, who recovers with dignity.)* Er, Scottish play — was received, at least by this admirer, with great acclaim.

(Irving bows and exits as Miss Terry lingers. Stoker enters.)

WATSON: As for Bram Stoker — what we thought to be the insane work of a depraved mad man was in actuality —

STOKER: — A book.

(Stoker displays the book to Holmes.)

HOLMES: *Dracula!*

(Stoker exits. Miss Terry rushes to Watson, revealing the latest edition of the Strand Magazine.)

MISS TERRY: *(Gaily.)* John, would you be so kind as to autograph this latest edition of the *Strand Magazine?*

(Watson gladly obliges.)

HOLMES: May we please proceed?

(Miss Terry exits.)

WATSON: As for Herbert, our stage door devotee at the Savoy Theatre, he prudently left his "temporary position" and, rather extraordinarily, published his story about time travel.

HERBERT: By Herbert George We —

HOLMES: *(Cutting him off.)* Just go by your initials — it's catchier.

HERBERT: *The Time Machine* by H. G. Wells! Righto, Mr. H.

(Herbert rushes off.)

WATSON: As for Ms. Hudson, our long-suffering landlady of 221B Baker Street made a tidy fortune from running the official Sherlock Holmes tour.

MRS. HUDSON: And if you look closely, ladies and gentlemen, you can see on this wall the very initials of our beloved Queen Victoria, spelled out in bullet holes by The Great Detective himself. Souvenir bullets are available in our lobby gift shop.

(She goes.)

HOLMES: This is all your doing, Watson. You know I do not condone such commercial merchandising —

WATSON: *(Cutting Holmes off.)* As for Richard D'Oyly Carte and the happy collaboration of Messrs. Gilbert and Sullivan and Company —

(Gilbert, Sullivan, and Carte pass through, in the middle of a heated argument.)

GILBERT:	SULLIVAN:	CARTE:
Yes, yes, yes, it's a musical problem! Grossmith cannot maintain his tone, Passmore cannot stay on pitch, and the chorus sounds decidedly lumpy!	No, no, no, no! Gilbert. Musical problem? There's no musical problem. The real problem is the feeble dialogue in your ludicrous libretto. Makes no sense at all!	Gilbert. Please. Sir Arthur! Gentlemen! Please! PLEASE! SHUT UP! It's like the damned carpet all over again!

HOLMES: *(Cutting them off.)* The less said about them, the better.

WATSON: And, as for Mr. George Bernard Shaw —

(Shaw enters.)

WATSON: Filling the void left by Jonathan McCarthy, he became London's chief drama critic.

HOLMES: *(Handing Shaw his once-pawned walking stick.)* — And however irresolute, destined for great success.

SHAW: My walking stick! Thank you, Holmes. And while I thoroughly enjoy my pulpit as critic, I am toying with a notion for a new play about an eccentric, systematic chap with unusual analytical abilities who lives quite cozily with his ex-military roommate.

HOLMES: A comedy, I presume? No matter. I plead guilty to the first charge, and as for the latter, well, I am happy to report that I am a confirmed old bachelor and likely to remain so.

(Music: Three bars of a familiar refrain . . .)

SHAW: Aha!

(A lightbulb explodes in Shaw's head and upon this eureka! moment, he runs off.)

HOLMES: Watson, you know this can never be published.

WATSON: I know. Besides, I should be obliged to recount *our* part in the business as well. It could hardly be termed legal.

HOLMES: I can see that some question remains. Would you be so kind as to permit me one more deduction?

WATSON: You just can't help yourself, can you? Very well.

HOLMES: You are an Englishman to the core comprised of all the noble facets thereof: stalwart, loyal, eminently fair, and invariably forgiving. You are also first and forever a doctor, and governed by a tradition of healing. Matching these intrinsically English, and ergo "Watson" qualities, your question is but a simple surmise — you are wondering why Eccles allowed himself to die. After all, had he taken his own antidote with the zeal he pressed it on others —

WATSON: *(Exactly.)* Yes, he might have survived.

HOLMES: We shall never know his truth. Some men are not only murderers but also judges, juries, and their own executioners and in those capacities they mete out punishments far more severe than their fellow men could devise. The West End Horror —

WATSON: *(Longingly.)* "The West End Horror" — Good title.

HOLMES: I think so — is a story for which the world is not yet prepared.

WATSON: Holmes, we could have lost the empire. You saved England and no one knows.

HOLMES: Watson, England is coming to the end of an era. *(Music in: "God Save The Queen.")* In two years time we will celebrate Queen Victoria's Diamond Jubilee, marking sixty remarkable years on her throne. Shortly thereafter, the world will step boldly into a brand new century, bringing us a new monarch and a modern method of crime detection. The ennui that enveloped me at the outset of this adventure stemmed from my misconception that all our enemies had been dealt with; that there were no new criminals. However, I can see now with ambivalent clarity that modern times will bring modern criminals and vigilance shall be our cry. *(Music finishes.)* No, no one must ever know, save for my dear friend and invaluable colleague, John Watson.

(Holmes crosses upstage. Watson resumes writing. Music: Chopin Nocturne.)

WATSON: And so it was that in the early morning hours of 3 March 1895, a fire broke out on a deserted mews, somewhere behind Whitehall, burning a police wagon and the four bodies within beyond all possible recognition. Sherlock Holmes had poured kerosene over it and I had laid on a match as we walked out of the spent night and into the new day.

(Holmes takes up his pipe and prepares to smoke as Watson puts down his pen, closes his journal, and looks at his friend. The music finishes and the lights fade to black.)

END OF PLAY

BIRTH

By Bless ji Jaja

For the ol' school grandparents,
Mr. and Mrs. Isaac N. Long, Sr. and Beatrice M. Long.
And Mr. and Mrs. M. L. Coleman and
Lucille L. Coleman-Coleman.
For whom, "till death did them part."
They don't make 'em like that no more . . .
though I wish they did.

PLAYWRIGHT'S BIOGRAPHY

Author, playwright, and director, Bless ji Jaja enjoys various accomplishments. Within six short years as a professional writer, he has two published books, two produced plays, contributed to several magazine articles, as well as directed for theater.

His first published work, *Love Awaits,* is a compilation of insightful interviews by black women speaking on love, life, and sex. In 2002, the follow-up and companion piece to *Love Awaits,* titled, *Understandings, for our sisters,* was published by Upstream Press. *Understandings* takes a look at various and *authentic* African-American men, as well as brothers abroad, giving their own personal insight on sex, life, themselves, and love — especially trying to love, be with, and deal with black women.

Mr. ji Jaja's playwriting credits include his very first produced play, *Birth,* being honored with inclusion in the Smith and Kraus anthology of *New American Playwrights, The Best of 2002,* and his first draft of his first dramatic piece, *Man Made God,* recently selected as finalist in the *Seventeenth Annual Theodore Ward Prize for African-American Playwrights,* Chicago. *Birth,* an aging comedy debuted in Phoenix, Arizona, at The Helen K. Mason Center for the Performing Arts on October 4, 2001, and has since been staged by The Billie Holiday Theater, New York; The Paul Robeson Theater, Buffalo; The Anthony Bean Community Theater, New Orleans, and The Inner Circle Repertoire Theater in Baltimore.

Another recent play by Mr. ji Jaja, *Barberdashers, Haircuts, and Male Grooming,* was produced by The Billie Holiday Theater in February 2003. *Barberdashers* is the poignant story of old versus young, community versus individuality, and life versus death.

Mr. ji Jaja's directing credits include in 1998 the Los Angeles Epiphany Theater Company's first company production of *Dangerous Liaisons,* Sarte's *No Exit,* and Sam Shepard's *Fool for Love,* in Washington, DC. He shares co-directing titles with Vera Katz for the nontraditional casting of *A Street Car Named Desire,* Washington, DC. He is the 1996 recipient of the Allen Lee Hughes Director's Fellowship at Arena Stage, Washington, DC, and has also apprenticed for the Tony Award–winning play, *Fences* at DC's Arena Stage.

Mr. ji Jaja is a consecutive two-time winner for Best Student Director at Howard University's Directors' Program where he earned his BFA and has guest written articles for *EM Magazine, Psychology Today,* and *The Nu School Magazine.*

Mr. ji Jaja currently resides in his native borough of Brooklyn, New York.

INTRODUCTION

I once asked my grandmother, Lucille L. Coleman, why she had never remarried. She simply replied that "another love of my life had not come along." We then explored what went into making marriages work and to what extent did those edicts still apply to today's unions. The findings were not too encouraging. Whereas her commitment to matrimony began and ended with love, many of today's pledges are undertaken with economy, complacency, and fad more-so factored in as the primary motivator; marriages treated as casual dates. "Oh, it didn't work out. We broke up, and now I'm engaged to this new person, Courtney."

There are also political marriages. Unions are made or allies come together in silent or explicit contract to prove or achieve something. And once gained, the contract may be discarded and disposed of, True love and convenient arrangements. What have we come to? What have we lost? What must we reclaim? These were the origins of *Birth*'s conception.

My goal as an African-American writer is to continue in our rich literary tradition of helping and healing, exposing and examining, inspiring and remembering, through words, who we are. And more important, why we *be*.

ORIGINAL PRODUCTION

Birth opened on October 4, 2001 at The Black Theater Troupe's Helen K. Mason Center for the Performing Arts. It was directed by Ben Tyler. The production manager was Denise Wilcox; stage manager, Cheves Samuels; technical director, Gabriel Martin; lighting design, Mike Eddy; sound design, Brian Burrill; and costume design by Carol Simmons. Production assistants were Jemelah Brown, Marquisha Brown, and Loretta Cantley. David J. Hemphill was executive director. The cast was as follows:

FRED MITCHELL	Harold Luther White
OLIVE MITCHELL	Joyce Gittoes
JONAS WELLINGS	Mike Traylor
SELAH WELLINGS	Fanta Shabazz White
VERA BLUME	Helen Hayes

CHARACTERS

FRED MITCHELL: sixty-five.
OLIVE MITCHELL: sixty-four.
JONAS WELLINGS: sixty-seven.
SELAH WELLINGS: sixty-six.

TIME

Spring and fall.

PLACE

Ditmas Park, Brooklyn, New York

SETTING

The main set is the home of Fred and Olive Mitchell. It's a complete, middle-class, private home with unseen driveway and two-car garage just outside their front door. On stage is a large living room, stairs leading to upper rooms, and a kitchen, or an entrance leading to it. There is a small portable wet bar, and an antique, sometimes working Victrola on display. Jonas and Selah Wellings's home may be in the downstage left area. An incomplete, cutaway structure of their home may be suggestive of the state of their union: fractured, deficient, flawed. A visual contrast between whole, decorated, and alive and the imperfect.

Birth

ACT I

The play begins at the house of Jonas and Selah Wellings. Lights up. Jonas sits in his easy chair. He is reading a newspaper closely with difficulty. Selah, his wife of over forty years, is on the telephone with Olive.

SELAH: OK, thanks. Hold on. Jonas. Jonas, Olive says your reading glasses are there.

JONAS: OK, good. Just hold 'em for me. I'll get them tomorrow.

SELAH: No, Olive, it's your anniversary, let Fred rest. *(To Jonas.)* Don't you think you need them now?

JONAS: No, no, I'm all right. *(He briskly turns the pages.)* Just checking out the headlines and then I'm going straight to bed.

SELAH: Uh-uh, look dear, before you go any further, I can't begin to tell you how many times I may have won a million dollars . . . Yes, now before you read from your script, let me read mine. First of all, if I've won anything, just send it. If a purchase is involved in order for me to obtain my potential million, you purchase them in my name, and when I receive said million, I'll be sure to reimburse you, plus a nice gratuity, OK? . . . But, those are my rules. Ta-ta. *(She clicks.)* Olive? . . . I'm sorry, one of those sweepstakes callers. You work hard all your life, and now with one foot in the grave, they wanna just give you the bank . . . Oh, Olive, wait, I don't believe this. *(She clicks.)* Hello? . . . Yes . . . Yes, sweetheart, I'm satisfied with my long-distance carrier . . . Five cents a minute? You don't say? . . . Well, I tell you, dear, the telemarketer sitting next to you may be sending me a cash prize. I authorize her to buy anything from you. Just deduct it from my winnings, okaaay, good niiight. *(She clicks.)* Olive? Oh, now it's you. We have to do something about these folks, but let me let you go . . . And again, lovely evening. May you and Fred have many more . . . OK, I will . . . Bye-bye.

(Selah hangs up. She takes a seat. Jonas becomes conscious of his close reading and puts down the paper. He then looks at the television. After a second he moves closer to the set. Another second he moves closer still.)

SELAH: Jonas, give it up. They're only across the street. Either go get your glasses, or go to bed.

JONAS: I'm finished, I'm finished. Just reading the box scores. You know how microscopic that copy is, but I can see.

SELAH: Of course you can.

JONAS: Well, I saw enough to see and ask, why is that Gail pregnant at her age?

SELAH: Well, that's between Gail her reproductive system, but more power to her.

JONAS: Yeah, yeah, Ungawa, I'm going on to bed.

SELAH: Jonas, I . . . we need to talk.

(Jonas, knowingly, takes a deep breath. They become even more isolated by two specials and the television light.)

JONAS: OK.

SELAH: Jonas. The newspapers. Television. Radio. Going to bed. Diversions. We can't go on like this. I can't go on like this.

(Silence.)

JONAS: *(Inhales and exhales.)* Avoidance. The antidote to conflict.

SELAH: And we've been avoiding this, ignoring this long enough . . . So, if we are to now finally speak at length . . .

JONAS: It's unfortunate that it, uh, has to be in the context of . . .

SELAH: A separation?

JONAS: *(Nodding.)* Which has long since occurred.

SELAH: And . . . So how do we go about this?

JONAS: Amicably.

(Jonas draws closer to Selah. They embrace. They hold each other with all the tenderness and care of all that they have meant to one another. Selah is the first to release.)

SELAH: Jonas, I would like to think that had I not brought this up . . . that you would have.

JONAS: Every day was supposed to be *the* day.

(Silence.)

SELAH: Uh, Olive wanted me to come back over for a minute. I'll get your glasses. *(Selah starts to walk away.)* Lynette. Marcus . . . We did do that right?

JONAS: We did most things right.

(Selah exits. Lights down. Lights up on Fred and Olive Mitchell. Fred is at the worksite of his disabled antique Victrola gramophone. He has been trying to repair it himself for some time now, but it refuses to cooperate with his efforts.)

FRED: Damn. What, what, what the hell could it be?

(Olive enters from the kitchen with a cordless phone. She is straightening up from the party.)

OLIVE: Yeah, Selah, I have his glasses right here. *(She looks through them.)* Whoa, you sure he doesn't need them now? Fred could walk them over, he's not doing anything.

FRED: What does this look like?

OLIVE: Yes, as I was saying, he's not doing anything.

(To that, he gives up completely. Fred sits in his chair dejected and frustrated.)

FRED: Well, now I'll really do nothing. And I'm sure if Jonas really needed his glasses, he would come and get them.

OLIVE: OK, I'll hold. Not without a seeing-eye dog. *(She goes to Fred.)* Fred, why not just take the Victrola to a professional to fix?

FRED: A so-called professional don't know nothing about gramophones. Take 'em a stereo, or DVD player, OK. But that there. They wouldn't know from a hole in the wall. If they did, I would have taken them that and my 8-track player. Which I'll repair next.

OLIVE: *(She laughs.)* You're funny. Yeah, Selah, telemarketer? How much this time? Oo, a million. Well, let me let you go. Oh, OK, I'll wait. *(To Fred.)* Fred, Selah's a millionaire. Maybe she can buy you a new, working Victrola.

FRED: I could have had *this* Victrola fixed had I not been working on repairing and restoring all your ol' stuff.

OLIVE: At least it's twentieth century stuff, as well as heirlooms, thank you.

FRED: A hairdryer?

OLIVE: No, I don't mean that, and some black duct tape around a frayed wire, gee thanks, Fred, I didn't mean to monopolize all your time for that.

FRED: Well how 'bout repainting the bedroom for tonight's anniversary. As if the party was upstairs in the bedroom.

OLIVE: Selah? *(To Fred.)* In case someone wanted to see the new spread. *(Back to Selah.)* Oh, aren't they the worst?

FRED: Spreads?

OLIVE: I get that all the time . . . Oh, not again . . . OK. Yes, Fred, the same as you showing Brian and Jonas just how fine a paint job you did.

FRED: All that hard work, shoot, someone is gonna appreciate it.

OLIVE: It's still been over a year with that Victrola, now, what's your excuse?

FRED: You, and the past plus years of fulfilling your request.

OLIVE: How long, Fred, how much longer until the thing is fixed?

FRED: With no interruptions?

OLIVE: With no interruptions.

FRED: Two weeks easy.

OLIVE: Selah? Oh, it's like you ever wonder what Jehovah Witnesses do after you don't answer your door. They go to their telemarketing jobs.

(Olive goes into the kitchen.)

FRED: Yeah, you go on . . . 'Cause what I need is total peace . . . You know the black man already has hypertension. *(He crosses to the Victrola.) Now. (He stares at the Victrola.)* Eh, later. Hey, Olive, can you warm me some of that pizza while you're in there, or how 'bout some potato salad?

(Olive re-enters.)

OLIVE: Fred, I'm already trying to clean up. And I'm on the phone. And the pizza is still in the oven. It's already warm.

FRED: I tell ya. The more anniversaries, the more they act like they ain't married.

(Fred gets up and goes into the kitchen himself.)

OLIVE: No, we just more and more realize that we're wives and not maids. *(To Selah.)* Ah, now there goes my phone. Hold on. *(She clicks over.)* Mitchell's. Hey, baby, hold on. *(She clicks.)* Selah? That's Gail calling to say they made it home safely . . . OK . . . Thanks, again, and I wish you and Jonas the same . . . And next time don't forget my cake mold . . . Talk to ya. *(She clicks again.)* Gail? . . . OK you made it home safely? . . . OK, so good night . . . OK, good night . . . OK, I love you too . . . Thank you. Yeah, OK . . . Uh-un . . . All right . . . Yeah, Gail, get the hell off my phone. I don't want to hear about all this wheat grass and wood root and Shea this. Where are you getting all this? I want you to give birth to my grand-child, OK, not a plant. Now just eat some okra and leave it be. *(Fred reenters with a plate of potato salad and sits.)* . . . OK, love you too . . . Right here, sitting down, taking a food break from all the energy he's exerted from working on his pet project . . . OK . . . I'll ask him . . . OK . . . OK . . . Hey, hey. Hey, Gail? Do you have any empty hangers in your closet? You do. Well, go hang this up. *(Olive hangs up on her daughter.)* Boy, that girl can talk.

FRED: And I wonder where she gets that from, I wonder?

OLIVE: She wanted me to ask you whether you ever heard of the word atrophy?

FRED: No, but I'll tell you, if after all this time, if I haven't slept with it, eaten it, or needed to bathe in it, then that word and Gail can kiss my you know what. And I think you know what word I'm talking about.

OLIVE: Atrophy means sitting there doing nothing but eating potato salad.

(Fred readjusts himself in his chair.)

FRED: There. *(Music from next door starts up.)* And now there he goes. I knew we couldn't get through the whole evening without him.

OLIVE: Well, we certainly could have used him earlier for the musical entertainment.

FRED: Not with the crap he plays. *(Fred rises and goes to the door. He opens it and yells.)* It's late! Now turn that mess down! *(He returns to his seat. The music is lowered.)* And I get plenty of exercise.

OLIVE: Lifting forks and remote controls don't count. If you ask me, your fingers are the only thing in some sort of shape.

FRED: All of me is in shape.

OLIVE: Hey, don't forget. I sleep with you.

FRED: All of me!

OLIVE: OK, then for starters, give me ten jumping jacks.

FRED: What! What are we, kids challenging each other? The black man already has poor circulation.

OLIVE: So, let's get it moving.

FRED: Just wanna finish me off?

OLIVE: Just ten.

FRED: Look, I just entertained company. *(He rises.)* But I'm a do it. But I just want you to know under what circumstances.

(Fred stretches and warms up.)

OLIVE: Well?

FRED: Just a minute, I'm warming up. Athletes warm up. OK. Here we go. *(Fred executes, with effort, ten near-perfect jumping jacks.)* Ha. (Winded.) Didn't think I could do it, huh?

OLIVE: Well, to be honest, no. I gave you six. Seven tops.

FRED: Well, there.

OLIVE: Oh, I knew you could do ten jumping jacks. I just want you to do it more often.

(Fred now feeling invigorated, starts moving to the music from next door.)

FRED: Oh, yeah?

OLIVE: Yeah.

FRED: Well, maybe I *will. (Bouncing around.)* That felt good. I don't know about that garbage they're saying, but that beat is the JB's.

OLIVE: Oh, so now you're up?

FRED: I'll let these moves do my talking.

OLIVE: Take it easy now, Fred. Remember the black man's circulation and all.

FRED: Oh, I got this. *(Fred begins to do his thing. A combination of old folks dancing, with a twist of what he believes to be current dance moves.)* Aw, shucks now. Give me room, give me room.

(Olive sits and observes Fred, who begins to work his creativity down to the floor.)

OLIVE: OK, now bring it back up now.

FRED: Yeah, OK, I'm bringing it.

OLIVE: Well, bring it. We're waiting.

FRED: I'm bringing it.

OLIVE: All right now.

(Fred takes a breath and with more effort brings his moves back up to a standing position.)

FRED: Yeah. Didn't think I could bring it back up, either, uh?

OLIVE: Well, it was a bit touch and go there for a minute.

FRED: And on top of ten jumping jacks.

OLIVE: *(Clapping.)* I'm impressed. *(Moving in on him.)* Now, do you think can you impress me some more?

FRED: What?

OLIVE: Well, I said that was for starters. Now how about a little anniversary after-party celebration?

FRED: Ah, now wait a minute. You should have made that clearer before this little jumping jack, dance contest popped off. One thing at a time. One thing at a time. *(He sits, winded.)* Un-un. Whew!

OLIVE: You need me to get you some water?

FRED: Uh . . . Yeah, you better.

(Olive retreats into the kitchen while Fred fans himself. She returns with a glass and pitcher of water. She pours Fred some relief.)

OLIVE: Well, you shouldn't have tried all that extra stuff.

FRED: I was just feeling it. *(Drinking.)* Umph! You could have brought some ice, Olive.

OLIVE: Well, I wanted to hurry and get you this. At least it's wet.

FRED: Yeah, water tends to be that. Thanks. *(Drinking more.)* But yeah, I was just going with the flow.

OLIVE: Well, next time go with the floor. Next time go with gravity and stay down there.

FRED: A little more.

OLIVE: Here you go? *(She pours.)* Drink slow, now.

FRED: OK. That hit the spot. Bless you.

OLIVE: You're welcome.

FRED: Yeah, buddy.

OLIVE: So, um, now you're ready?

FRED: Hell, no. Calm down. Feel my heart. *(Olive does so.)* You know the black man has existing heart conditions. I said had I known where you were headed with this, I would have conserved more energy.

OLIVE: It wasn't planned. *(She starts to caress his chest.)* It's just that you looked so sexy, with your moves and all.

FRED: I said feel my heart, Olive, not fondle my chest.

OLIVE: I'm sorry. It's just that when you went down. Umph. I felt that.

FRED: Yeah, I felt it too. Just in a different place.

(They laugh and enjoy themselves.)

OLIVE: Fred?

FRED: Yeah.

OLIVE: Do you think we do it enough?

FRED: Yeah, I think I do it enough.

OLIVE: Although, this is relatively speaking.

FRED: Yeah, it is.

OLIVE: Yeah, like, compared to, say, an Asian elephant that mates once a year. In that case, we do it enough.

FRED: Yeah, so?

OLIVE: Yeah, so we're not Asian elephants, Fred.

FRED: Well, what are the stats? For your average couple? And mind you, the average couple our age?

OLIVE: Two to three times a week.

FRED: What! Two to three — That's a lie!

OLIVE: No, it's not.

FRED: Yes, it is. Who'd they ask, men only? 'Cause you know that ain't nothing but male ego talking. Average couple my foot.

OLIVE: Well that's what the report said. And I personally feel up to two to three times a week.

FRED: *(Laughs.)* You? Two to three times a week?

OLIVE: Yeah.

FRED: Well, where was that two to three, thirty, forty years ago?

OLIVE: Well, you know my upbringing. Those were different times.

FRED: Ain't this a bitch. And now super freak comes out. Two to three times. But then again, I'll tell ya, today with of all these artificial implements and whatnot, OK, two to three, three to four, yeah, if I'm using artificial limbs and paraphernalia. *(Giving a mock interview.)* "Yes, sir, I'm hooked up so that by squeezing my left cheek, pow, I'm good to go. And for the highlight, well, I just squeeze the right cheek and, bam! Thank you, Techno-sex-tronics." Shoot, if I had a hydraulic pump up my hind-part, I'd go three and four times a week also. Read the fine print, Olive, read the fine print.

OLIVE: It's two to three, and maybe it's one of those pumps you need.

FRED: Don't you go there.

OLIVE: Well, how 'bout one of those new pills?

FRED: I'd be damned. Do you hear the end of those commercials. When they try and speed read all those sides effects right by you. *(He rapidly imitates the commercial voice-overs.)* Side effects may include nausea, bloating, vertigo, weight gain, weight loss, loss of memory, farting, hunger, thirst, appetite, no appetite, consult your doctor before taking . . . No, ma'am.

OLIVE: You and that TV.

FRED: Yeah, and let me tell you something else. *(Fred holds out his hand as if offering it to Olive to shake, but his fingers are spread wide.)* You see this thumb? This thumb represents the male member at thirteen, fourteen. *(Next door's music has grown louder. Fred interrupts himself, goes to the door, opens it, and yells at the neighbor.)* Will you turn that noise off! Turn it off! *(Fred waits. It's actually turned off and he then comes back inside to continue.)* Now, this thumb is young men at puberty!

OLIVE: Fred, he turned off the music, you can stop yelling.

FRED: *(Pointing to his thumb. Calmly.)* Puberty. Straight up and down at any indiscriminate time of the day. I've taken a lot of zeros in class 'cause I didn't want to stand up. Shoot, it's not that boys are hard of learning; it's just that we ain't try'n to embarrass ourselves. With the exception of crazy Darryl Williams back in the seventh grade. Remember when Mrs. Waters asked who knew the math answer. Now not only did that fool stand up, but he was the first to raise his hand. The only one to raise his hand! We're thinking, wow, Darryl knows the answer, wonders never cease. But no, that fool just wanted to stand up and show off his little newfound pubescence.

OLIVE: It wasn't that little.

FRED: Excuse me?

OLIVE: I said, I guess I fell in love with and married the wrong classmate.

FRED: Yeah, OK. Who knows how that fool turned out. And being that he wasn't one of the brightest stars in the galaxy, I'm surprised that with the one talent he had, I've never seen him on any of the four adult channels.

OLIVE: Four uh? You got 'em all down pat, don't cha?

FRED: Well, you, know, as I channel surf. And they're all back to back. And then when I see a black couple, come on, you know you've snuck a peek, once or twice. Compared notes. Moves. Agility.

OLIVE: See, that's why we don't do it enough. You exert all your energy on the TV with all their manufactured fantasies.

FRED: I know you're not downing fantasies. What about you lately?

OLIVE: Well, mine are for us. Which, bringing it back to the issue, this is our anniversary. I was just trying to include a little romance.

FRED: I know and I understand that.

OLIVE: So, then how about tomorrow morning? Can I look forward to that? You know. When you wake up. And you have that little morning sunrise thing going on.

FRED: Yeah, back to my issue. Now the pointer finger is man in his twenties and thirties. The middle finger, his forties. The ring finger, his fifties. You see where we're going here. You see how we're heading south. And so this pinky is our sixties. No longer up here where the thumb is.

OLIVE: So what exactly are you saying?

FRED: I'm saying, that the sunrise you *used* to see, well, Olive, baby, the sun has set. I'm saying that at sixty-six, three and four times a week is against nature.

OLIVE: You're sixty-five and it's two to three times a week, and I don't think it's the study that's flawed.

FRED: Whatever. Folks are lying. But if it's two, three, four times a week you want, well, OK, I can hook you up.

OLIVE: With who?

FRED: Not with who, but with what? But first are you allergic to Teflon?

OLIVE: You're funny, Fred, but no thank you. You just try and make it a who. Like I wonder what Darryl Williams is up to these days.

FRED: OK, OK, enough of Darryl Williams.

OLIVE: Well, you brought it up. I guess you just can't keep it up.

FRED: OK, OK, Olive.

(Silence.)

OLIVE: Well, are you still hungry? You still want me to get that pizza for you? You know how spicy tomato sauce gets you revved.

FRED: Oh, boy.

OLIVE: Yeah, and then we can play a little game of restaurant, to keep the excitement going. We can go into the kitchen and play Home Delivered Pizza. Served right on the table.

FRED: *(Holding up his spread fingers and hand.)* So the finger thing meant nothing? Just bounced right off your ear. Just me talking to the air.

OLIVE: Yeah, but I know how you are about the foods you like. How it inspires you.

(Fred shakes his head.)

FRED: My mother always said you were a freak. And here you are proving her right.

OLIVE: OK, so she's looking up here at you saying, "I told you so." Now what are we gonna do about it?

FRED: Looking up? Are you trying to say that my mama's somewhere wishing she had an ice-cold drink? Are you trying to say my mama's in hell? 'Cause I don't let nobody talk about my mama. My mama was a good, one-third Christian woman.

OLIVE: Did you just say your mama called me a freak?

FRED: No! She just said with all that quiet reserve, I just better watch out. And that's exactly how it turned out. Closet freak.

OLIVE: Well, all I'll say is it takes one to know one and leave it alone.

FRED: Yeah, you better leave it alone.

OLIVE: Fred! Are we going into that kitchen or what?

FRED: *(Laughing.)* And this is the same woman who was waiting until her wedding night? Saving herself for Jesus?

OLIVE: And you should have been trying to do the same.

FRED: Save myself for Jesus, impossible.

OLIVE: OK, tell him that at the gate.

FRED: I will and he'll understand.

OLIVE: You better stop that.

FRED: I'm serious. Unlike you, I couldn't save myself for Jesus because I'm not gay. *(He laughs.)* Get it? I'm a man. He's a man.

OLIVE: OK, Fred. You've had your moment.

FRED: OK, OK.

OLIVE: Now. The kitchen. The table. Or are you gonna introduce another delaying tactic?

(Fred twists and turns in hesitation and avoidance.)

FRED: But on the table? Where we have to eat? Call me anal, but you know . . .

OLIVE: OK, well, some clothes have to be washed. How 'bout the washing machine instead of the table?

FRED: In the basement? The cold, dank basement. You know black folks don't like cold. And you know what coldness does to the male member.

OLIVE: I'm washing whites.

FRED: The hot cycle! Won't that burn the skin?

OLIVE: We're not getting in the machine, Fred. But I also have mixed colors which means warm water.

FRED: You've got all the answers, uh?

OLIVE: Yes, 'cause this is our anniversary, and you're gonna have to really convince me that you're not able.

FRED: Well, you got any other fantasies in mind?

OLIVE: So you are willing? You are able?

FRED: A little something. Anything for the anniversary. But I'm also hungry. So, something's stirring. I'm not sure which.

OLIVE: Well, let's combine the two.

FRED: The wash and eating?

OLIVE: Fred.

FRED: OK, OK. Go get the pizza.

(Olive goes into the kitchen and retrieves the pizza and also returns donning a chef's hat.)

FRED: Umph, umph, umph. You should have told me this was what you wanted. I wouldn't have gotten you that anniversary jewelry box.

(She returns and walks to the door.)

OLIVE: Right, next time just get jewelry. But I thank you. Now I'm gonna go to the door, like a delivery girl.

FRED: Wait a minute before ringing the bell. I want to prepare my mind. Since they do say ninety percent of this stuff is mental. *(Fred walks upstage, holding his head, chanting.)* Lena Horne, Lena Horne. Pam Grier, Pam Grier. Janet Jackson, Janet Jackson. *(Fred comes back downstage after retrieving and donning a pair of dark sunglasses.)*

OLIVE: *(Warningly.)* Fred.

FRED: *(Gleefully, moving his head as if blind.)* Janet? Is that you? With my pizza with extra sauce?

OLIVE: Fred take those sunglasses off. Now, I'm going outside to ring the bell.

FRED: Shucks, and it was working.

(The doorbell interrupts.)

OLIVE: Who the hell?

(Olive opens the door and in steps Selah.)

FRED: Selah! Come on in.

SELAH: Hi, Olive, Fred. Olive, I'm sorry, but if you have a minute.

OLIVE: Uh, sure.

SELAH: Unless it's a real bad time? It can wait. I know this is your special anniversary evening and all —

FRED: No, no, you can come on in. I was just going upstairs to eat a little of this pizza. So, you two go right on and do what you two do. Good night.
(He starts upstairs.)

OLIVE: Fred. Save me a slice. OK.

FRED: Sure, sure.

OLIVE: See you in a bit.
(Fred exits upstairs.)

SELAH: Uh, Olive, you're sure it's not a bad time?

OLIVE: Well, Fred and I were just about to have some food sex, but other than that, no, not a bad, bad time.

SELAH: Oh, I'm sorry, Olive. Why didn't you give me some sort of sign?

OLIVE: Like what?

SELAH: Like, Selah can you come back in thirty minutes?

OLIVE: Thirty minutes? You overestimate Fred. And I see that once again you didn't bring my cake mold.

SELAH: Oh, Olive, I'm sorry.

OLIVE: Selah, it was only the last thing I mentioned on the phone.

SELAH: I know, Olive, I'm sorry.

OLIVE: And I'm not coming over to get it. You came over to borrow it, you come back here with it. So if you're waiting for me to say forget it, you can keep it, you can forget it, it's not gonna happen, I want my cake mold.
(Selah is overcome with withheld emotions. She begins to moan in pain.)

SELAH: Mmmm, oh, God, Olive!

OLIVE: OK, OK, you can keep the damn thing.

SELAH: No, no, no. It's not that. It's nothing about the cake mold.

OLIVE: Well what is it, Selah?

SELAH: Olive, Olive, Jonas and I have, our marriage has run its course. We're separating. We finally admitted the obvious. We handled it with civility and proper decorum, but, inside, Olive, I'm going through it.

OLIVE: Of course you are, Selah. My God, what can I say?

SELAH: Olive, I'm so sorry to come back here like this. With this news, especially it being your anniversary, I'm so sorry.

OLIVE: No, no, it's all right. Of course you needed to come over. I'm glad to be here for you. Is there anything I can get you?

SELAH: Anything, thank you.

OLIVE: Oh, Selah, my heart goes out to you. How did this happen? Run its course? This is like all so sudden. At least it appears to be. Tonight, you and Jonas appeared, so comfortable, so as one.

SELAH: Thanks to having mastered deception so well. Oh, I can't believe this either, but again, Olive, I'm sorry for the intrusion, and I do thank you. You have always been there for me. Such a good friend. Even back when I was so aloof. So many times you could have told me where to go.

OLIVE: I did.

(Selah laughs.)

SELAH: Yeah, you did. Glad I didn't listen.

OLIVE: Selah, I'm the one that's sorry. *(She hugs Selah.)* I can only think if this was Fred and how I'd feel. And as of late with so much of our romance going I don't know where, I mean we used to have a very healthy and active love life, and now, it's like the passion has gone, which is what, a sign that the love is diminishing?

SELAH: Well —

OLIVE: And it seems as if much of what Fred does is out of obligation. This evening for example. It's our anniversary, and he had sooner gone to bed, and, and —

SELAH: Olive, Olive, calm down. I'm sure you and Fred are all right. At this stage diminished lovemaking can be for several reasons. One being age, and we can stop there. I see you and Fred's love. There are no illusions there, so just stop it.

OLIVE: Oh, Selah, I'm sorry, I'm supposed to be consoling you, and here I am letting my own insecurities get in the way.

(The front door bell rings.)

SELAH: And now, I'm sure that's Jonas.

OLIVE: Should I send him on his way?

SELAH: No, no, just as I came over for you, I sure he's here for Fred. Why be selfish?

OLIVE: I'll let Fred get it. Lord knows he needs the exercise.

(The bell rings again. Fred comes down in his bathrobe, carrying a slice of pizza.)

FRED: Olive, what's the problem? *(The bell rings again.)* What, what, who is it!

(He opens the door, revealing Jonas.)

JONAS: Good evening, Fred.

FRED: Jonas, hey, how are you? You looking for Selah?

JONAS: Please, no. I've, I've come to see if you had a minute?

FRED: *Yeah. (Chewing.)* Excuse me, though. I was just getting ready for bed with my nightcap here, you want a slice? There should be some left in the kitchen.

JONAS: No, no thanks.

FRED: Well, have a seat. Here's your glasses. Now what's going on?

(Jonas rises and paces the room.)

JONAS: Fred, you and Olive, you really have a nice home here. Really warm. Complete. You two are really a class act.

FRED: Thanks. But, uh, I get the feeling that's not why you're here.

JONAS: No, no, it's not . . . May I sit down? *(Fred gestures.)* Fred, just, this evening Selah and I finally admitted that for some time we have been drifting apart . . . And that continuing the facade does neither of us any good.

FRED: So, what are you saying, Jonas?

JONAS: I'm saying that Selah and I are separating. We've uh, come to this conclusion. So, yeah, I guess I am here half-checking on Selah and half-seeing if I can burden your shoulder.

FRED: Well, Jonas, I'm shocked. I'm sorry to hear this. I don't know what to say.

JONAS: But I didn't mean to come put you in any awkward position. *(He rises.)* Maybe I'll just go on.

FRED: No, no, Jonas.

(Just then Olive and Selah enter.)

OLIVE: Fred, Selah and I are going to take a quick drive. You need anything while I'm out?

FRED: No thank you. I'm OK.

OLIVE: All right then, I'll see you later. Jonas.

JONAS: How you doing, Olive? Hello, Selah.

SELAH: Jonas.

(Olive grabs her pocketbook and the women exit. The men are alone.)

JONAS: When Olive gets back, I guess you can compare notes.

FRED: This is quite a blow.

JONAS: Yeah. And with everything being motivated by the fact that I've met someone.

FRED: Now you're not saying that —

JONAS: No, no, it's not an affair. It's not that. But more a situation which has allowed me to realize what Selah and I don't have. Haven't had.

FRED: And Selah is aware of this?

JONAS: I think so. I can assume. I mean, she knows my habits, and just by virtue of a change in routine, a change in our communication, she has to notice something.

FRED: Jonas, tell her.

JONAS: Yeah . . . It's just a case of one of those easier-said-than-done situations. But, uh, again, thanks for letting me bend your ear with this.

FRED: You want a beer?

JONAS: No thank you, Fred, I think, I better —

FRED: Do, you want a beer?

JONAS: Thanks, I'll have a beer.

FRED: You want anything stronger? A little Hennesey?

JONAS: No, the beer is fine.

FRED: OK, then.

> *(Fred retrieves two beers from the portable bar.)*

JONAS: Thanks.

FRED: No, problem. *(Fred sips while Jonas takes a big drink.)* What can I say?

JONAS: Fred, I just thank you for the company.

> *(Silence.)*

FRED: Well, Jonas, I would like to ask you something. Not to be indifferent to the news you just told me this, but, uh, maybe to take your mind off of things for a moment.

JONAS: Please, I welcome it.

FRED: Though it is in the area of relationships. And though you say, you're not involved in any affair, but, uh, well, how can I put this? Jonas how's your sex life?

JONAS: Fred, Selah and I aren't going through any of this because of bad sex.

FRED: No, no, of course not. I'm just talking. Drinking, talking. *(Silence.)* But what I'm trying to get at is, uh, how is your ability? Your efficiency?

JONAS: My ability is good, why do you ask?

FRED: Good, uh? You ever participate in any surveys?

JONAS: Fred what's your point?

FRED: Well, Jonas, on average, you'd say your efficiency is what?

JONAS: Two, three times a week. Is there a problem, Fred?

FRED: No, no. I don't think so. At least I didn't. But you say up to three times a week? Due to what? What are you on? Implant, pill?

JONAS: I'm on a willing desire. Fred, if you're having a problem —

FRED: Well, I don't look at it as a problem.

JONAS: Yohimbe.

FRED: Pardon?

JONAS: Something you should take. It's called Yohimbe.

FRED: Oh, I don't go in for all them drugs.

JONAS: No, no. It's not some synthetic drug. Nothing pharmaceutical. It's totally holistic. Homeopathic. All natural.

FRED: And I ain't hear a natural word in all of what you just said? You sound like Gail. This new woman ain't my daughter, is it?

JONAS: No, her name is Vera.

FRED: And that could be an alias.

JONAS: Well, Fred, barring any real physical impediments, Yohimbe should help you out. Think of it like vitamin C. Just a little something to aid and assist your natural abilities.

FRED: Yohimbe, uh?

JONAS: Ask for Power Max 1500. Unless this has been some long-standing occurrence?

FRED: No, I wouldn't say long-standing.

JONAS: Well, let's be more specific. Are we talking about lack of interest or lack of ability? There is a difference. Is this, uh . . . erectile dysfunction?

FRED: Oh, hey, watch you mouth! Don't be cussing in my house. But to answer your question, no. Noo.

JONAS: Well, then what are you saying?

FRED: Well, to be honest with you . . . A little loss of attraction may be the case.

JONAS: Which is natural. As long as you haven't said loss of love.

FRED: But I don't want to only be turned on when Olive becomes a lost traveler, or pizza deliverer.

JONAS: Fred, what you're saying is that after more than forty years of the same thing, you've found yourself jaded. So what else is new? Of course you'll be turned on by Olive and a fantasy. That's the enticing variety of life.

FRED: Then how come Olive doesn't need me to be a traffic cop or a school teacher?

JONAS: 'Cause women go on love and familiarity. And we go on lust and variety.

(Silence.)

FRED: Yohimbe, uh?

JONAS: Can't really hurt.

FRED: So, it doesn't come with a thousand side effects. I don't have to worry about nausea, dizzyness, or excessive flatulence?

JONAS: No, none of that.

FRED: But, hey, let me avail you of something. *(Fred holds his hand out to Jonas, as if for a handshake, fingers spread as with Olive.)* You see this thumb?

JONAS: Yeah, yeah, I know. We're supposed to be the pinky and I don't buy it. Fred, supplements can help, but more importantly, it is all about the state of mind. That along with the usual suspects of rest, diet, and exercise. And of course, removing yourself from those situations which no longer serve your best interest.

FRED: Yeah, well I also know we have one natural factor working against us. And that one factor is woman, herself.

JONAS: Women?

FRED: Yes, women. Check it out. Let's start with the primary years. Let's say from age eighteen and for the next twenty or so years all they do is just basically lie there. Lie there while we do all the hard work. So, that means for twenty years, they're preserving strength. Occasionally faking it, preserving more strength. And then when they don't fake it, but instead do that multi-orgasmic thing they can do, well that only all the more saps our strength. So while they're preserving, conserving, and gathering steam, what does that do for us?

JONAS: Interesting.

FRED: Yeah, wait, it gets better. They also go through their "tear it up" phase. That "hurt me, work it out, give it to me stage." And you know we can't tear nothing up. Eight-pound babies come out of there, so what damage are we really doing? And they encourage this. I tell you it's a conspiracy. That's why the black man has high blood pressure. "Tear it up, tear it up." But do our egos tell say, "Hey, look here bro. Let's reconsider this." No, the ego says, "Let's tear, pound, and pulverize it!" Yeah, right. So, now there's age forty. We're starting to go down hill, *(He waves his hand, fingers spread.)* OK, and woman are now at their sexual peak. How? Why, all that preserving of strength. Now they want it more than ever. Now that we're drained and depleted, here they come, complete with elaborate shows and fantasy. I tell you, I'm on to something. Why else do women have longer life expectancies? It ain't all pork and beef. I tell you they can add choochie to that list too. Yeah, so, hey, now I ration it out.

JONAS: You've really thought this out.

FRED: I looked at the obvious facts. Now I'm the one with the headaches. It's either that or some surrogate sex-mate I've been reading about.

JONAS: Fred, what's your technique?

FRED: Come again?

JONAS: Your technique. Your particular style. What's your motion? Show me.

FRED: Uh, without showing you, it's in and out like most people.

JONAS: Now, you talked about this sapping of our energy and strength. I'm gonna show you how to retain it. How to keep it.

FRED: Yeah, by claiming headaches. Why should they have exclusive rights to that? Or I'll claim sore back. You know them back things are hard to prove.

JONAS: Fred, what's your motion?

FRED: You're serious, uh?

JONAS: It's all science.

FRED: *(Fred pauses, then begins.)* Science? Well, Jonas, my motion is smooth.

JONAS: Smooth?

FRED: Yea, works for me.

JONAS: So, I would imagine like so.

(Jonas demonstrates ordinary, tepid thrusts.)

FRED: Man, would you put a little more style and rhythm to that. Move. Observe.

(Fred joins Jonas in demonstrating a few rhythmic thrusts of his own. Jonas stops and observes. Fred begins to enjoy his own demonstration and begins to show off. Jonas retrieves a pillow from the sofa and tosses it to Fred.)

JONAS: Hold that to your pelvis and continue. I'll refine that for you.

FRED: *(Holding the pillow to his pelvis and continuing his demonstration.)* Yeah, see, style and rhythm, just like a dance.

JONAS: Uh-un. Just as I thought . . . Sixty-five and don't know what the hell he's been doing all these years. First off, it all begins with how you even hold the pillow. *(He takes it from Fred.)* You don't hold it like its some wild animal trying to get away. You hold it like a newborn. Gently. The end isn't the goal. The goal is the journey. You don't work yourself into an intense frenzy. You wanna lead her to it. So, it's about constantly switching up, pacing, and alteration. *(Jonas goes through several motions, all of which appear to be of some epileptic nature. He completes it with half-crazy leg dance.)* But the art is in the control. Experiencing all the nuances. Slow. Attentive. Gentle but firm. Control. You don't let the goal manipulate you. You are in command. That way she peaks, but you don't. You keep control. You keep your composure.

FRED: *(Fred crosses to the door.)* Man, let me lock this door. I can see it now. Olive walking in here and you freak'n her pillow. Man, you looked as if you were fending off two midgets. What was that leg thing? Man, I'll stick to my headaches. Or I know I'll have to look better than that.

JONAS: See, that's our problem. Always having to look good. Where's the mirror, where's the mirror? I'm talking about technique, and you're auditioning for GQ.

FRED: And wait a minute. Did you say "she peaks, but you don't?"

JONAS: Yes, you keep your orgasm within. You direct it inward. But I guess we should forget the whole thing, you're obviously not ready.

FRED: Keep it inward?

JONAS: Fred, I thank you for the beer, and for momentarily taking my mind off of my situation.

FRED: Are you saying you never actually, outwardly climax? You keep it in inside?

JONAS: Yes, Fred, that's the practice.

FRED: Maaannn!

JONAS: Fred, that's how *you* conserve energy. That's how man can learn discipline. That's the true art of lovemaking. You learn that, you learn how to be a true lover. The point is to make love to your mate, not yourself.

FRED: And not reaching the finish line is the point of it all.

JONAS: Thanks to us, women have been unwillingly doing it for years.

FRED: Not my Olive.

JONAS: I believe I can make a case that even when we're with a woman, we're still only masturbating.

FRED: And you're the one getting a separation.

JONAS: Love and sex may be twins, but they're still two different entities.

FRED: Whatever. Sex, lovemaking, I'm gonna cross my finish line. I wanna see the evidence of all my hard work and good effort. Who wants to keep that inside? That ain't even natural. You'd be done messed up your internals. End up impregnating myself. Be the first man in history listening to you.

JONAS: *(Offering his hand.)* Fred, thanks, again. Thanks for your time. The lovely evening earlier. Everything. I wish you and Olive the best. May you have many more.

FRED: Thank you, Jonas.

(They give a sincere hug.)

FRED: OK, not too long now. *(Fred breaks the hug.)* You've been keeping your stuff inside. I don't want no accidents up in here.

JONAS: Goodnight, Fred.

(Jonas exits and Fred is alone.)

FRED: Keep it inside, that's a first. Shoot, not the kid. No way. That'll hurt. *(He crosses back over to the sofa and sits. He turns up the volume on the remote. An old late-night movie is on. He mutes the volume, puts down the remote, and contemplates a pillow. Finally, he picks it up. He stands and holds it to his waist. He begins the same technical gyrations as instructed by Jonas, leg and all. He too appears epileptic. Mid-performance, Olive enters.)*

FRED: Uh, it's not what it looks like.

OLIVE: And you call me a freak.

FRED: I can explain.

OLIVE: Don't even bother.

FRED: No, I —

OLIVE: Ah, ah, I don't want to hear it. But don't you ever mock my fantasies, call me over zealous or anything. Don't say your mama knew this, your mama said that, don't you say nay word. You are busted.

FRED: No, let me explain —

OLIVE: Ah! Ah! Just know that your mama was watching.

FRED: I was doing it for you!

OLIVE: *(Laughing.)* What?

FRED: I was doing a, a, a pelvic thrust exercise. A proven scientific technique.

OLIVE: Scientific technique?

FRED: Yeah, according to — you know that Jonas is an interesting character.

OLIVE: Jonas?

FRED: Uh, yeah, of course we spoke of and discussed what he and Selah are going through, ain't that a shame? And then to help ease his mind, we spoke of more trivial issues. Amongst them, male virility, and he, was, uh, giving me a few pointers. This technique. An exercise to practice so the next time you're in one of your moods and want to hang from the ceiling or armoire, I'll be in some sort of shape to oblige you.

(Olive just stares and shakes her head.)

FRED: No, really.

OLIVE: Whatever, Fred. I'm going upstairs.

FRED: Olive.

OLIVE: OK. As my mama used to say, I believe you. And now I'll be leaving you. But just remember, next time I want to hang from the ceiling, I want to see the results of this scientific technique, OK? *(Fred pouts.)* Now don't roll your eyes and walk away. Here, take your little girlfriend with you. *(She throws the sofa pillow after him.)* Good night.

(Olive departs. Fred picks up the pillow.)

FRED: Well, it was a bit softer.

OLIVE: *(From upstairs.)* I heard that. And I got your soft.

(Fred mimics Olive. Lights fade. We shift to Jonas and Selah. Selah has entered the house. A moment passes before either speaks.)

JONAS: Hello.

SELAH: Hi.

JONAS: How was your outing with Olive?

SELAH: Reassuring, thank you . . . And your time with Fred?

JONAS: Good . . . I told him —

SELAH: Yeah, well, it's not official until the neighbors know —

JONAS: Even before our own children. Should we call them now?

SELAH: No, I'd rather we tell them face to face.

JONAS: Which should alert them to something, being that it isn't Christmas or any holiday. *(Silence.)* So, where did you and Olive go?

SELAH: To Trinity's Sanctum . . . I needed to be reminded of just how cherished women are. You know, it's very comforting to know that we are treasured. Or at least we should be . . . Jonas, is there anything you have to tell me?

JONAS: Selah, it's getting late. Can we continue this in the morning? We've already acknowledged something very difficult and painful.

SELAH: Jonas, is there anything you have to tell me?

JONAS: it's late, Selah.

SELAH: Jonas!

JONAS: OK! . . . I've met someone.

SELAH: Well, thank you for not making me say it for you.

JONAS: There is something with whom I converse, nothing else, but converse, and it has no bearing on what you and I have come to.

SELAH: No?

JONAS: No, it has no real relevance to *us*.

SELAH: What's her name?

(Silence.)

JONAS: Selah.

SELAH: Name, name, what do you call her? I'm sure she's aware of mine.

JONAS: Her name is Vera, and if she didn't exist, we would still be faced with our reality.

SELAH: But there is. This Vera does exist.

JONAS: Selah, I don't want to fight. Maybe we should give this more time.

SELAH: I gave it all the time I could waiting for you to say something about this person with whom you say you only converse. I doubt I'll be any less incensed at some later date.

JONAS: Selah, why did we marry? Although never stated, why did we marry? 'Cause we both knew we had something to prove. Young and ambitious, and all the fairy tale reasons had very little to do with it. We saw in each other the opportunity to achieve and accomplish, and we went for it, but Selah, now what? Yes, we care about each other —

SELAH: I grew to love you.

JONAS: And I, you.

SELAH: I fell in love with you! I fell in love.

JONAS: *(Quietly.)* And, Selah . . . that's all I want to do. I'm not saying it's Vera. The hell with her. What I'm saying is . . . I've always respected you. Selah, I love you, and damnit, this does hurt. But, Selah, I'm hurting knowing that I never fell in love. Never fell in love. So what do I do? Now, after all these years? After the fulfilled accomplishments what do I do? What does Jonas do for Jonas? Shut up and go with it? Another ten, fifteen years, till death do us part? . . . Or do I finally be honest?

SELAH: And you come with this after you've found someone with whom you can talk.

JONAS: It just happened.

SELAH: Nothing just happens.

JONAS: We've only just met, and she doesn't —

SELAH: She does matter! Did she ask you to come to me about this?

JONAS: Yes.

SELAH: And her motives were to just be a supportive, good, talking friend? . . . Well, I'll tell you what. Let's all talk. *(Selah picks up the phone.)*

JONAS: *(Gently taking the phone.)* Selah, why is this necessary?

SELAH: You don't get it, or you're just not trying. Now either you'll make the call or I will. Since you're not in the habit of erasing numbers from the Caller ID.

(Selah leaves the room. Jonas remains. Lights fade. Fade up on Fred and Olive. Olive comes downstairs. Fred is asleep in front of the television which is broadcasting the Spanish weather. The gramophone is dismantled even more than before. Olive turns off the television and stands before Fred shaking her head.)

OLIVE: Umph, umph, umph. Would you look at this. And your mama tried to talk about me. Well, mama Mitchell, look at your son. Lady, look up here from your fiery depths and get a load of your son. *(Fred stirs, smacking his mouth, but doesn't awake.)* Fred . . . Fred. Fred, wake up!

FRED: I'm up. I was just praying. Uh, Amen.

OLIVE: Come on, go to bed.

FRED: You off the phone already? What did Gail want this time?

OLIVE: She's now thinking about a birthing tub.

FRED: Delivering the child under water?

OLIVE: That's the idea.

FRED: So, now she thinks she's a fish.

OLIVE: Lord, I don't know what Gail's thinking. But she's mainly now complaining about Brian and his wants and needs.

FRED: Well, what does he want?

OLIVE: What do all men want? Correction, what do most men want? He wants what got them into this situation.

FRED: Well, tell her to go on and give the boy some.

OLIVE: She's eight months pregnant, Fred.

FRED: And?

OLIVE: And she's uncomfortable. She's bloated. No, that's too close to home. So now Brian is suggesting more of their other options.

FRED: Hey, hey, hey, OK. I don't need to know that. Now how am I gonna kiss my daughter with you telling me information like this?

OLIVE: Well, she kisses you, knowing your information and habits.

FRED: Olive, what are you discussing with our children?

OLIVE: Well, she asked what would I do?

FRED: And how do you get to me from "what would you do?" You tell her your business, not mine.

OLIVE: But you should be proud, Fred. You know it's not everyone that can, say, eat corn on the cob. Take your brother for instance. You've seen him at reunions and how his corn looks. As if a rat's been thrashing and gnawing at it. I mean, I feel sorry for his wife, Deloris. Whereas, your corn. All nice and neat and professional. Baby, you know how to eat some corn.

FRED: Well, thank you very much.

OLIVE: You're welcome, baby.

FRED: *(Yawns.)* Well, this sure has been one good, long, eventful, memorable, and unfortunate evening.

OLIVE: Oh, yeah. Isn't that just too bad? Let's say a prayer for Selah and Jonas before we turn in.

FRED: Of course. You want me to get the Bible?

OLIVE: No, don't get the Bible. I said just a prayer, not a sermon. You can't make church each Sunday, but you're always ready to deliver a sermon.

FRED: I don't go to church because I ain't forgot that Reverend Cunningham still owes me sixty dollars.

OLIVE: Oh, boy, here we go.

FRED: Yeah, here we go. And I know he remembers. How can someone car breakdown, along comes one of your church members; *loans* you sixty dollars for the tow truck; then you see that very same congregant come Sunday morning, and all you can say is, "Good morning, Brother Fred, praise the Lord," then turn your attention to the next member. How can someone do that? Hell, that man ain't gett'n another dime out of me. I should have known he wasn't all that righteous. I mean, the man don't rightly smile right. He don't show no teeth. And a reverend that don't show teeth while smiling, I can't find him all too trustworthy. And I *don't* want to hear that he's just serious and solemn and all. That man don't show teeth 'cause he ain't right. Like he's hiding something. And showing teeth is the only reason worth smiling. Now he don't, and so I don't deal with him.

OLIVE: Maybe he has bad teeth and he's self-conscious.

FRED: Well, he need not be. He has my sixty dollars to help contribute towards getting get 'em capped, cleaned, and spit-shined.

OLIVE: Just a quick prayer, Fred. That's all I asked. Not for you to get into your personal vendetta against Reverend Cunningham.

FRED: And maybe he's so tightlipped because he has bad breath due to talking all that bullsh —

OLIVE: Fred!

FRED: Dear heavenly Father, on this day where you have blessed us with being able to celebrate forty-five years of love, life, and togetherness, we give you the highest praise. Lord, we humbly thank you for guiding us thus far, and may you guide us for another forty and forever more.

OLIVE: And hopefully have the Victrola fixed by the time forever gets here.

FRED: Anyway, Lord, I ask that you see my daughter, Gail, through to a safe and healthy delivery, wanting to have a child at her fool age, and now wanting to deliver the child in an aquarium. Lord, it's said that you look after fools and babies, so please look out for this new baby and its fool mother.

OLIVE: Fred.

FRED: Yeah?

(Olive taps Fred's forehead.)

OLIVE: Jesus said turn to your neighbor give him that. Now, Selah and Jonas, Fred, Selah, and Jonas.

FRED: And heavenly Father, whereas you have guided others to see fit to part company and go their separate ways after so many years in matrimony, Lord, may they do so in peace and within your ever-loving arms. We ask this in your name, your most humble servants, Fred and Olive Mitchell. Amen.

OLIVE: Amen, and may they find their joy. And Lord, please assist me in my effort to have my husband be more, outgoing, adventurous, and uh, efficient. Thank you, Lord, Amen.

FRED: Efficient, uh?

OLIVE: Happy anniversary, Fred. I love you.

FRED: Happy anniversary, Olive. I love you too.

(Blackout.)

END OF ACT I

ACT II

Act II begins with sounds of hip-hop coming from the next door neighbor. The lights come up on Fred tinkering with his Victrola. His frustration of not yet having repaired it is fueled by the music. He angrily goes to the window and shuts it, deadening the outside sounds. He crosses back to his work.

FRED: How can anyone concentrate with all that ungodly noise? Boy, you can take them out of the projects . . . *(He tinkers for a few more seconds, cranks it, and to his surprise the Victrola plays.)* Ah, ah, Olive! Olive!
(Olive comes from the kitchen where she was preparing dinner.)

OLIVE: I hear it, I hear it.
(Fred extends his hand for them to dance. Olive accepts, but the Victrola dies just before they can celebrate.)

OLIVE: Aww. But I heard it. It was playing. Well, tomorrow is another day. And there's always the radio and the oldies station.

FRED: Yeah, yeah, yeah.
(Fred picks up a hammer and reels back.)

OLIVE: Fred!

FRED: Well, that's what I feel like.

OLIVE: But that's a sign that's it's almost fixed. Just some more fine-tuning and we'll be slow-dragging the night away.

FRED: If not for that noise next door disturbing my concentration, I could have long since had it working.

OLIVE: What noise?

FRED: Sure, it's not there now, but he was blasting it earlier.

OLIVE: Come on now, don't blame across the street.

FRED: All I'm saying is I could better concentrate without it.

OLIVE: Well, somebody must like it. It afforded him the nicest house on the block.

FRED: *I* don't give a hoot. It's still noise. And they get up there at those award shows thankin' God. As if He inspired that mess. As if Jesus wants to hear that over a good Jimmy Cleveland. Then they can't spell half of what they're saying and can't correctly pronounce the other half. Them funny ways they spell their names. It's a reason for that, you know. It's called ig'nence. Gaudy jewelry and all. Yeah, nothing represents our meek and humble Savior like a diamond-filled platinum cross. Talk about what would Jesus do? Not that.

(Fred sits and reaches for the television remote.)

OLIVE: There you go. If it's not the Victrola, it's the TV.

(She joins Fred by sitting on the arm of the easy chair.)

FRED: Well, the two go hand in hand. Television and music. TV brings us the world. And music, the reverberating soundtrack.

OLIVE: I don't know if you're a worst repairman or poet.

FRED: Well, that's not my quote. That's the cable program on channel six hundred and eighty-nine.

OLIVE: OK then, just a poor taste plagiarizer.

FRED: Shh, come on now, I'm trying to see what's on the Hawaiian news.

OLIVE: *(Olive mutes the TV cutting off the news's intro music.)* How 'bout we go out and see the world? Fred, let's take a third honeymoon.

FRED: Now there you go.

OLIVE: Will it be more appealing if I call it a relaxing, hand down your pants, TV watching, bungalow get-away?

FRED: *(Laughing.)* Hey, well then I'm already on vacation. Wanna go fetch me a piña colada?

(Olive is not amused.)

FRED: Come on, I'm retired. This is what I'm supposed to do.

(Olive turns the television off all together.)

FRED: Hey, come on now, Olive.

OLIVE: You come on. I want us to do other activities. I don't want us getting bored. Not with life, or each other.

FRED: I'm not bored with life.

OLIVE: And?

FRED: Oh, nor with you, honey. I like you and I like this. Come on, we've been to the Bahamas. You've been to one island you've been to them all. And with all these immigrants here, it's like we've been everywhere from Haiti to India, from Korea to Mexico. Guam to Lithuania. Just go outside. They're here and they bring all that stuff with 'em. The smells, the clothes, the accent, I tell ya, it's like we're at the Olympics.

OLIVE: I still want to be on different land. I'm still bored.

FRED: Is that my fault if after sixty-four years, you can't entertain yourself?

OLIVE: Oh, I can entertain myself. With you, I've had to learn . . . Look, Fred, if you can fix the Victrola, I'll even take that. Listen to the good ol' sounds for an evening.

FRED: Yeah, see.

OLIVE: And if not, we're going to a jazz club.

FRED: I'm working on it, I'm working on it.

OLIVE: So get ready for an evening out. I'm giving you one more week.

FRED: Umph.

OLIVE: Well, I think I'll go upstairs. There's a working CD player up there. You care to join me before I start dinner?

FRED: No, I see where you're headed.

OLIVE: What?

FRED: What we tried last week.

OLIVE: Last week?

FRED: Yeah, last week. Remember. Happy anniversary last week.

OLIVE: Man, ain't nobody studying you. I'm talking about listening to some good ol' music.

FRED: OK, 'cause I may as well warn you, there ain't much in the insurance policy.

OLIVE: Don't worry, I know. So now that that's out of the way.

FRED: Well, all the same, no thanks. I'm trying to catch up on my international news.

(Fred looks for the remote.)

OLIVE: Here, Fred. *(She gives him the remote.)* You are a poor excuse.

FRED: And then I wanna work on the Vic. You say I only have a week. Oh, I see. This is part of your distraction plan. Invite me for other things so I won't have time to fix the Victrola, and before I know it, I'm out in some smoke-filled room listening a poor imitation of Bird and Coltrane. No thanks. I'll work on the originals here. After the Hawaiian news.

(He hits the remote and the television comes on. The sound is low.)

OLIVE: Yeah, the news. What you should be on. The world's most pathetic couch potato.

FRED: Um-mm, yeah. Although this is what you need to be paying attention to.

OLIVE: Yeah, when I get old and run out of ideas like you.

FRED: Go 'head, disrespect informative news. And especially knowing how it transformed your life.

OLIVE: Transformed my life?

FRED: Yes, your life.

OLIVE: Oh, yeah it has. It stole my husband. I'll be upstairs.

FRED: Hold on there a sec. *(Fred mutes TV.)* Did not television change your everyday comings and goings? And I'm not talking about silly product commercials.

OLIVE: What are you talking about, Fred?

FRED: Did television not change your life for the better?

OLIVE: Not that I can readily recall.

FRED: What! Oh, how soon they forget. Did not television bring our people our civil rights?

OLIVE: If you say so, Fred. Now, see ya later.

FRED: No, no, hold on 'cause you think I'm just blowing hot air. Now allow me to make you gain some respect so you can stop disrespecting this vital piece of culture here. Now, let me take you back to early 19 and 63. Birmingham, Alabama and the local police commissioner, Bull Connor. Picture attack dogs, fire hoses, mace, and swinging batons. Scenes of brutality and racial intolerance. Now when those scenes were finally shown on what, the television! The tel-e-vis-ion did things start to change? Yes, they did. Decent Americans saw it, folks worldwide saw it, and all were outraged. The Kennedys saw it. And all saw it via television. And with it came all the moral outrage, sympathy, and support. By spring those televised demonstrations led to national legislation, which led the de-seg-re-gation of restrooms, water fountains, lunch counters, theaters, and more importantly for you, what? I know I don't have to remind you. What? What were you celebrating? The desegregation of what?

OLIVE: *(Sheepishly.)* Fitting rooms.

FRED: What? I didn't hear you.

OLIVE: Fitting rooms, OK. Fitting rooms.

FRED: Fitting rooms! So you wouldn't have to buy a dress, come home, try it on, have it not look like it does on those anorexic window mannequins, and then you not be able to take back. No wonder you're such a good seamstress. And so, to what do we owe the end of that indignity? Tel-e-vision. So what do I have in my living room? What do I sit in front of to pay tribute and commemorate those hard-fought achievements? Not a fire hydrant. Not a dog leash. But what? A big screen, remote control, picture-in-picture, Technicolor, tel-e-vision.

OLIVE: You finished?

FRED: Not quite, I'm on a roll. My television keeps me informed. It let's me know what struggles are still to be fought.

OLIVE: Struggles to be fought? I can't get you to walk to the corner store so what modern-day struggle are you marching in, Mr. Sharpton?

FRED: Ain't marching. I didn't say anything about marching. Today, it's all about where to write, fax, and e-mail my letters of condemnation.

OLIVE: E-mail.

FRED: Yes, I've been to the library. They have computers there.

OLIVE: And that phonograph as my witness, I know all you did was stare at the machine, looking for the remote control or handle to crank it.

FRED: Ha, ha. I've have you know I recently e-mailed our Congressman and Senator. And next I'm taxing the governor.

OLIVE: Umm-um.

FRED: *(Pressing his remote.)* I stay informed. There's "60 Minutes." Tony Brown's "Journal." "To the Contrary." "McLaughlin —

OLIVE: Oh, and for you, most importantly, don't forget what?

FRED: Like It Is?

OLIVE: Oh, come on now.

FRED: Oh, World News Tonight?

OLIVE: Try again.

FRED: The North Pole News channel?

OLIVE: Fred, please.

FRED: Well, help me out here, I must be having a senior moment here.

OLIVE: Fred, you know you live and breathe for what? Some Soul Train and that Soul Train dance line at a half past.

FRED: More like forty-five minutes.

OLIVE: Yeah, so I see the importance of your television. To make sure you don't miss those half-clad body parts shaking all over the place. You oughta e-mail Don Cornelius. Get you some type of Diligent Twenty Year Viewer's Award.

FRED: Hey, I wonder if they have e-mail? 'Cause whatever happened to that Asian sister with the long hair? And that tall, lanky fool with the cane?

OLIVE: I give up.

FRED: Good, thank you.

OLIVE: I'll be in the kitchen.

FRED: Look, I don't harass you about what you're always caught up on.

OLIVE: What I'm caught up on?

FRED: Yes. The phone. Sometimes I have to remind myself that's not an ugly earring hanging from your head, but the phone. But do I say anything? No. So, I have my television, and you have your telephone. Perfect marriage.

OLIVE: All I know is we better be going out somewhere soon.

(Olive turns to go into the kitchen.)

FRED: Moderation. Everything in moderation.

OLIVE: And since it's dark, lock up and put the chain on the door. I'll be in the kitchen and you'll be out there sleep.

FRED: *(Doing so and under his breath.)* Yeah, yeah, I'm not even sleepy. You just go on and cook my dinner.

OLIVE: Excuse me?

(Heading to the door to lock it.)

FRED: Nothing. I just said, why do we even bother with this flimsy, little chain? Like it's gonna do something.

OLIVE: Just put it on.

(She exits into the kitchen.)

FRED: If they can get through all these dead bolts, this little chain is not going to do anything. And what's with opening the door with the chain on? An eight-year-old with a swift kick can make his way in. Shoot, yell through the door if you want real safety. Who is it! What do you want? No, go away!

(Yelling from the kitchen.)

OLIVE: Maybe it's intended to slow down an intruder! You ever think of that?

FRED: Oh. Slow 'em down. Sure, give him a sore shoulder and really piss him off.

OLIVE: Just sit down and let the TV watch you.

FRED: I told you I be praying.

OLIVE: Well, you need to ask for help. And I heard that "fix my dinner" comment. Unlike you I haven't lost most of my faculties.

(Fred laughs. From the kitchen, Olive joins him in laughter. The lights fade and comes up on Jonas and Selah. We switch to Jonas and Selah. They are awaiting Vera's arrival. Selah pours herself a drink.)

SELAH: Is she usually late?

JONAS: Selah, what do you wish to accomplish?

SELAH: Is she usually late?

JONAS: The time it takes to determine that as some little quaint habit has not yet passed.

SELAH: Well, has she ever been late before?

JONAS: That's your third drink, Selah.

SELAH: Have you ever known me to be uncultured or uncouth in the presence of company? Haven't I always been the perfect socialite? The perfect hostess.

JONAS: Selah, considering the understanding we've come to, what do you wish to accomplish? Can you avail me this evening's intentions?

SELAH: You'll be availed, Jonas.

JONAS: Selah . . . You know I love you.

SELAH: Jonas, please.

(Awkward silence. They find their own space and wait. The doorbell rings. Selah and Jonas are frozen. It rings again. Jonas crosses to the door and answers it. Vera stands in the doorway.)

JONAS: Good evening, Vera. Thanks for coming. Please come in.

VERA: Thank you. Sorry, I'm late.

> (*She crosses inside. Selah takes in the figure that has just entered her home. A late-fortyish white woman. Selah is dumbfounded.*)

JONAS: Vera, my wife, Selah. Selah, this is Vera Blume.

> (*Silence.*)

VERA: Selah, I know how awkward this all is, but I did also want to meet you. I know this a very sensitive situation, and I can't possibly begin to relate how in no way do I mean to be an interloper or some unknown intruder. I too wanted to meet in order to come to an understanding, and to make known that although Jonas and I are just friends, I will disassociate myself until there is total clarity between all of us. I —

SELAH: Please shut up. Just please stop . . . Vera, first of all, I had no idea. Now we can say, in this day and age, what's the point, but believe it or not, it is still no less shocking, and I simply have to take this in.

VERA: That we are of disparate backgrounds, OK, but ultimately, what?

SELAH: Vera, I know your intentions are to come off as decorous and as well meaning as possible. But, please, let me ask you to leave before it becomes otherwise.

VERA: And I understand.

SELAH: Vera, there is much I'd like to say to you, but there is even more I'd like to say to Jonas.

JONAS: I asked why was this necessary?

SELAH: So, was I never to know! Were we to go our separate ways and that's the end of it?

JONAS: Of course not, Selah. Though if that is the case, are we not entitled to continuing living? And do so without consultation? I was trying to put time and healing between this situation. I had nothing to hide.

SELAH: Nothing to hide! —

VERA: Excuse me, Selah.

SELAH: No. Vera, we will talk. But, no, now will not be the time, good evening.

> (*Jonas opens the front door.*)

JONAS: I'll be back shortly.

SELAH: Jonas . . . I always knew you were a little less committed to the cause, but I never thought I'd respect you less than a white man . . . Good night.

> (*Selah turns and walks away. Lights fade. Lights up on Fred and Olive. Fred is in his lounge chair fast asleep with a beer bottle in hand. Olive comes down. Sexy R&B plays from next door. Olive takes notice of Fred and shakes her*

head. She bypasses him and goes to the window, closing it, deadening the music from next door.)

OLIVE: Fred.

(Fred only slightly stirs. Olive moves to shake him, but then stops herself. She gets an idea and excitedly hurries back to the window. She opens it, allowing the music to pour in. Olive begins to move to the beat and dances her way back over to Fred. She stops before him and loosens her bathrobe. She takes a deep breath and begins soft gyrations and delicate undulations. She dances her way around Fred, until finally sitting in his lap, rubbing her body against his. Fred finally awakens.)

FRED: What the . . .

OLIVE: Hey, Freddy.

FRED: I'm dreaming.

OLIVE: No, you are not dreaming.

FRED: Yes, I am. Either that or I'm drunk. Tipsy at best.

OLIVE: You're neither. You had your one Bud-lite hours ago.

FRED: Well, I gotta be something. And what the hell happen to your breast?

OLIVE: It's called a push-up bra.

FRED: Olive, what is going on?

OLIVE: Nothing. I'm just waking you for dessert. Now just be open, Freddy.

(Olive rises and again begins her dancing.)

FRED: Olive, Olive, Olive.

OLIVE: Yes, Freddy, Freddy, F-Daddy.

(Just then the phone rings, but Olive ignores it.)

FRED: The phone is ringing.

OLIVE: I don't hear it. I only hear music.

(Fred moves to get the phone, but Olive grabs it and answers.)

OLIVE: Hello, we're not in right now, don't call back.

(She throws the phone onto the sofa.)

(Fred rises and crosses to the window to close it.)

FRED: Yeah, I'm going through something, 'cause as sure as the sky is blue, I'm now watching Jonas leaving his house with a white woman.

OLIVE: *(Olive crosses to the window.)* No.

FRED: Yes. My wife prance'n around, cutting off the circulation in my leg, and now here's Jonas leaving his house with a white woman. And you say I'm not dreaming?

(Fred goes to the door and opens it.)

FRED: Hey, Jonas!

OLIVE: No, Fred. Oh, my God, they saw me.

FRED: Now I don't know if that's his lawyer or the woman he was telling me about, but I'm gonna find out. Jonas. Hey. Come on over.

OLIVE: Fred!

FRED: Well, go on upstairs, this is my dream anyway, banish. I'll tell you all about it when I awake.

OLIVE: *(Heading up the stairs.)* Fred you just can't leave well enough alone. It looks like we were snooping. I tell ya —

(Olive goes as Jonas and Vera enter.)

FRED: Jonas, come on in. Come on in. I want to see this part more up close and personal.

JONAS: Excuse me?

FRED: Jonas, I'm just here dreaming that Olive was giving me an adult dance show, and now you're standing here in my living room with a, with a European woman —

JONAS: Vera.

FRED: Named Vera . . .

VERA: Vera Blume.

FRED: Nice to meet you. Frederick K. Mitchell.

JONAS: Uh, Fred, we'll have to do this another time, we really must be going.

FRED: OK, OK. But one second, please. *(Fred returns to his sofa.)* In case this really is a dream. *(Fred lies back and closes his eyes. After three seconds he opens them to the same scene.)* OK, so this is real.

JONAS: Fred, Vera is a friend of mine.

VERA: Nice to meet you.

JONAS: Yes, and so maybe another time we can make it more formal.

FRED: I'm sorry if you got a glimpse of my embarrassed wife, otherwise she too would have greeted you. I apologize on her behalf.

JONAS: Well, that's quite all right, but it's late and we must.

FRED: Yeah, OK then, good night.

VERA: Good evening, Mr. Mitchell.

JONAS: My regards to Olive.

FRED: OK, then. We'll talk.

JONAS: Yeah, I'll give you a call.

FRED: Goodnight.

(Fred and Jonas shake hands, then Fred appeals to Vera.)

FRED: But just in case this is a dream, and it may be the Bud-lite talkin', but, Ms. Blume, I, uh, from time to time like to solicit public opinion, and I was just reading an interesting article, before falling asleep, before this dream here started, and, uh, I was just wondering, what's your take on surrogate partners?

JONAS: Fred.

VERA: Excuse me, Mr. Mitchell?

FRED: Fred, please. But your opinion.

JONAS: Vera.

VERA: No, no, why stop the train now? And I am amused. But firstly, Fred, I would suggest an open and frank discussion with your wife, then maybe with a professional therapist who can help discern what's best for you both, and hopefully resolve can be gained from there.

FRED: Oh, well, then that may be a problem.

VERA: I'm sorry?

FRED: Oh, you see, well, us black folks don't go in for all that sit-down and let's-talk-about-it doctors. We read *Ebony* and *Essence* for that.

VERA: Well, in that case I wish you the best.

FRED: Thank you. Good night, Jonas.

JONAS: Fred.

(*Jonas holds the door for Vera and they exit. Fred immediately heads upstairs.*)

FRED: Olive! Olive, you won't believe this.

(*Lights fade. Lights up on Jonas and Selah's home. Olive and Selah are seated over a pot of tea.*)

SELAH: Olive, it was like something out of elementary school. Boys bringing their Christmas toys to class to show off. And there's lil Jonas.

OLIVE: Oh, Selah, I'm sure that wasn't the case.

SELAH: Olive, please. I'm sure that is the case. I don't care how old he is. Some things people will take to their graves.

OLIVE: No, Selah.

SELAH: Yes. You hold on to your secret dream long enough, and one day you will eventually awaken to it. And what the hell does she really want?

OLIVE: Honestly, Selah, why can't she simply want what you want? And see what you see in Jonas? Feel what you feel?

SELAH: Because what I feel took time, dedication, and sacrifice.

OLIVE: But Selah, it doesn't work like that. The love I have for Fred didn't take work. There is no sacrifice. It never should be.

SELAH: Oh, I just need to forget this.

OLIVE: No, Selah, quite the opposite. Don't forget it. You have to deal with it. Endure it . . . Selah, have you ever cut loose? I mean really let go?

SELAH: What do you mean?

OLIVE: I mean, you go to the edge, but then you don't jump off. You're obviously and understandably affected by what's going on, and yet you've maintained this dignified displeasure. I say no. You can't keep stuff like this locked inside. You can't forget it when it's right there. Selah, let it go.

SELAH: There's no need to give them the energy.

OLIVE: No, not them, Selah, this is for you. You need to purge for you. Exorcise all this bull. This is a long time coming so we need to go back to visiting what our grandmamas and great aunts had to resort to. Selah, I want you to start shoutin'!

SELAH: What?

OLIVE: That's right. You heard. I want you to shout. Exorcise. Purge.

SELAH: And shout what exactly?

OLIVE: Hell, anything. It's not so much what you yell, just so long as you yell. Now, Selah, we're gonna deliver the new you. We're gonna give birth to why this very separation has happened, 'cause it's deeper than just this white woman. God only delivered her as the motivation. Selah, yes this separation is sad and unfortunate, but this separation is also a new beginning . . . Now what's your favorite cuss word?

SELAH: Oh, Olive.

OLIVE: Yes. What's your favorite word to use when swearing? Like can you throw a damnit on that God you're often retreating to?

SELAH: Well, that wouldn't be my favorite.

OLIVE: OK, so what is?

SELAH: I'm sorry, Olive, but I've never chosen a favorite.

OLIVE: And that won't stop us. Now which one sounds good to you?

SELAH: I imagine whichever one best suits the situation.

OLIVE: Well, for the worst situation, which would that be?

(Brief silence as Selah considers.)

SELAH: OK. I would have to say the sugar-honey-ice-tea one or the MF one.

OLIVE: There you go! 'Cause the MF one is a personal favorite of mine. Accept no substitute. When having to tell a Mofo off, nothing else will do. Now all you have to do is say it with all the energy and vitality it deserves.

SELAH: Olive, I don't know. I wouldn't feel right yelling such a thing.

OLIVE: So let's go a little less harsh. How 'bout the sugar-honey-ice-tea? Can you go there?

SELAH: I think that's more manageable.

OLIVE: Good! Now that's what I wanna hear. And afterward, if you don't feel like a new woman, you haven't let go. You haven't jumped. Now remember, we're getting rid of all the filth. All the negative, nonaffirmative, baggage. The luggage and the tonnage.

SELAH: The bullcrap.

OLIVE: Oo, there you go. And most of all, you're letting go for Selah. All right?

SELAH: All right.

OLIVE: OK, then. And ain't no preliminaries. You just jump right on in. Purge and shout. Sugar!!!

SELAH: OK.

OLIVE: OK.

(Silence. Selah gathers herself and then lets loose.)

SELAH: Sugar!!!

OLIVE: There you go.

SELAH: Honey!!!

OLIVE: Honey!!!

SELAH: Ice!!!

OLIVE: Louder!

SELAH: TEA!!!

OLIVE: LET IT GO!

SELAH: SUGAR!!!

OLIVE: Purge! Release!

SELAH: HONEY!!!

OLIVE: Give birth to Selah!

SELAH: ICE TEA!!!

OLIVE: That's right, come on!

SELAH: SUGAR! HONEY! ICE TEA!

OLIVE: LET GO!

SELAH: YOU NO GOOD, MF, SUGAR! HONEY! ICE TEA!!!!!

(Selah collapses into Olive arm's, crying, releasing, purging.)

OLIVE: It's OK. It's OK.

(Selah continues to sob. Olive holds her, soothes her.)

OLIVE: It's OK. All right. You're gonna be all right . . . Just like grandmas and Sunday mornings.

(Lights fade. Lights up on Jonas and Vera on a park bench.)

VERA: You can feel winter coming.

JONAS: You can feel it in your bones too?

VERA: *(She laughs.) No,* I mean you can feel it in the air.
(Silence.)

JONAS: You know there used to be a beautiful sugar maple right over there. And the colors it would make this time of year, God you would love to see it. I wanted tie a rope and tire to it. Give the kids the real feeling of swinging. Instead of all that chain and iron.

VERA: That would have been nice.

JONAS: Yeah, but they uprooted it before I ever had a chance.

VERA: Jonas, I'd like to talk to Selah again.

JONAS: Why?

VERA: Because we really didn't have the chance the first time. I know there is much to clear up. Much to express.

JONAS: Vera, why are you spending more and more time with me? On one hand, I tell myself, I don't want to get older just to be able to pay half-fare on the bus or enjoy reduced movie prices. I want more than that. That's why at a museum I would say something to a younger, beautiful you. Which then begs the question, what is a younger, beautiful you doing with me? We haven't been intimate, and that is not what I'm looking for . . . Vera, I really love that we can converse. That I can talk to you about a whole new world, and you're with me every step of the way. Vera, I'm very clear on why I enjoy spending time with you. I even told myself, and it may sound pathetic, but am I also trying to live out some silly, repressed fantasy? Something I couldn't do once upon a time.

VERA: Well, then . . . maybe we would be even. (*Silence.*) And, Fred, we have been very intimate. You have been very intimate sharing your thoughts, ideas, introspections, fears. And if you don't recognize that . . . well, then mister, you don't know what true intimacy is. But I do, and I enjoy sharing it with you . . . And I look forward to even more.

(Lights fade and up on Olive coming into her home. She hums to herself.)

OLIVE: La-di-da, la-di-da, Mofo. La-di-da, la-di-da, mofo.

(Fred comes into the room.)

FRED: What's that?

OLIVE: Excuse me?

FRED: What's that you're humming?

OLIVE: I was humming la-di-da, la-di-da, mofo.

(Silence.)

FRED: Any particular reason?

OLIVE: Liberation.

FRED: Oh, thanks for clearing that up . . . Uh, is everything all right with Selah? I kinda heard the two of you over there raising sand.

OLIVE: I think everything will be.

FRED: OK, good . . . So, am I to expect many more of these hollering fits?

OLIVE: That would be up to Selah. As she needs it.

FRED: And how 'bout you? Because I don't think it'll bode well, me yelling at

DJ Noise across the street, and my wife is over here sounding like one of those very same rap records.

OLIVE: Well, you don't have to worry about me, *(She puts the chain on the door.)* I'm liberated . . . Fred, it's a nice, clear night.

FRED: Yeah, it is, ain't it?

OLIVE: Why don't we go out star gazing anymore?

FRED: 'Cause we moved to New York. Too many city lights.

OLIVE: Not at the parks. There's Central. Prospect.

FRED: OK, so you'll make sure the safety chain is on, but won't think twice about star gazing in a New York park.

OLIVE: OK, then Long Island. Westchester. I say we pick a spot and go before the cold weather sets in.

FRED: OK, sure.

OLIVE: Now you just said, OK. So later on I won't have to fight you about this?

FRED: I said OK.

OLIVE: OK.

FRED: OK.

(They both settle into the sofa.)

OLIVE: When?

FRED: Before the cold weather sets in. *(Silence.)* Olive?

OLIVE: Yes, Fred?

FRED: We've been together a long time.

OLIVE: Yes, Fred, we have.

FRED: How come you never asked whether I've ever had any marital indiscretions?

OLIVE: *(Laughing.)* Indiscretions. You even put an "S" on the end, how cute.

FRED: Well?

OLIVE: Fred, I knew of every surprise birthday party, surprise gift, and surprise news you ever tried to spring on me.

FRED: And?

OLIVE: Man, you can't keep a secret. I wouldn't have to ask. You'd leave a trail from here to the pet's front door.

FRED: Oh, you think so.

OLIVE: Yeah, I know so. Whereas you would be totally in the dark. Such as with your good and late friend, Otis.

FRED: Otis! What about Otis? What do you mean, what are you saying?

OLIVE: Calm down, Fred.

FRED: I know you ain't have an affair with Otis.

OLIVE: No, Fred. Otis and I never had an affair.

FRED: Then what am I in the dark about?

OLIVE: About how much he wanted to have an affair. About how much he used to hit on me, and you had absolutely no idea.

FRED: What! Well, why didn't you tell me?

OLIVE: Because I had it under control. Otis was harmless. Otis was your friend. Otis was just being a man, and it was no sense in getting it all blown out of proportion.

(Fred rises and crosses to the wet bar for a bottle of water.)

FRED: *(Mumbling.)* Some friend, I oughta go spit on his grave, that mofo.

OLIVE: That's right, that's how it's said. And Otis was your friend. That's just how you men do. But it was up to me to put him in his place, let him know what's what, and that was the end of it. Case closed. Now, unlike Tonya Sheldon and the crush she had on you.

FRED: Tonya Sheldon had a crush on me? Tonya with the enormous, healthy, uh, lungs?

OLIVE: Yes, Tonya. And, now, see it's different when a girlfriend wants to get with your husband.

FRED: How so?

OLIVE: Because we women are smarter. We're more crafty, and you men are so weak and easy. Tonya would have had you before you knew what was going on. That is had I not smelled her heat and sent her on her way.

FRED: Umph. Healthy-lunged Tonya . . . Boy, when you're in the dark, you're in the dark. Well, why couldn't I smell her heat?

OLIVE: Don't worry about it, Fred. And I'm not gonna teach you now.

FRED: Oh, come on. You know after all this time, I'm committed only to you. Shucks, and with your crazy family, did I really have a choice?

OLIVE: What are you talking about?

FRED: Oh, come on now. Second to loving you so much, with your belligerent family, I know better than to cause you any heartache.

OLIVE: Belligerent family?

FRED: Yes, belligerent. Your family that waits for folks after church just so they can have a physical word with them. Shucks, I know if ever I became their target, they'd be over here with spiked bats and sandpaper. Uh-un, no thanks.

OLIVE: Well, all I can say is that family had it coming. They were ducking and hiding from us for so long, church was the only place we could corner — uh, confront them, I mean.

FRED: Umph, umph, umph. Just like some true thugs. And at a church no less. And over money.

OLIVE: Yes, money, and I'm sure you can understand, mister, "I ain't going back to church 'til Reverend Cunningham pays me my fifty dollars."

FRED: It's sixty. But I decided I am going back. I figure I put in ten dollars each service, so, I'll just stay away for seven Sundays. That works out to seventy dollars, plus interest. I get my money back and I ain't gotta say two words to the right Reverend.

OLIVE: That's a shame. And I would like to think that it was our love that kept us dedicated for all these years, and not my family.

FRED: Oh, it's been love. *(They kiss.)* But let's just say your family's the added incentive.

OLIVE: Anyway, let me go finish pruning these plants upstairs.

FRED: Hold on a minute. Uh, one more thing.

OLIVE: Yeah?

FRED: You know you never explained that exotic dancing while I was asleep thing.

OLIVE: Never you mind. Like you said it was a dream.

FRED: No, no it wasn't. Now come on, Olive. I know it was just another attempt to titillate me.

OLIVE: Yes, yes it was. I've gotten a few pointers from that cable television of yours.

FRED: Aha! I told you, you be sneaking a peek. But! But, I commend you. That's variety, I like that.

OLIVE: What are you up to, Fred?

FRED: Nothing. Nothing at all, I'm just drinking, talking. Drinking, talking. And, you know, I've been thinking of some of my own creative ways of titillation.

OLIVE: *And? (Defensively.)* I'm listening.

FRED: Well, there's something I'd like to propose. It's kinda new. Different, but consistent with what we've been going through lately. Something to enhance, you know, titillate, and bring more excitement to our love life, sex life. And you do encourage me to be open. I even think the new *Essence* even had a favorable article on it.

OLIVE: *(Suspicious.)* Go on.

FRED: It's something many couples are into and have tried with great success. *(Olive is now only silent and folds her arms.)*

FRED: Well, remember you jokingly talked about you and Darryl Williams. *(Fred begins laughing, but then decides to turn serious to help his case.)* You know, there exists . . . there's something for today's couples, ordinary, every-day couples like ourselves. Like you read in your surveys. And I was just thinking. Just thinking what are your thoughts on surrogate love mates, and uh, possibly including one with us? You know, just a passing thought based on all this new information. You know, to help enhance things? Love life. What do you think about that?

(Silence.)

OLIVE: Fred, first of all there's nothing loving about that. Secondly, I guess it would be you and I and another woman, right? Not a man but a woman, 'cause since you've never any indiscretions, how perfect it would be to have your wife sanction it, all under the guise of helping our so-called love life. Well, Fred, I don't need a surrogate third wheel to help me make love to my husband, and I'm offended and appalled and insulted that you can even fix your mouth to say such a thing. I, I . . . Good night, Fred, I have nothing further to say to you. *(Olive stares at him a moment, before turning her back and making her way upstairs.)*

(Fred can only watch.)

FRED: I sure hope this doesn't means she's gonna call that crazy ol' family of hers.

(Lights down. Lights up on Selah. The doorbell rings. She answers. It's Vera.)

SELAH: I'm glad you could make it.

VERA: I'm glad we're able to try again.

SELAH: I guess that's the wonderful thing about being self-employed.

VERA: And I guess I have my parents to thank for teaching all of their chil-dren to be more independent and self-reliant.

SELAH: As well it should be. My parents weren't as insightful. Though they did instill the whole educational, matriculation ethic, but what one really learns is that that only trains you just well enough to work for others. May I get you anything?

VERA: No, nothing, thank you, I'm fine. And maybe, Selah, your parents were thinking more self-esteem, that you could attend and matriculate in any arena.

SELAH: My self-esteem would have been helped by having a business to inherit. You see, I've noticed a little something about financial autonomy. It gives one the feeling that they can acquire anything. Have anything . . . wouldn't you say?

VERA: I would say that you're an astute woman, who's done quite well.

SELAH: But I realize I could have done better. Where are your parents from?

VERA: My parents are from Poland. Mother Belarusian. Father Jewish.

SELAH: And how did they find the adjustment?

VERA: They came over with some exploitable skills. It helped them fairly well.

SELAH: Such as?

VERA: My father was very good with numbers, which was put to use as book-keeper. My mother, a seamstress.

SELAH: And your education?

VERA: Rutgers.

SELAH: Any masters?

VERA: Yes . . . arts and cultural humanities.

SELAH: Congratulations. So, does that qualify you as a JAP?

VERA: No, I don't think so. I'm just regular Vera Blume.

SELAH: OK, so now that takes care of the obligatories, my first question is why? . . . Why did you not first come to me?

VERA: I have no answer to that. At least not a sufficient one.

SELAH: I'll accept anything you've got. Give me selfish. Give me indifference. Give me something.

VERA: I'm sorry.

SELAH: Have you ever been married?

VERA: Yes.

SELAH: Divorce?

VERA: Death.

SELAH: Sorry to hear that.

VERA: Thank you . . . Selah, it is my understanding that you and Jonas have made your peace. So, what exactly is it you want from me?

SELAH: I want for you to not exist, but since that's not possible, I would at least like to know what is it you want? From Jonas, from coming here again, since your conscience is clear with the understanding of where Jonas and I stand, what is it you now want?

VERA: I want you to know that this whole situation was not intended to be malicious, deceitful, or secretive.

SELAH: Then why weren't you here weeks ago or for however long this whole situation has existed! . . . Vera, I asked a question. Why? Why not weeks ago?

VERA: I was afraid, OK! . . . I was afraid.

SELAH: Of what?

VERA: Of loneliness! . . . Of continuously being alone. Of growing . . . afraid of loneliness.

SELAH: And Jonas is the only person who can keep you company? What about my loneliness? What about the time investment that I've put into this marriage? Has Jonas made you aware of our history together?

VERA: Yes, he has.

SELAH: How strained things had become?

VERA: Yes.

SELAH: How our union wasn't exactly born of love, granted there was Philios and Agape, just not Eros. Our coalition turned marriage having more to do with fulfilling an American dream, over anything deeper or more spiritually fulfilling, I'll admit that. And how because of that, twenty-four hours were taking much longer to go by? Were you informed about all that? *(Silence.)* With silence comes consent, but how about this. How about me being willing to sit, and wait, and stay together counting those seven hundred and twenty minutes. Me being willing to getting to know and explore all of what we didn't share. Me being wide open enough to fall in love. Did he talk to you about that?

VERA: But it takes two, Selah.

SELAH: Yes, there was a two, and I was trying to have us be just that, but along came a spider. You all are so alike.

VERA: Yes, isn't it so easy to condemn the whole if for so long you've never stopped to look at and get to know the individuals.

SELAH: Ruthie Bryers. Elementary school. Test day. My friend, Ruthie whispers, Selah, question six? Ruthie needed help. My friend needed help. So I tilt my paper in compliance. A moment later, Selah, question eight. And it would have continued had not our teacher, Mrs. Lieberman intervened. Now here's the picture. Two girls. One black, one white. The black girl's paper is tilted. So now who's helping whom? Is Ruthie looking at my paper in order to supply answers? Or am I doing the supplying? Of course the little black girl is accused of cheating. And does my individual friend, Ruthie, confess and state otherwise? . . . I'm sorry, but individual acts like that does tend to leave an impression. And here we are again. So are you here to help me, or are you helping yourself?

VERA: I was only trying to resolve. And is it selfish for me to see in Jonas what you *now* see? Want, what you now want? And if it does take two, then why did your husband approach me? Jonas first spoke to me.

(Selah's body begins to rock. She starts to moan as for the time, she holds it within.)

SELAH: Mmmmmmmmm. Mmmmmmmm.

VERA: Selah?

SELAH: Mmmmmmmmm.

VERA: Selah, are you all right? Is there anything I can do?

SELAH: Out. Mmmmmmmm. Oh, God. Mmmmm.

VERA: Selah.

SELAH: Mmmmmm . . . Just go.

VERA: How can I help?

SELAH: GET OUT!

(Vera retreats.)

SELAH: GET OUT! GET OUT! GET OUT!

(Lights up on the Mitchell's living room. Days later. Fred is sitting in his Lay-Z-Boy. Olive enters from the kitchen with two pots of cooked food. She re-enters the kitchen. Fred tries to ignore the pots, but the aroma is too great. He eases over to the table. He lifts the lid, inhales, and melts. He spoons out a portion of food, eats, and melts even more. He returns the lid and starts back towards his Lay-Z-Boy, but the food calls. He has to have one more mouthful. He steps back to the table, hand over the pot, as Olive re-enters. He begins waving his hands.)

FRED: Shoo, fly, shoo. Didn't want 'em, uh, getting in your food.

(Fred then turns and heads back to his chair. Olive carries one plate, one fork, knife, and dinner rolls. She sits and says grace. Fred tries to ignore her, but ends up making faces while Olive blesses her food. She begins to eat, loudly smacking for effect. Fred rises and goes over to the table. He grabs the phone and dials. He walks away for privacy.)

FRED: Hello, Young Chow? Yeah, I'd like to order a uh . . . yes, this is Fred Mitchell . . . Yea, the wife is fine . . . Gail is fine too . . . No, the baby hasn't been born yet, look I would like to place an order. And this time pack some food in there . . . More food, bigger cartons, I don't care what you have to do . . . What do you mean, order more? I'm already paying too much, you give me equivalent portions . . . Now, I want chicken wings . . . Shrimp and lobster sauce and an extra side order of rice. No, no hot sauce, the black man already has thyroid problems. OK, thank you. I'll be there shortly. And, uh, Chow. *(He turns and whispers.)* Do you guys have any buttered rolls? *(His low tone forces him to repeat himself.)* Buttered rolls. *(Again.)* Rolls. *(Now loudly.)* Rolls! Not butter the bowls! Do you have any buttered rolls. Rolls that you put butter on! . . . No? Well, I'll see you soon anyway . . . Bye.

(Fred hangs up and exits, leaving Olive who has been steadily enjoying her meal.)

OLIVE: I could have told you they didn't serve rolls. Do you want me to save you one of mine? Oops, I'm sorry. I forgot, I'm still not speaking to you. So maybe you can get your surrogate partner to butter your rolls.

(Olive bites into her roll and lights fade. Lights up on Jonas. He has two suitcases and is preparing to leave. A car horn blows and Jonas grabs his luggage. Selah enters.)

JONAS: I'll get my other things later this week . . . I left the hotel number on the dresser.

(Silence.)

SELAH: Good-bye, Jonas. And don't forget your glasses. So you can see where you're going.

(Jonas retrieves his glasses. Puts them in his top pocket. He crosses to Selah in an effort to kiss her good-bye, but she turns her head, refusing him. Jonas picks up his cases and exits. Lights fade. Lights up on another night at the Mitchell's. Fred is sitting in his Lay-Z-Boy. Olive enters from the kitchen with one plate and one fork. She is on the phone.)

OLIVE: Yeah, girl, I made these rolls, melts in your mouth.

FRED: Olive? Olive!

OLIVE: Yeah, girl. OK, talk to you later.

(Olive ignores Fred and prepares to eat. Just as she folds her hands for grace, the phone rings.)

OLIVE: Good evening. Hold on. Fred.

(Fred takes the phone.)

FRED: Good evening, Young Chow? Fine, fine, and you and yours? Good . . . No, not yet, but when she delivers, you'll be the first to know . . . Yeah, I was just getting around to it . . . No, not the usual. Uh, what's the special today? OK, I'll give it a try. OK, see ya in fifteen minutes.

OLIVE: I see he now has my ugly earring on speed dial.

(He hangs up. And sits quietly. Olive enjoys her meal in silence. After a moment, Fred jumps up.)

FRED: Olive, I'm sorry. And I'm not apologizing because Young Chow has our personal home number, we're on a first-name basis, nor that I'm sick and tired of eating takeout. I'm apologizing because I made a stupid and insulting proposition to my wife, and I have no excuse other than senility. I'm sorry and I beg your forgiveness.

(Olive takes a deep breath and lets him stew for just a moment.)

OLIVE: Sit down, Fred. That's all I wanted to hear. *(Olive rises to embrace Fred and accidentally knocks over a glass of water. It spills on to the table and floor. The phone rings.)* Get the phone, I'll get this.

FRED: Yeah, it's probably Chow. *(He answers the phone.)* Young Chow, you can cancel my order . . . Oh, hey, Gail, how you doing? . . . What! You are? . . . OK, she just went in the kitchen, hold on. Olive! Olive, the phone.

OLIVE: OK, OK, where's the fire? *(She takes the phone.)* Hey, baby . . . What! Oh, my God! Oh, my God, Gail's water just broke. OK, OK, everybody just calm down! . . . OK, you are calm. You called, uh, uh, what's your husband's name? . . . Yeah him. You called the doctor? You called everyone. OK, OK, so we'll meet you there. How do you feel? . . . Good, good . . . Well, no, we were just about to eat, but now I'll put the food in the car and get in the kitchen. I mean put the car in the kitchen and get in the food.

(Olive starts putting the food from her plate back in the pots. Impatient, she then gathers everything by taking the ends of the tablecloth and lifting, capturing everything. She then begins to walk to the front door with the bundle. Fred grabs her and takes the phone.)

FRED: Gail it's me, Daddy *(He guides Olive away from the front door and into the kitchen.)* She means she's going to put the food in the kitchen and then get in the car. We'll meet you and Brian at the hospital . . . OK, dear . . . See you shortly. I love you too. Bye.

OLIVE: *(Reemerging from the kitchen.)* OK, I'm ready. I should have known. The water spilled, of course that meant her water broke. We're given signs like that from God to prepare us. It's how things work —

FRED: Yeah, yeah, here's the key. Start her up for me and I'll be right there. On second thought, give me back the key. Just sit in the car, I'll be right there.

OLIVE: OK, hurry up.

FRED: I'll be right there. I just gotta call Young Chow and tell him the good news.

OLIVE: WHAT!

FRED: Just kidding. Just kidding. See how cool I am. Cool. Calm. I just gotta run to the bathroom. Now, go on, I'll be right there and we'll take off.

(Fred goes upstairs. Olive exits. Fred reemerges at the top of the stairs, peeking down. He sees that Olive has indeed left and he runs down and into the kitchen. We hear pots clanging. He soon re-emerges chewing with one mouthful of food and two dinner rolls. One already half-eaten. He stands by the door, peeking through the window at Olive. The car horn blows, but he holds his ground. He finishes the half-eaten roll, and places the other in his pocket. The car horn blares. He then exits. Lights fade. Lights up on Olive. She's on the phone in a jovial mood with daughter, Gail.)

OLIVE: OK, OK, I got one. What do you call a woman who knows where her husband is? . . . A widow. How 'bout this one. What do you call a smart, honest, intelligent man? A female impersonator . . . Here's another. Why does it take a million and one male sperm to reach one egg? 'Cause at least a million will get lost and have to stop for directions . . . No? . . . My own daughter, a tough crowd. Well, try this one on. Why don't women blink during foreplay? . . . We don't have time . . . Ah, you like that one . . . Oh, know you have one . . . OK, why do men become smarter during sex? *(Olive laughs.)* Because they're plugged into a genius, that's a good one. Yeah, well, let's leave these poor men alone.

(Olive absent-mindedly fiddles around with the disabled Victrola as she talks.) Let's just say we all have our issues to work out . . . The men have theirs and we have ours. So, if you have any issues, mother-daughter, woman-man, whatever with whomever, make sure you address them now before they address you, and they will come after you . . . Yes, don't take anything to your grave or that'll be the very thing to put you there . . . Hey, now, I'm no mechanic, but I know a loose wire when I see one.

(She connects it and the Victrola begins to spin. Olive jumps back in surprise.) Oh, shit. *(She places a record on and it plays.)* Oh, my God. I fixed the Victrola. I fixed the phonograph! Oh, my God . . . Oh, no! *(She takes the record off.)* I have to unfix it . . . Well, you know your father's ego. And we just made up. This it'll set us back a hundred years . . . Nooo, doing this won't help . . . I have to undo it. But then it'll never get fixed . . . Leave it alone? . . . Un-huh . . . Un-huh . . . Good idea. But what if he first tinkers with it and disconnects it again, then it'll go back to being broke . . .Well, we'll see I convinced him to go and try something new . . . Golf . . . Yeah, we'll see . . . OK, let me go . . . I'll think of something. So, kiss Kima, Karla and what's that newborn's middle name? . . . What? . . . Once more. Daaaa-ude. Daa-ude. And you're giving him his first name, when? . . . Uh-un . . . See what I mean about addressing issues? You ain't do none of this stuff with any of the others . . . Yeah, well OK, you kiss him for me anyway. See you soon, depending . . . Love you, too . . . OK . . . Yeah, Gail you got hangers in your closet? Then, don't make me go there . . . Bye.

(Just as Olive hangs up, we hear Fred drive up. Olive returns the record and is indecisive about her next move.)

OLIVE: Oh, God, give me at least two minutes.

(She hesitates between going back to the Victrola, the door, and running upstairs. She decides to run to the door and put the chain on. Fred tries to enter.)

FRED: Olive! The chain is on the door!

OLIVE: Uh, who is it?

(She still vacillates between the door and Victrola.)

FRED: It's meeee.

OLIVE: Meeee whooo?

FRED: Jehovah Witness, Olive, who do you think, open this door.

OLIVE: Well, you said a small child can lean his way in. Let's see if it's really that flimsy.

FRED: Olive!

OLIVE: OK, OK. *(She decides to leave the Victrola as is.)* I'm just funning.

(She releases the chain and Fred enters.)

OLIVE: Good evening.

FRED: Good evening.

OLIVE: So, how was it?

(Fred pulls out one bent and badly damaged club from his golf bag.)

OLIVE: Oh, my goodness. How'd that happen?

FRED: Don't ask. But let's just say a tree is one of nature's sturdiest pieces of furniture.

OLIVE: Well, you gotta give it a chance. Did you ask for a guide?

FRED: An instructor.

OLIVE: Well, an instructor. A coach. A lumber jack. Did you ask for anyone to help you chop down the trees?

(Fred stares at Olive.)

FRED: I don't get it. For something that looks so boringly simple, I just don't get it. I think my moral conscious won't allow me to get the hang of the game. I think I'm just offended on too many fronts. For one, the folks are badly dressed and so they offend my good fashion sense.

OLIVE: Still not a good reason to call it quits.

FRED: Well, then there's my sociopolitical senses that are offended. All that real estate just to hit a little ball in a little hole. All that land while home-lessness and overcrowded housing abounds. Explain that?

OLIVE: Well, I'll give you that one.

FRED: Yeah, I think I'll fax our governor come tomorrow. No wonder those trees kept attacking my clubs. Playing that game is a sin against mother nature. She's bound to retaliate.

OLIVE: Well, dinner's almost done.

FRED: Thanks, I am starved.

OLIVE: Good. And afterwards Gail and Brian wants us to come over.

FRED: Did they give the boy a name yet? 'Cause I ain't going if my grandson ain't named.

OLIVE: She says they have to let him decide.

(Silence as Fred gives a look.)

FRED: OK, now how is that going to happen?

OLIVE: She says, the idea is to study his personality and see what he looks like. See what name suits him. Or say a name and see what he responds to. Like you know, you don't really look like a Frederick. When the teacher first said your name, "Frederick," it was only out of kindness that I didn't outright laugh. But it's not your fault, it's a parental thing. But you do look like a Fred. Just plain, ol' Fred. So, to avoid another mistake like that, they'll wait until he names himself.

FRED: You better live forever 'cause my mother is gonna have a few choice words for you.

OLIVE: No, I don't have to live forever. Remember, I just better not go to the extremely warm place. *(Olive indulgently laughs at her joke.)* Whoa, I'm hot today. OK, OK. No more mama jokes. But I couldn't resist. We know your mama is up there sitting at the right hand of God.

FRED: Well, I don't know about the right hand. I mean, mother did have a vice or two so she's probably down near the end, next to Saint Jude or somebody.

OLIVE: OK, fair enough. So we'll eat and head on over.

FRED: And why are they calling the boy Do-Doo if that ain't gonna be his name?

OLIVE: That's his middle name, Daude. And they don't call him that to his face. Fred, I really just want to go out. Enjoy the drive. My once a week new class is not enough. So after we eat, we either go see our newest grandson, or we go out dancing? Your one week with the Victrola is up.

FRED: *(Moans.) Agh.* I just got in. I'm tired from golf.

OLIVE: The boringly simple sport?

FRED: Besides, I should have some grace days. Like for when Gail interrupted my evening by having lil Buddha.

OLIVE: Fred. Daa-ood. *(She takes his hand and places his fingers to her lips as if he was blind and/or deaf.)* Daa-ood. Long "A," short "O," "E" silent.

FRED: Daa-ood. They-odd.

OLIVE: Well anyway, you have from now 'til when dinner is served. That's your grace period.

FRED: Mmm.

OLIVE: Fred, I have full confidence in you.

(Olive goes into the kitchen. Fred moves away from the Victrola and sits in

his chair. He turns on the television. He starts to relax, placing his hand in his waistband. Olive yells from the kitchen.)

OLIVE: Fred!

FRED: Yeah!

OLIVE: Are you working on the Victrola or are you in your chair with your hands down your pants?

FRED: Yeah, yeah, I'm getting to it. Just quickly checking the news. *(He turns off the television and trudges over to the Victrola.)* Why she always wanna do something? We had our time. Now it's time to just sit back and relax. Think about all that we've done. Let them young fools do all that stuff. *(He only looks at the Victrola from various angles, deciding on which part to attack first.)* And I work hard on this thing enough without having to be blackmailed into it! . . . *Daa-ude.*

OLIVE: What's that dear!

FRED: Nothing, *daar-ling!* . . . *(Mumbles.)* Just fix dinner.

OLIVE: What?

FRED: Nothing! I'm looking at the dindrode on the Victrola!

OLIVE: OK, dear.

(Finally, he gives it a few whacks and then hits the on switch. The table spins. Fred is momentarily stunned.)

FRED: Ooo. *(He grabs a record and places it on the table. It produces music.)* Ah, ah, Olive! Olive! I fixed the Victrola. I fixed the Victrola! *(Fred begins to do a victory dance and strut like a king.)* I. FIXED. THE. VICTROLA!

OLIVE: How? What'd you do?

FRED: Uhh, well I, I, the dindrode I mentioned. That was the main problem all along.

OLIVE: What, it was burnt out, let me see it.

FRED: No, don't touch it, you'll break it. *(Olive looks at the audience.)* It, it wasn't burnt out just not connected right. It was a bad fit that I corrected. And the magnet wasn't properly aligned. I had to realign it. And the belt needed tightening and a little lubrication. And a spring was off, and the needle misaligned. It was the combination of everything. That why it's taken this long. But voilà, music. Music! Real music!

OLIVE: My hero.

(Fred picks out another 78. He removes the first.)

FRED: At long last. Now I can play something for DJ Noise over there. Something original. Something originally composed, conceived, written, and produced. I give you music. *(Fred puts on Nat King Cole's "Unforgettable."*

He turns up the volume. He goes over to the door and opens it.) Hey, DJ
Noise! It's on now! *(He turns to Olive and walks to center of room.)* May I?
*(Olive pirouettes into Fred's embrace as together they dance. Olive breaks away
on a dance spin and closes the door. She returns to Fred.)*

OLIVE: Fred, I would like to formally apologize.

FRED: Oo, come on now, nuff said. We already made up.

OLIVE: No, I was not being fair. I know you wouldn't intentionally hurt or
embarrass me, and I overreacted. I became vindictive. Dinner and all, and
I would just like to say . . . I just want you to know that I cherish you
deeply.

FRED: Aw, and I you, Olive, you know that. And I promise, we'll go out more
often.

OLIVE: Ohh, I love us.

FRED: I love us, too.

OLIVE: And, and what about romance?

(Fred puts the safety chain on the door.)

OLIVE: Un-un. Aw shucks now.

FRED: Whoa, whoa, hold on. I just wanna give you my making-up gift.

OLIVE: Oh, you didn't have to?

(Fred retrieves a hidden shoebox-sized gift box from under his easy chair.)

FRED: Well, you got me the golf clubs. I just want to keep it balanced. Keep
the romance going. Here you go. Surprise, I got you a brand new cordless phone!

OLIVE: Oh.

FRED: Psyche. Open the box.

*(Olive takes the top off the box and takes out a much smaller jewelry box.
She opens that box which reveals a pair of earrings.)*

OLIVE: Oh . . . Fred, not a phone, but some real live, ugly earrings.

FRED: *(Dejected.)* What?

OLIVE: Psyche you too, I'm just funning. Fred, they're lovely.

FRED: And you can wear them tomorrow night when we go out.

OLIVE: Oh, Fred.

FRED: That is if you still have enough strength, after tonight.

OLIVE: Excuse me?

*(Fred turns off the main ceiling light, but the lamp remains, creating an
amorous effect. He offers his hand to Olive.)*

FRED: My dear.

OLIVE: *(She takes hold of Fred's hand, and they embrace.)* Oo, now don't tell me my apology has acted as some kind of aphrodisiac? Or my — Oo . . . Oo, Fred, is, that you?

FRED: Well, it ain't my pinky.

(Fred passionately kisses Olive.)

OLIVE: Mmm. And all I had to do was make a sincere declaration of love to turn you on?

FRED: And now all you have to do is shut up or you'll turn me off. But don't worry, you'll be vocalizing soon enough.

OLIVE: Ooo.

FRED: Tonight, we're gonna create our own music.

OLIVE: Oooo!

(Olive runs upstairs. Fred goes to the bar and forgoes his lite beer. He grabs a bottle of champagne and sings.)

FRED: "Unforgettable." *(Lights fade.)* "That's what you are."

(Fred ascends the stairs. Blackout.)

END OF PLAY

UNEQUALIBRIUM

by Alexander Lyras and Robert McCaskill

What if some day or night a demon were to steal after you into your loneliest loneliness and say to you: This life as you now live it and have lived it, you will have to live once more and innumerable times more; and there will be nothing new in it, but every pain and every joy and every thought and sigh and everything unutterably small and great in your life will have to return to you, all in the same succession and sequence — even this spider, and this moonlight between the trees, and even this moment and I myself. The eternal hourglass of existence is turned upside down and you with it, speck of dust!

Would you not throw yourself down and gnash your teeth and curse the demon who said thus? Or have you once experienced a tremendous moment when you would have answered him, "You are a God and I have never heard anything more divine."

— Friedrich Nietzsche
The Joyful Wisdom

PLAYWRIGHTS' BIOGRAPHIES

Robert McCaskill has worked professionally as an actor, writer, and director. He has developed and directed nine one-person shows. Mr. McCaskill lives in New York City where he earns a living as an acting coach. Clients include Bernadette Peters, Montel Williams, and Alexander Lyras.

Alexander Lyras has written and performed in New York City since 1993. His two other solo plays, *desperelics* and *All Gods Creatures,* have been produced in New York and Los Angeles. He has worked as an actor on stage, in film, and in television and has collaborated numerous times with Mr. McCaskill.

ORIGINAL PRODUCTION

Unequalibrium opened on January 18, 2002 at the Gene Frankel Theater in New York City. It was performed with three separate soundtracks. The playbill listed the characters and time of occurrence:

Monologue	Character	Hour
STREAM OF CONSCIOUSNESS	Jonathan	11:34 PM
THE STEAMROLLER	Theo	5:34 PM
DISENTAGLED	Isaac	11:34 PM
THE NOMAD	Manny	11:34 PM
EKSTASIS	David	12:34 AM

TIME

Friday night and Saturday morning, December 14 and 15, 2001.

Unequalibrium

Stream of Consciousness

Cardboard moving boxes frame the stage. The lights rise on Jonathan: wool socks, torn jeans, FDNY T-shirt, mustard flannel, beer in one hand.

JONATHAN: It wasn't exactly a nightmare. It was more like a foreign film, I was showing myself in my sleep. Big party, guys all bow-tied, women floating around like sirens, plunging necklines, breasts everywhere . . . Musta been three hundred perfectly sculpted busts at this thing, I'm telling you, the grillwork was fucking phenomenal.

And people are congratulating me and my parents are toasting me and the women huggin' on me and I'm like *I know some of these are silicon, but I don't care, it's a dream.*

And then you came up to me. And as you pulled away? You had no eyes, David. Empty sockets. And I'm like, *Dave, where are your eyes?* And you're like, *They're in my pocket, John.* I'm like, *Don't put 'em fafafa you're gonna get lint on 'em!* And . . . you just stood there. And I said, *Dude, put your eyes back in your head and look at all these boob jobs!*

. . . And that was it. I woke up, an apartment full of boxes, not a breast in sight. Obviously an anxiety dream, come on. It's been three months! You realize you're going on three months of not speaking. Twelve weeks of silence? I mean, HEY! It's been cool. I've gotten alotta reading done! But honestly, we gotta have some kinda conversation before you go, cause I'm starting to take this personally.

Turn that down! Dave? Can you lower the radio, please? They're reporting this like we've never had a blizzard in Manhattan.
(Jonathan pulls a large silver sword from inside a box.)
This is technically both of ours, you know that. You can take it, I'm just saying . . . Can you imagine the fourteenth century? Hitting someone with this like . . . deliberately?
(Picks up a New York Rangers hockey jersey off the floor with the sword and drops it into a box.)
You're gonna need more boxes, look at all this shit. The Union Square Staples is open till midnight, I think, isn't it? Dave? *Dave? Union Staples . . . Open till midnight?*

— Say something . . . I'm serious, man. Say anything. You know, you're really starting to piss me off. Scratch that. I'm fucking ANGRY AT YOU! You're gonna move back home to Ithaca tomorrow, I'm gonna be left in a half empty apartment arguing with you in my head, cause you're doing some narcissistic monk routine?

DON'T FUCKIN' WALK AWAY FROM ME, DAVID! I don't understand why you're doing this. You didn't even see them fall, Dave. I'm the one that saw the planes hit. One and two. I'm the one that saw the fuckin' Jumpers . . . and I can still talk.

All right, I really didn't wanna resort to this but it's become painfully obvious to me the only thing that'll help you at this point are mind-altering drugs! And fortunately as your best friend, I baked you some.

(Reveal the pill.)

Methylenedioxy methylamphetamine. This one's mine. Yours is by the beer you haven't touched. Look at it. It's good shit. I should know, I made it today in the lab at the high school. My students are doin' an iodine experiment, I'm in the corner cookin' contraband with a Bunsen burner, like, *can one of you kids gimmie a hand over here!* It'll loosen your screws a little. That's why they call it Ecstasy. Cause X is, well, stasis as I teach my seventh graders, is like having equilibrium, like how something static is unchanging — Don't lift that by yourself! — So stasis is *stability* and ex is OUT OF. So, EX-*stasis* is NOT STABLE or OFF BALANCE, sort like you right now, movin' outta town cause school was four blocks from Ground Zero, you got ten years of shit to pack, we're outta boxes, Staples closes in twenty-three minutes, YOU'RE ECSTATIC! Hence this pill is perfect for the occasion!

Wait, whoah, whoah, David. I'm serious! It's not like I'm trying to dose you! It'll open your mind. It will! Did I tell you about the one time I ate mushrooms? David. Yo! If you're not gonna talk, at least listen.

Penelope and I, in college, go hikin' along the Appalachian trail about an hour from campus. She breaks out some Celestial Seasonings Mandarin Orange tea, puts in a few caps, a few stems, a sprinkle of dust. It actually tasted amazing. And we're tossing a Frisbee back and forth, waiting for the neo-tryptamines to kick in, talking current events, you know, like maybe picketing the next WTO conference, as young lovers will . . . ha ha! When slowly, the backs of my knees start tingling. My instinct was to sit, but Nells was like, listen, we gotta move. So we stash our gear and we start to hike this trail and in less than two minutes, David, like someone had cleared away the cobwebs . . . It HITS!

COLORS! The colors started POPPING out at us — 'cause, I totally forgot to mention — we'd each taken an extra thousand milligrams of vitamin E 'cause like, my lab partner told me it enhances the atocopherals in the retinal fluid and colors become brighter and more intense? It totally works!

The trees are GREEN and the sky is BLUE and the clay is BURNT SIENNA. Eight o'clock in the mornin', sixty-five degrees out, me and Penelope are about to become Smurfs. Everything is so fuckin' ALIVE. Why can't the earth be THIS beautiful all the time?

— I get ahead of Nells a bit 'cause I'm like a little kid, and I end up at the stream first, which is our destination. This deep stream cascading down from the mountain, meandering and babbling and dumping out into the Water Gap I think, and when Nells finally catches up to me, she somehow ends up on the *other side* of it, so the stream *split* us which I found very symbolic, sort of like, man and woman and water in between, you know? Well at the time, it made perfect sense.

I end up sitting on this huge rock in the middle of the brook, and the water rushed right towards it and split right at the base and as far as I'm concerned it's the most exciting divergence on the planet. Talk about population differentiation. The biodiversity alone was amazing: all oxygenated and oligotrophic? You've never in your life *seen* a healthier riparian ecosystem, in operation, perfectly balanced.

And you know I'm not religious . . . but I have this revelation that we live in a pantheistic world where God is every thing in the universe and every thing in the universe is God. I mean, everything. He is us and I am it and we are all the walrus, kookookachoo. And . . . through the surface of this eddy, just beneath the foam, I notice a brook trout staring back at me from under a rock. This little dude with eyes up here and this mug, and he's checking me out, you know politely curious. I lie on my stomach to get a better look and . . . I can see his whole aquatic setup. He's got a rock house with a slanted roof, the equivalent I'd say of a decent one-bedroom, a hole in back he can dash into for safety from the nasty crayfish, a surplus of macro-invertebrates to snack on and bro, it blew the Discovery Channel away.

I look to his left and I see this crumpled Coke can he's swimming around and it sort of kills my buzz. It's like; *aw man, why does THAT have to be there?* Although I liked it cause it was very RED and SHINY. I make eye contact with the trout — and David, I report this as accurately as I am able — the fish starts TALKING! Don't gimmie those eyes, OK, I wasn't hallucinating! I know what I heard . . . This was some rare form of ichthyological telepathy, cause the trout tells me, he says to me, he's *distraught.* I'm like, *No way! Why?* He says: OPEN YOUR EYES AND LOOK AROUND, JONATHAN!

And I look upstream and I see a TIRE sticking out and it's rotting. And beyond the tire, a corroded MILK CRATE, the rust discoloring the silt bed. And suddenly, as I take in the full scenario for the first time, I can see it's sort of all over the place: little bits of garbage. And I get this . . . feeling. This compulsion inside me, David. That I've been sitting long enough. Here on this rock, I've been sitting long enough. And I STAND UP. I plunge my arm into the water and I grab that Coke can, the Kit-Kat wrapper, the bottle cap. I wade up stream against the current, stuffing my pockets with debris and I get to the tire, and I heave it over my shoulder and it's filled with mud! But I'm on a friggin' mission now. I yank up the milk crate, it splits apart and slices my forearm open and *that's a whole thing when you're* BOOMING! Lacerated epidermis and bisected capillaries, platelets, and plasma . . . LIFE, oozing outta me.

Turns out it's not fatal. And if I wasn't already, now I'm totally committed to purifying campsite sixty-four. I climb onto a mud bank to unload all this shit and get back for more, and I loop around this bush, and I come into a clearing, and I swear to you David, there is garbage EVERYWHERE. There's litter in the trees and bushes and . . . in holes dug into the ground. I start to hyperventilate because, aside from the shock of the size of the mess, I am officially tripping my balls off.

There's no way in I can do this alone. I turn and face Penelope, who at this point is singing Crosby, Stills, and Nash to a flock of Canadian geese and they're loving it. And I scream to her, PENELOPE! I NEED YOU! She tilts. I nod. We connect. And though it's never occurred to me since, at that instant, I knew I wanted children.

Penelope crosses the water — which is full circle on the symbolism — and we work together to clean this place. I find an industrial storage cylinder we use as a central garbage hub. We fill it. I'm jumping up and down on it to make more room. Recyclables accumulating alongside it. Glass, paper, plastic. Five hours, Dave. Our hair's in knots and we're exhausted and we're proud and we're finally coming down, when Penelope asks, *what do we do with it all now?*

And I realize, we're seven miles up a mountain, there probably isn't a garbage route nearby. And . . . it's a sobering blow. All this work for nothing. I become nauseous. I spiral down into this vacuum of hopelessness, when Penelope says: *maybe they can haul it all out in a boat.* And we look at each other like, a boat! Because, it's a river.

The guys at base camp are so thankful for our efforts, not only do they schedule a Monday morning pick up but the head guy pulls open a drawer in this old oak desk and hands us deputy Ranger patches. Right there, baby.

That experience, was the birth of my life in science. The drug, the pill, totally opened me up. Let me see what was right in front of me. Take this with me, David. Let's learn something new . . .

— Is that a nod? You're nodding, what does that nodding mean? Does that mean yes? Yes! Beautiful!

— Go to Staples, get your boxes, you got thirteen minutes to get there, I'll take care of the rest of this shit.

Wait a second! Wait! Take that before you go. Don't worry! It takes thirty minutes to kick in, you'll make it back in time.

We're going on a journey, pal. Ready? Here goes!
(Pop pill, finish beer. Fadeout.)

The Steamroller

A man in a wrinkled tuxedo, fat pillow underneath his blue tuxedo shirt, tie undone around his neck, wedding ring, cell phone in the pocket, Greek worry beads in one hand, a handkerchief in the other. This is Theo.

THEO: HEY! Saw you over here. Saw you. I don't believe! Hang one sec. THEO*? Kerthisa, levendimou! Tha pire ola! Ker-thi-sa!*

— *Am I being loud? I'll keep it down!* How the hell are YOU? I'm blanking over here, don't tell me — TIM! TIMOTHY! I'm terrible with — I haven't seen ya since the reun — I know, you believe it?! Unbelieve, this guy. It's good to see someone from home. Can you just? Just hang on, Tim, hang one sec — *Not you! I don't even know you guys! You guys get outta here!* Just wait, Tim.

I'm coming! Can you hang onto those chips for me? I'm right over here at the bar. Guys, I'm workin' on the barkeep over here, I'm gettin' everyone a drink, give it a rest.

THEO! GRIGORA*, pethakimou, let's get to the city! But before the snow, Theothoro! The snow!*

What? I'm celebrating over here? Sorry my jubilation vexes you. Still try-

ing a drink! This bartender's like my wife. I keep givin' him money, he keeps telling me to shut up.

I don't even gamble, that's the amazing thing! I don't even gamble, over here! NO! I was working the casino here, finished the contract early, how often that happen? I play a couple tree-four hands, I start winning! These guys going crazy over here! I bought the tux, you know, the hell of it! How 'bout you, come to A.C. often? — First? This your first time? No shit! Well, welcome to Atlanti-City, my friend. It's like ya died but got to stay in New Jersey!

You know, I see yer dad every so often? YABSOLUTELY! Comes into the shop in the city. I gotta plumbing shop West Twenty-second Street: ALL AUTOMATED PLUMBING. Kiddin'? I just converted the entire casino to hands-free toilets and urinals. Got 'em in my home!
(Touches one button on the cell phone.)
Business? Business is great, knock on porcelain. — I almost lost it ALL about four hours ago! — WHEW! Where'd your life go wrong? Right? My legs are still shakin'.

— Still busy. Six bucks a month for call waiting, she's gonna tie BOTH lines.
(Redials the cell phone.)
How 'bout you, ya married? Good! Never get married, my friend: they chew ya cock right off. I mean, she, she, she, she, doesn't unnerstand . . . This is a form a meditations for me, over here, you know? I ain't just trowin' money. I use a system when I play, and it works. The key to unlocking this particular system is just . . . having a little faith.

God dammit! It's gonna go now from busy to machine. *Apistefto!*

She doesn't want me to come home, is what it is! I'm stranded over here. Refuge in A.C. And now she thinks she's not gonna let me see the kids. WHEW! The kids are my home, over here, you know.

Theo! Fevgome, parakalo!

You 'member Theo? — Come on everyone 'members Theo. He was a senior for like six years. He's a Theo, I'm Theo, we got your dueling Theo's here!

Feelaraki! Keeta! Look who it is!

He doesn't 'member you.

Po pas, vre? — *I thought we were going to the Garden, see a show! Sovara?*

Look, look at this cocktail broad he's with. WHEW! A girl like that puts the ass in class, if you know what I mean. He's gonna disappear now, three days.

'Scuse me, barkeep? I'm still trying to get a drink, over here. You believe this kid? I coulda bought the ice and liquor, blown my own glass, and poured the drink by now . . .

Hey, what's a matter, I'm not tipping you? I'm tipping, that's paying rent. I expect you to adulate over here. Can I get another Campari soda, and —

Come on, one drink, catch up 'ole times. You want an aperitif or what? How 'bout a shot a ouzo? No? How 'bout a beer? They got the Stella Artois! You want a Stella?! Stella. STEELLAAA!

I'm calm! What? That's not me, that's you.

It's him right? Wait, where you goin' we're gonna drink a drink, right? Come on, drink a drink!

No respect for the service industry these kids. It's all part of their system. Slow service the bar keeps you at the tables . . . There's a whole SCIENCE how they manipulate.

That's why you gotta have a better system if you expect to control the odds. Wanna know mine?

The system as it is known, is called THE STEAMROLLER. What the Steamroller does is break blackjack down into calculable units. If the dealer shows a 2 or 3 on his top card, YOU hit till 12: cause algebraically, those are your strongest odds.

If he shows 4, 5, or 6, then all you need is 14. If he gets a 7, 8, or 9, hit till you got 17, and full stop! Only if he lands an ace or a face card, do you go for 21's all the way. Black Jack's just the name of the game. You don't need it to win.

— Two tips beginners always forget: one: never apologize for winning a bet, and two: under no circumstances do you ever play A.C. as a gamble. Atlanti-City is not a gamble, my friend . . . It's an investment.

Last night, thirty thousand dollars in a hole! I'm practically hemorrhaging money. My balls are in my throat, but I stick to the system, which at this point, I'm doubting. DON'T DOUBT THE SYSTEM.

— I go for cash advance? Wife cancels the card! Friggin' cancels! I gotta wait the ATM withdrawal limit resets at midnight, nip a smidge from the college fund. Hey . . . I was having a premonitions, you know? I could FEEL it coming on. Slow/surely, win a few thou back, light at the end of the hard-aways. Couple hours: seven thou, eight, knock another nine, I'm only down fif! My balls drop down to my stom. Seven hours, Tim, back, forth win, lose, win, win, WIN. Suddenly I'm only down a

sawbuck! Feel like I'm gonna make it out, you know? Ten grand I bal-
ance-transfers to the Capital One card.

So it's very early this mornin', I can tell cause the waitresses got
French-Vanilla Coffeemate — and that's when real magic starts. I'm not
doin' a thing diff, Tim, but I win twenty-sev of the next thirty-two and
POOF: I BREAK EVEN! Ding!

Everything inside says go home, kiss kids. But I stay . . . I don't even
know why? It's an awesome thing to ponder, that your whole, entire life
really boils . . . two, tree big decisions. I was about to walk outta there
like ever other boufo/malaka swallowed by the sys, but I stay and I start
KICKING A.C. ASS. My chips forming a skyline on the felt, I'm not
even thinking about money! A crowd circling around me, cheering after
every win! I hit sixty-four thousand dollars right as the seafood buffet
opened for lunch, shrimp scampi's wafting the sweet smell of success.
WHEW BABY! It's like a-po-theosis, over here! I'm feeling guilt, you
know? I'm putting in their toilets over here! I turn around over here —
(Sings like Sinatra.)
Luck be a ladyyyyyy!
And luck, Tim, *luck is the residue of design.* Nice one, right?
(Touches one button on his cell phone.)
Who said it first? Emerson? Get outta here. Emerson, huh? Was he in
our class?

Stupid woman won't answer the friggin' phone. — Don't go, Timmy.
I'm getting a bottle of champagne. HI HONEY! *I love your anger!*
(Wink at Tim.)
*Ella de loukomimou! I'm a winner! Kerthisa, kataleve? You don't care? Sixty-
four thousand dollars! Zitas signomi apomena? Are we ever gonna work this
out, Eleni? Eleni! — Hello. Apistefto!*

She still loves me. Tim? Where'd he go? Timmy? Looks like I'm going
to the city by myself.
(Blackout.)

Disentangled

*Scattered about the stage, ski pants, sweatshirt, a thick flannel, duck boots,
running shoes, ski goggles, a wool hat, a long winter coat, a warm-up pullover
with gloves in the front pouch, a CD Walkman, keys, and a small cardboard
box overstuffed with office supplies. A man in sweatpants rolled up to his knees,*

a synthetic orange tank top, socks, and wool slippers, holds a phone with a
long cord stretched across the apartment to his ear. This is Isaac.

ISAAC: Good-bye! It's late. I'm tired! You're great! Good-bye. I'm not mad! No, I'm not coming over tonight, Kassandra. — I'm NOT coming over. Kassandra? Kassandra? Kassandra? Why are you torturing me? I'm NOT mad! Can you hold one sec?

(Isaac puts the phone on hold. He walks to a box and pulls out a nine iron. He smashes a small cardboard box to death with it. Feels better. Returns to the phone and picks it up.)

I'm back. Fine, I'm mad! I'm FURIOUS AT YOU! — Because it was our friend's recital, our FRIEND! And you're talking and you're whispering, and you're *(ffiffk!)* during the performance, like you're in a bar! And I tell you to *shhh* and you SHHH me back LOUDER! That face you make! The whole thing was interrupted! And you're with ME, Kass, PEOPLE KNOW YOU.

Everyone's a potential client at this point, a very needed client, you know that. The LAST thing I need at this point is to lose a design because my girlfriend's being a cunt. — Hello?

(He hangs up.)

I gotta watch my fucking language now?

(He redials.)

Trouble in paradise. Hi . . . It slipped! I'm sorry. I promise I will never use that word again. I promise! — OK . . . I'll come over.

(Isaac puts both duck boots on.)

Yes now, I'm putting my Timberlands on. You know, can I just say, that you are my greatest joy and the only source of misery in my life.

Well, why are you being like this, now? I need you to be supportive right now and you're on a rampage!

(He puts the flannel shirt on, accidentally buttoning it over the phone cord.)

I AM trying to! What do you think I'm doing everyday? The market's not what it used to be, darling, and right now web masters are a notch below typewriter repairmen!

I can't answer that. — No, because, there is no answer, OK? There is no SYSTEM for figuring this out. You can live your life like you think there is — like the corporate winners who downsized me — but it's a lie. Because the truth is: NOBODY KNOWS ANYTHING.

I'm putting my jacket on!

(Isaac puts on the winter jacket. Notices the phone cord in his shirt. Pulls it out.)

These people? These corporate people are all scared to DEATH to take a gamble!

(Isaac begins to search for something. Pulls stuff from pockets. Shakes out the clothes and shoes on the floor.)

Their entire philosophy of life is predicated upon the idea of RISK AVERSION.

God, if I hear that term again I'm gonna put my fist through a shower curtain. These people can't take a piss without figuring out if it's risk averse or not. And all the MDA's and LMM's and whatever other initials I don't have, that they get a salary in perpetuity for, are nothing more than a form of insurance, it's all insurance!

(Isaac searches elsewhere on the set.)

— I'm trying to find my keys, Kass. When I do, I'll walk out the door! You're like them, you realize that? Demand! That's what they do. They demand that big money-making idea! But make a mistake and you're fired. These people will never understand that mistakes are the only time anything interesting ever happens.

You know what these people gave me after six years and four months of work for them, Kass? Know what they gave me? A cardboard box with my belongings in it.

(Isaac searches underneath the beaten cardboard box.)

— I'm not *indicting* anyone! I'm saying I have to reinvent everything from scratch now, on my own, with no help and therefore I have a different form of stress, WHICH YOU ARE NOW EXACERBATING!

(He finds the keys!)

No, I'm NOT coming over! Cause I'm not waiting forty minutes for the F train, that's why!

(He takes off duck boots and winter jacket.)

— I can't afford a taxi to BROOKLYN, Kassandra. You want to hear me say it? I CAN'T AFFORD THAT.

(Rips off flannel shirt.)

This isn't about what I want, I asked what YOU want! That's how we started this however many hours ago — Fine, you wanna know what I want? I want to stop you mid-mood swing, 'cause I have problems too. I want my severance check without having to sue somebody. I want the other five hundred thousand losers who got laid off to stay out of MY Starbucks cause I can't get a seat. I never wanna have to eat at Gray's Papaya again. — I want a break! I want a break FROM ABOVE 'cause I deserve it! And if I don't get it right this second — NOPE, DIDN'T GET IT! — Then RIGHT NOW what I want to do is to go for a long run and get all this hostility out.

(Pulls jogging sweatshirt on backwards and inside out.)

— I know it's snowing out, I like to run in the snow.

(Fixes sweatshirt.)

— Where do you get that from what I said? — So I'm subconsciously running away from you? I run when I'm stressed that means we're breaking up?!

(Puts on running shoes and all-weather pants. The phone cord, between his legs, gets wrapped into his pants without him realizing it.)

OK, I'm gonna say something now, I don't want you to get mad. No more Ricky Lake. No more. Because you get this swivel-chair psychology and honestly — (Laugh.) I have no place to put it.

(He paces with phone cord caught inside his pants.)

— OK, Kassi, don't start that! Kassandra, Kassandra, Kassandra . . . Stop crying.

Kass? Kassi? Please don't cry. — Shmushy? Who's a mushy? Who am I gonna smush with?

If I come over, you'll stop crying? Yes, I'll come over.

(Pulls off sweatshirt and running shoes, puts on duck boots.)

— I AM serious about us! Do you really think we would have combined CDs if I wasn't serious?

Go, if you have a suggestion, we're communicating here.

(Puts on flannel.)

— What about my ego? — Well, whose ego *should* I worry about, darling, my fellow man; I refuse to help my fellow, my fellow man just LAID ME — I'm sorry, did I interrupt you? Egomaniacal? It's egoMANIA-CAL now?

(Takes off flannel. Puts on one running shoe.)

— Uhuh, well . . . the only part of you that's grown in the past four years is your ability to fight. I'm convinced you need to feel pain! I'm convinced you like it. HEY, MAYBE I COULD START SMACKING YOU AROUND LIKE YOUR FATHER DID, HOW'S THAT SOUND?!

— Hello?

(He hangs up.)

Oh, that was a genius move. *Smacking you around like your father did?*

Why don't you just offer to dig her mother up from the grave while you're at it?

(He redials.)

— I feel terrible for saying that. That was unfair for me to say. Please pick up the phone. Pleeeease?

— HI! That was way outta line for me to say. I didn't mean that. That's not what I meant! — What? Don't say that.

(Hops around with one shoe, one boot. Puts jacket over tank top.)

— OK, I'm coming over. I coming right now! I'll take a cab. I'll run down to the Garden and hire a limo! — Kass, don't do it! Because you've been dry for two years, don't throw it away.

I DIDN'T MEAN IT, I JUST SAID, WHY DO YOU PUT WORDS IN MY MOUTH! BUT YOU KNOW THAT'S NOT WHAT I MEANT, CYNTHIA! I mean Kassandra!

— Hello?

FUCK ME!

(He hangs up.)

Kassandra . . . Your girlfriend's name is Kassandra.

(He redials.)

That was an accident. I didn't mean Kassandra — Cynthia! . . .I meant Kassandra. Please pick up the phone?

Hi . . . Because you're reminding me of her right now. — Because Cynthia had no context for the world outside of her own emotions. The only thing that didn't bore her, was her!

That IS why I'm with you! Oh, my god! You've had an impact on my life, OK! I'm dented!

Why are you acting so irrational? Yes you are! Is it that time of month, did your dream catcher fall, what?!

You're gonna blame this on the pill again? You're gonna blame this on the pill? THEN STOP TAKING IT! — You did? When? — What does that mean? — I don't understand, every other day, every other day is not how that works. It's every day, Kassi. Everything in this world is every day. Are you pregnant? Well don't you think you should check?

I don't under — you telling me you're fucking someone else? Are you FUCKING someone else? *Blawawawa? Waum um* what? You're gonna stutter on that response? OK, you know. Don't answer. Now I'm DEFI-NITELY not coming over!

(He attempts to put the running shoes on. Gets entangled again in the phone cord.)

No, hang up, I won't call back! I'm putting *Rage Against the Machine* in my Walkman and running straight to fucking Chappaqua and you won't have to worry about it 'cause you'll never be close enough to hurt me again. *(He hangs up. Puts on full running gear.)*

Good! I'm free. I can finally have sex with other women. Yes! I'm gonna get so laid! That Asian girl in 2B is definitely gonna hear from me. *(He clears the stage of everything. Sits. Thinks. Has a nervous breakdown. Cries. Heads to phone. Redials.)*

Oh, pick up the phone, Kassandra. PICK UP THE PHONE AND ACT LIKE A, A — WOMAN!

HI . . . I have one last question for you: Will you marry me? — I am nothing but real. Will you marry me? — It's not because you're pregnant, well maybe it is, I just wanna start a home with you.

Here's what I propose to do. It's sixty-four blocks to your place, I'm gonna run there. And when I get there and propose in person, I will hear my answer. — Don't say anything. I'm out the door!

. . .What?

(Blackout.)

The Nomad

A figure in an olive-green suit and a purple oxford sits on a tall stool holding a pool cue. A huge gold ring. Slicked back hair. In the suit pocket a pack of Dunhill Reds. This is Manny.

MANNY: I'm an attractive guy. I'm not talking about my appearance. I mean literally. I'm attractive. Throughout my life I've found people cling to me like socks. Like I'm something for them to hold onto. My therapist says, I gotta magnetic personality, know what I mean? — Go 'head. You break.

Tonight after work a few of us go over to TGIF's for happy hour. The place's so jammed, we gotta push our way in.

They got the Rangers and the Knicks on two huge TVs, and for once, they're winning! Cherry on top is, they got a promotional thing happening, so all cocktails made with Dewer's are free! So I'm sipping a scotch margarita, watching a little Knicks, little Rangers, why choose? But after a few minutes, I notice that aside from the bartendress and promo girl, there ain't another woman IN the place. It's giant fucking sausage party, when . . . like it's out of a *Dawson's Brook* episode, this girl walks in.

— Must a been about nineteen years young, hair swirling into her face, bead a sweat on her neck, drop-dead gorgeous. And out of the entire bar, Nicky — bar filled with guys — she stops in front of me and she says all hysterically, comma, *I need an honest man's help.* Swear to God, Nicky. *I need an honest man's help,* she says, her bottom lip aquiver. *A scalper stole my money, he won't give me the ticket.*

Now whenever I hear of such a gross injustice, I consider it my personal responsibility to correct it so to speak, it's why I became an attorney. — See, the universe is constantly coming at us with questions in the form of people. I never let 'em go unanswered.

I throw my jacket over the bar stool, tuck my tie in my shirt, and I head outside and see this dirtbag holding tickets, counting a wad a cash. He looks up at me, sees my suit, my shoes, probably figures I'm some yuppie taking my cell phone for a walk, no problem. But see this is me, I'm your worst fuckin' problem.

And before he gets a chance to size me up a second time, I'm in his FACE. And he smells like shit, he's got snot on his lapels, he's been drinking. He's a class-A-lowlife-scumbag-jerkoff-asshole, y'know the type a guy I defend.

— And I just GRAB THE TICKETS outta his hand like SWOOP. I got 'em. I'm staring at him eye to eye like, *what are you gonna do about it?* Guy doesn't bat a lash.

— I turn to head back inside . . . and I don't know what happened? It was like a switch inside me FLIPPED and I spin around and just CRACK this guy!

He didn't know WHAT hit 'em. It was me, ten times hard in the face. BAM BAM BAM BAM, proppin' him against the chain link, BAM BAM, with both hands, like Tie Domi. BAM BAM BAM.

I'm gettin' ready to go back in . . . you know, maybe get a little lucky after balancing the scales a justice; until I sawr what I did.

It must a been really cold out or maybe it was my ring, but I had totally opened up this guy's face. His fuckin' heartbeat was squirtin' outta gash in his head. I'm like, holy shit, *I just fuckin' killed this homeboy.*

I look to see if I caused a scene there's a million people around, it's cocktail hour in Manhattan: NO ONE noticed. This guy's lying on the pavement, literally forming the shape of a question mark, people are walking past with Macy's Christmas bags.

I hail a cab.

I pick the guy up off the ground, one of his teeth bounces out, I'm trying to pick up the tooth while propping him up, like they're gonna screw it back in. He's dripping blood off his chin, down his shirt. Cabby takes one look at the guy and pulls away! I'm like *get back here ya fuckin' Towelhead!*

— I hail another cab, it's no problem this time except that it's bumper-to- bumper traffic all the way to Roosevelt Hospital right as the snow started getting heavy.

We get to the emergency room, we need a doctor quick, the guy's seriously injured. This nurse is there; little white hat, right, she hands me a clipboard, says *fill this out.* I'm like, *the man is bleeding to death! Look at him!* She says, *we can't look at anyone till we have the forms filled out.* She's a little hottie, but she's got attitude, you know? I'm trying to get a drink from the water cooler, no cones in the cup dispenser, I can't quench my thirst. I go up to the desk to ask for cup, nurse sees me coming, slides the window shut, Nicky . . . like I'm a dog. It's true! The cute ones think they can be rude to people.

— Nice shot. My dad taught you that one. —

I'm trying to fill out the triplicate, no idea any of this guy's information, I'm making it all up as I go, thank God I'm a lawyer. But I can't concentrate 'cause there's this Polish hot dog vendor watching a *Benny Hill* rerun with an ice pack on his crotch. He's laughing and then keeling over in pain. He's like, *AHCHXaahhh!* I'm like one, it's not that funny, you know, Benny Hill over here? This guy's laughing like it's a Jackie Chan picture. I'm like, two, if it hurts you, change the fucking channel!

I give everything to the nurse, she starts to peck away at the computer, like this, with one finger, I'm like great there goes another pint of scumbag's goo. I'm starting to feel really guilty about all my aggression, when I hear this yelling. The whole hospital can hear it cause it's REALLY LOUD! It's scumhead! He's conscious for five seconds, he's in a shouting match with Polish Benny Hill.

This security guard, more like a LINEBACKER comes over. Scumbag sees him, puts his dukes up like he's ready to rumble. Security guard says, I'll never forget this, he's like *I will restrain you.* Just like a command. Scumbag takes a swing at him and Security TACKLES him. OH-hoo! This guy coulda played professional ball, or did, scumbag's not having a good night. They go careening into the water cooler, it shatters into a million pieces, now I'll never get a drink. I'm like, where is the Dewer's broad when you need her?

Nurse comes over, tells me, *I dropped these;* it's the TICKETS. She asks me, *what are they for?* I have no idea. I'm on this urban odyssey, I don't even know what I'm busting my balls for?

I finally look at these tickets, Nick, four of them, at the Garden, for Yanni. FUCKING YANNI, right? — The nurse is like, *You have Yanni tickets? It's been sold out for a year! I never miss them!* I'm like, *You wanna come?* She's like, ME? And I'm like, *yeah you and bring two friends!* You know, increase the ratio. I give her three tickets, tell her meet me at Beefsteak Charlie's in twenty minutes. The nurse is like, WHO ARE YOU? — That's the essential question isn't it, Nicky? Answer that one, you're home free.

I stop by at the bar, my jacket's gone; thousand dollar suit, I'm officially miffed. It's sleeting out, the city's gray and gross, last thing I wanna do NOW is entertain Miss General Hospitals, but it occurs to me that if I don't, I might not have a place to crash tonight, my fuckin' keys are in my jacket! — I walk outside. No free cabs: always when you're in a rush. I gotta run in the street through the traffic, I finally get to MSG, finally get to Beefsteak Charlie's? IT'S GONE; as in defunct as an establishment. She's not there.

I jog the circumference of the Garden, I got sweat-cicles hanging off my nipples, I finally find her standing in front of Penn Station. She tells me *her friends couldn't get off,* we got two extra tickets.

—Nice bank — As I settle down, I hear people asking around for tickets. A girl and guy right behind me pay a hundred fifty bucks each, 'cause the show's about to start, people are scrambling to get in. I figure if I sell two, I cut my losses for the suit.

This is where it starts to get juicy.

I make eye contact with this guy in front of the newsstand. Nicky, he's wearing a wrinkled tuxedo, he's got a bottle of Dom Perignon in each pocket, tells me he just came from Atlantic City, and tonight is his big night! I'm like *in that case, tickets are five hundred a pop.* Guy whips out a roll a Franklins could a choked a pterodactyl.

I got paranoid I'm being set up, right? So I sort of turn away to stall a minute, and who is standing there in my suit jacket but the Dawson's Stream girl! I'm like, I FOUND YOU!

She gives me a huge hug, hands me my jacket, keys are in the pocket, instant karma's gonna get me! I swing back to the tux, sell him the last ticket, HE tries to hug me. I'm like *never touch me in public, pal, I just met you.*

We all zip inside and the girls are creaming their panties 'cause we're third row center, ten feet from the stage, Mr. A.C. pouring us all champagne as the lights fade for the first song and let me tell you this Yanni guy? Fucking AWE-SOME. And you know me, I hate classical music. But YANNI, swinging his hair around, it's like he conducts with his hair! He's got the mustache you could shovel a driveway with. A Mediterranean Michael Bolton, this guy. I think he gets electrolysis. I heard.

(Light a cigarette.)

After the show, Mr. A.C. suggests the new Brasserie for a nightcap. We go sit down and if I tell you this guy gets *liquored.* Four hundred fifty dollar bottle of Chateau Lefite Rothschilds, he's talking to the girls about hands-off toilets and urinals and some shit. I swear to god, I felt bad for the guy.

    Check finally comes, it's a thousand something; I'm fishing around for my wallet, you know . . . I'm like ah, ah . . . A.C. throws down with twelve hundreds. Bop bop bop, eight ten twelve. Leaves three for the tip. — I go to put my wallet back and I feel something jangling around in my pocket. I pull it out: it's Scumbag's tooth. The tooth.

    And somethin' comes over me, Nicky. I get this idea . . . I decide to send the girls home which wasn't easy, my friend . . . If anything was a sure thing that was. I woulda taken BOTH those girls back to my place for a manage a dos like ya read about; still subscribe to *Forum?* — Well, I sacrifice it.

    Because . . . I drop the guy off in front of this fancy-pants plumbing shop on West Twenty-second Street. He's so shit-faced, he can't open the door, slipping up and down on the ice like Charlie Chaplin. I help him inside to a back office. He thanks me, I leave. But I notice . . . he doesn't shut the office door all the way, so I peak in and I see this guy pulling MONEY from every pocket. I have no idea, maybe seventy-five, eighty? And the thing is Nicky . . . he puts it all in this dinky, little safe that would make you laugh. You could open this thing with your eyes closed.

    I'm like, I'm getting Nicky in on this one! The guy's passed out over there, begging us for an answer. Without a hitch, the job's half an hour start to finish. That is . . . if you're up for it. — That's what I love about you, Nicky, you think outside the box. You drive, I'll ride shotgun. I'm back in the family fold, right? And hey, you should turn up the radio when you go out, some asshole'll think you're still home.

    — You know, my father, may he rest in peace, always used to say to me, "Son, life's a bumpy road." *I know Pops, I'm paving it.*

(Blackout.)

Ekstasi

A figure in a technicolor jacket, scarf, pointy fleece hat with a ball on the end of it, a fuzzy warm long-sleeve shirt, two sopping wet pant legs, and wet hair. His glasses are also beaded with water. This is David.

DAVID: I'm inside the Union Square Staples when I start freaking out.
(David jiggles his jaw back and forth.)
All I need are the boxes and they're nowhere to be found. Pyramids of products on display at every turn. It's like a giant Andy Warhol installation. The store is an assault of materialism. I go through four floors of this place, Jonathan? No boxes. It's exactly what I deserve for waiting till the last minute.

Wow. My tongue feels weird after not talking for three months.

I exit through the basement cause the fascist security won't let you leave where you came in, like terrorists have Staples on the top of their list, and lo and behold, there in the bowels of the building along with the rest of the storage supplies, are cardboard boxes. I look at them, they're twenty-nine dollars for four and they're this big. I'm gonna need five hundred thousand dollars worth to pack all the rest of this shit.

And then I remember on Twenty-seventh Street, the wholesalers throw out hundreds of boxes everyday, I'll get 'em for free! But see, it didn't occur to me right away because I've been conditioned like the rest of society searching for the meaning of life in a merchandising franchise.

I finally walk outside: it's like a dream. The snow has covered everything. It's reflecting the orange street lamps so it looks like it's just after sunset, but instead of New York's normal hustle/bustle chaos, the city's like Siberia. No people. No taxis. The wind whipping down Broadway.

I start to walk up town. I get to Twenty-second Street when this jogger runs pass me. He's listening to *Rage Against the Machine's* first album, I can hear "Bomb Track" blasting as he runs by. Middle of the night, a snowstorm that shut-down the city, this guy's out for a jog in ski gear. I follow him onto Twenty-second when I hear an alarm trip. Up ahead, two guys walk out of a plumbing shop in the middle of the street. They get into a car waiting at the curb and they try to pull out, but the wheels are spinning on an ice patch in the gutter, they're stuck. They're trying to rock it off the ice, throwing it in reverse and back into drive.

And the runner, I guess, couldn't hear the alarm . . . 'cause he gets to the car and he starts pushing! He's helping them get free! When the passenger-side door pops open, a guy gets halfway out, and —

(Two gun shots.)

I cross the street. I can hear the jogger moaning, sort of . . . softly. It sounded less like pain than it did like someone having sex.

I clear a car, and I see him, on his back, blood steaming into the snow. But as I came to him, it seemed like he was OK. His eyes were bright and he was looking at me kind of . . . competitively.

I clear my throat and I say to him, "You're gonna be OK." My first words in three months . . . and it's a lie.

This man in a tuxedo appears at my side. He has this sweet cologne on reminds me of my father. We crouch over the jogger as he starts to mumble. I can't make it out, Kass, Kassi, some woman's name.

— Head back, mouth open, snow flakes melting in his eyes. I think . . . a snowstorm's the only time the city ever really dreams. I lean back against a mailbox . . . one I dropped love letters into years ago.

I feel myself leave my body. I float up to a street light, hovering above the scene. I look down at myself, the man in the tuxedo, the snow accumulating on the corpse . . . Then I float higher. I can see the grid the city's built on. Geometric order.

The police are all in a rush for information. I keep looking at the jogger. His eyes focused on some fascinating question. And . . . I understood . . . I understand.

It isn't the Ecstasy, Jonathan. I'm telling you. It's not my perception on some synthetic drug that's freaking me out; it's reality! — It's NOT the X, I just said, John. Jonathan? I never swallowed the pill.
(Reveal the pill.)
I never swallowed the fucking pill, John. I palmed it. I didn't want to leave you hanging on our last night, but I just, I wasn't in the right head!

— I feel like I'm tripping now, though. I feel like I'm on a trip. I wanna be this awake, all the time . . . and I know it's gonna fade. Why does that happen?
(Takes off the coat.)

A month ago, you told me we'd do whatever I wanted on my last night here, didn't you? Well there is something I want to do, if you're willing. I want to stay awake till dawn, and I wanna unpack all this shit.
(He retrieves the silver sword from the cardboard box.)
This is definitely home.

Um . . . about tomorrow, Jonathan? We're ah . . . we're gonna need to get rid of all these boxes.

END OF PLAY

PROFESSIONAL SKEPTICISM

by James Rasheed

The play is dedicated to
Michael Murray and Brandeis University.

PLAYWRIGHT'S BIOGRAPHY

James Rasheed understands the ups and downs of a financial statement. A certified public accountant, he recently earned his MFA in playwriting and now has first-hand knowledge of scripts, which he puts to work in his new play *Professional Skepticism.*

The drama is a dark comedy that takes place in a large accounting firm. It follows four auditors as they compete against each other to become partners in the company. "It's about back stabbing, law bending and greed," says Mr. Rasheed who wrote the timely play before the Enron and Worldcom scandals.

Mr. Rasheed, who has always loved writing, returned to Clemson University to study playwriting and theater after seven years of working as an accountant. At Clemson, his play *August Flight* was highly acclaimed and produced at the state Kennedy Center/American College Theatre Festival, where it was nominated for advancement to regional competition.

In May 2001, Mr. Rasheed graduated from Brandeis University with an MFA in playwriting. *Professional Skepticism* was awarded Brandeis University's Herbert and Beigel New Play Premiere and was given a full production by the theater department. Brandeis also honored *Professional Skepticism* with the 2000–2001 Harold and Mimi Steinberg Prize for Best Original Play. During the spring semester of 2002, Mr. Rasheed taught a playwriting course at Brandeis University.

In July 2002, *Professional Skepticism* received its first professional production as a world premiere at the Wellfleet Harbor Actors Theater in Wellfleet, Massachusetts.

—Glenn Hare, Director of Marketing
and Communications at Clemson University

ORIGINAL PRODUCTIONS

Professional Skepticism was first produced professionally by the Wellfleet Harbor Actors Theater in Wellfleet, Massachusetts in 2002. It was directed by Jason Slavick with the following cast:

LEO	Robert Pemberton*
PAUL	Chris Faith*
GREG	Yaegel Welch
MARGARET	Marianna Bassham

Professional Skepticism was workshopped and produced on the college level at Brandeis University in Waltham, Massachusetts in March 2001. It was directed by Candice Brown with the following cast:

LEO . . . . Augustus Kelley
PAUL . . . . Chris Faith*
GREG . . . . Darius Omar Williams
MARGARET . . . . Marianna Bassham

Members of Actors Equity Association, the union of professional actors, stage managers, and choreographers.

INTRODUCTION

One of the fundamentals of playwriting is to write about what you know. During Brandeis University's winter break in 1999, 1 was sitting on my Aunt Lucy's front porch at Pawley's Island, South Carolina, trying to come up with an idea for my next play. I kept thinking about the time I worked as an auditor for a Big Five accounting firm. I remembered the long hours and how I felt trapped. The accounting world had engulfed every aspect of my life at that time. A picture started developing in my mind, but did I have a play here? Over the next two months, I explored many facets of my auditing experience as I pieced together a fictional story.

The following February I brought the first draft of *Professional Skepticism* to the graduate playwright's workshop. At the time it was a short one-act, only thirty-five pages. The response was encouraging. It was a solid beginning. A few months passed before I picked up the script again. Then came the hard part, rewriting. Once again I read over everyone's feedback and began incorporating some of their suggestions. For instance, in the initial draft, the character of Margaret was never seen, only talked about. One of the comments was that there was too much testosterone in the play. So Margaret arrives to break up the boy's club and to show us a successful woman in the field.

In November 2000 the play was presented again in the workshop. This time I wasn't sure if it was a one-act because it had grown to over seventy pages. Once again the workshop was an integral part of the process, helping me to flesh out the characters and their relationships to one another. I began meeting with Professor Michael Murray on a regular basis to further develop the play. He stressed the essentials. "Up the stakes. Keep things open. Build on the tension. What are these characters doing to each other? Show specifics. Don't rush the process." The rewriting process continued into the rehearsals.

Candice Brown, who directed the Brandeis production, and I would discuss scenes that she felt needed tweaking. We would then talk with the actors. As you can see, it was a collaborative effort.

In the audience at one of the performances at the Brandeis productions was Jeff Zinn, producing artistic director for the Wellfleet Harbor Actors Theater on Cape Cod. He was asked to attend by Marianna Bassham, who played Margaret. It was a great idea to add Margaret to the play! About ten months later, shortly after the Enron scandal hit the news, I received a call from Jeff. That July 2002, *Professional Skepticism* had its world premiere at the Wellfleet Harbor Actors Theater.

CHARACTERS

LEO: thirty-one, a senior accountant.

PAUL: twenty-six, a second-year staff accountant, should always be played as a Southerner.

GREG: twenty-three, African American, a first-year staff accountant.

MARGARET: twenty-eight, a senior accountant.

TIME

August 2000.

PLACE

All scenes take place in a conference room in a Big Five accounting firm in Charleston, South Carolina.

Professional Skepticism

ACT I
Scene One

At rise. Early Tuesday afternoon. Leo is sitting at the conference table review-ing an audit folder. Paul and Greg enter.

PAUL: *(To Greg.)* How about three on Sunday?

GREG: Three? That should give us enough time.

PAUL: If we eat around 12:30, we'll be fine. I'll call in a few minutes . . . Leo, have you heard anything else about the merger?

LEO: *(Annoyed.)* Why didn't you wait on me?

PAUL: We looked for you. Where were you?

LEO: Here.

PAUL: Here, where? I couldn't find you. I thought you went to lunch with Diane.

LEO: No.

PAUL: Sorry about that.

LEO: Where did you eat?

PAUL: Aaron's Deli.

LEO: Hah.

PAUL: Did you eat?

LEO: No.

PAUL: We didn't leave you on purpose.

LEO: *(To Greg.)* Hand me the accounts-receivable folder.

GREG: It's on the table over there.

PAUL: *(To Leo.)* Are you hungry?

LEO: What?

PAUL: Let me go get you a Coke and some crackers.

LEO: I'll eat tonight.

PAUL: You like those peanut butter crackers.

LEO: Forget it.

PAUL: It's my fault, please.

(Leo doesn't respond.)

PAUL: *(Continues.)* I'm buying you a pack of crackers and a Coke . . . Greg, you want a Coke.

GREG: Sure.

PAUL: Two Cokes and a pack of peanut butter crackers.

    (Paul scrounges around his area at the table looking for money.)

PAUL: *(Continues. To Greg.)* Lend me a few dollars.

GREG: All I have is a twenty.

PAUL: Do you have any change?

LEO: *(Pulling out his wallet.)* Here. Now go!

    (Paul takes the money.)

PAUL: I'll pay you back tomorrow because this is my treat.

LEO: Go!

PAUL: I forgot to run by the money machine this morning.

    (Paul crosses to the door leading to the hallway.)

LEO: *(To Paul.)* Did you leave any audit folders at the client's?

PAUL: No. We brought everything back to the office. I packed the trunk myself.

LEO: Then where is the inventory folder?

PAUL: *(Crossing back to the table.)* I was using it this morning.

    (Paul hands Leo the inventory folder.)

LEO: *(Army drill tone.)* I want all the folders, in order, in the audit trunk.

PAUL: OK.

LEO: I can't find a goddamn thing!

    (Paul starts gathering audit folders.)

LEO: *(Continues.)* What a mess! . . . This isn't finished.

PAUL: I said I was still working on it.

LEO: What the hell were you doing at the client's? All of this should have been done by now.

PAUL: We're on schedule.

LEO: No, we're not.

PAUL: When's our deadline?

LEO: I talked with Luther this morning. The client would like the financials issued on the eighteenth.

PAUL: That's not even three weeks! I'm still waiting on bank confirmations. And accounts-receivable confirmations.

LEO: Luther promised the client.

PAUL: There's no way we can issue these financials on the eighteenth. Not with an unqualified opinion. Seventeen days?

LEO: I'm on this audit to speed your ass up.

PAUL: Luther shouldn't have promised Mr. Gilreath anything before consulting with us.

LEO: I told him it wouldn't be a problem.

PAUL: Leo?

LEO: Aren't you going somewhere?

PAUL: Oh yeah. Sorry, Leo.

> *(Paul exits the room.)*

LEO: What are you and pinhead planning on Sunday?

GREG: Racquetball after church.

LEO: Where do you play?

GREG: Paul's a member at Windsor Country Club.

LEO: Windsor? That's a shitty golf course. You play golf . . . Tiger?

GREG: Yeah. Haven't played around here yet. Paul's not a golfer.

LEO: I wouldn't be hanging out with him. You know what I mean?

GREG: I've been to a driving range a few times.

LEO: Diane and I are members over at Crescent.

GREG: I've heard it's a nice place.

LEO: It is. . . . I can get you in. *(Referring to Greg's race.)* It wouldn't be an issue.

GREG: I'd like to play there.

LEO: Good. This weekend, I'll take you over. Show you the course.

GREG: I can't this weekend. How about next?

LEO: Your loss. So, how do you like it here?

GREG: It's been OK . . . I really do want to play at Crescent.

LEO: We'll see. You getting any?

GREG: What?

> *(Leo laughs.)*

GREG: *(Continues.)* Leo, pass me the audit manual.

LEO: *(Handing Greg the audit manual.)* How much did they start you out at?

GREG: Huh?

LEO: How much are they paying staff accountants this year?

GREG: Thirty-eight.

> *(Paul enters with a pack of crackers and two Cokes.)*

PAUL: *(To Leo.)* There you go. You really shouldn't skip lunch. *(To Greg.)* Here Bubba.

GREG: Thanks.

PAUL: *(Pulls out a little pocket notebook and begins writing.)* I owe Leo four dollars.

LEO: Greg was telling me they started this year's group out at thirty-eight.

PAUL: No way. Last year I started at thirty-four.

LEO: Too bad.

PAUL: They must be adjusting.

LEO: Thirty-four thousand wouldn't pay my grocery bill.

PAUL: Even with my raise this year, I'm not making thirty-eight.

LEO: I started around thirty-eight. Four years ago!

PAUL: I'm making enough. It's not like we're living in Boston or New York.

LEO: You should have negotiated.

PAUL: I didn't want to negotiate.

LEO: Why not?

PAUL: I wasn't going to mess up my opportunity to work for a Big Five accounting firm.

LEO: Luther makes over three hundred thousand a year.

PAUL: None of us want to work for a small firm.

GREG: I wouldn't.

PAUL: Leo, you're always making fun of guys working at small firms like Jordan and Company.

LEO: They're all a bunch of losers.

PAUL: You want to hear something worse? A friend of mind was let go at Peat. He just accepted a job with the IRS.

LEO: Fuck that.

GREG: *(Overlapping.)* No way.

LEO: You sold yourself short.

PAUL: I don't care. Working for Edwin and Wyndham is prestigious.

LEO: Whoo Wee. They pay us crap.

PAUL: Managers make pretty good money. Eighty thousand is decent.

LEO: You have to wait almost five years.

PAUL: I'd be happy with eighty.

LEO: Who says you're going to make it to manager?

PAUL: *(With conviction.)* I'm going to be a partner.

LEO: Bullshit. If this merger goes through, you'll be out of here by the end of the month. This place will just be a blot on your résumé.

GREG: Leo, what have you heard?

LEO: It's called downsizing. Some of you will be "deselected."

(Paul pulls out his little pocket notebook.)

PAUL: Pierce and Hawthorne has twelve staff accountants to our ten.

GREG: *(Overlapping.)* They're not going to eighty-six any of the first-year staff accountants.

LEO: *(Patting Greg on the back.)* Don't let the door hit you in the ass on your way out.

PAUL: *(Directed at Leo.)* Well they also have five seniors.

LEO: Stop fucking around and get back to work.

PAUL: *(Quietly.)* Three managers and two partners . . . Where's my ruler? Did someone take my ruler? *(Finding his ruler under a stack of folders.)* Never mind.

LEO: Thirty-four thousand. Hah. Oh well.

PAUL: I had other offers. Arthur Andersen in Atlanta offered me more money and better benefits.

LEO: So?

PAUL: I prefer living here.

LEO: Ahhhh. Pauley likes Charleston. Sweet . . . So sweet.

GREG: Leo. Leave him alone.

LEO: *(To Greg.)* I'm surprised you're not living in Atlanta.

GREG: Why?

LEO: *(Homosexuality reference.)* You just seem like a *Hotlanta* kind of guy . . . Luther originally offered me thirty-three. I thought to myself fuck that. I said, "No, thank you." Then he asked, "What would make you happy?" *(Lets out a slight laugh.)* What would make you happy? *(To Paul.)* Too bad you got a lousy deal.

PAUL: *(To Greg, picking up the phone.)* I'll reserve the racquetball court for Sunday.

LEO: Guys, I wouldn't make plans for this weekend. Your butts are in here until this audit is completed.

PAUL: Leo, I have already made plans.

LEO: Team is not spelled with an "I."

GREG: On Sunday, I can't be here until after one.
(To Paul.)
You're still planning to go to church with me?

PAUL: Well . . . We'll talk later.

LEO: Where do you go to church?

GREG: Riverside Baptist. You and Diane should join us.

LEO: *(Laughs.)* No.

PAUL: Leo's Catholic.

GREG: My mother was Catholic . . . until she was saved.

LEO: You drink?

GREG: Yes.

LEO: It wasn't lemonade you were sipping at the office party.

GREG: I drink in moderation.

LEO: But I thought all Baptists abstain from alcohol?

GREG: *(Adamantly.)* That's an ignorant misconception.

LEO: *(Smiling.)* Whoa! . . . So it's an ignorant misconception? I have missed the boat . . . Here's what I think. You drink, you just hope no one from your little church group catches you.

GREG: I have nothing to hide.

LEO: You look like a closet case to me. *(To Paul.)* Pauley, I thought you were an Episcopalian. What the hell happened? *(Putting a cigarette in his mouth.)* Pauley. Pauley. Pauley. You disappoint me, man. You're letting Greg drag you to a goddamn fundy church.

GREG: Most Baptists are not right-wing fundamentalists.

LEO: *(To Paul.)* You better practice saying, "Praise the Lord! . . . Yes, Jesus! Who wants to come up here and be saved . . . Yes, Jesus."

GREG: *(Overlapping.)* There are extremists in every other mainstream Protestant denomination. Including the Episcopal church. You are so full of shit.

LEO: I hear you, brother. Let's get fired up. *(Leo picks up his crackers and drink. He begins singing Daniel L. Schufte's "Here I Am, Lord.")* "Here I am, Lord. Is it I, Lord? I have heard you calling in the night. I will go, Lord, if you lead me. I will hold your people in my heart."

PAUL: Just ignore him.

(Leo returns to the door.)

LEO: *(Imitating the television evangelist, Ernest Anglsley.)* Amen. Can you say, "Amen?"

(Leo exits.)

GREG: Asshole . . . At Sunday school, they say we should pray for people like Leo.

PAUL: Right now?

GREG: I'll have his name placed on the prayer list.

PAUL: *(Relieved.)* Oh, good.

GREG: Bud, did you hear about Margaret?

PAUL: What's the matter?

GREG: She received her grades in the mail this morning.

PAUL: Already?

GREG: Yeah.

PAUL: The dreaded CPA exam. How did she do?

GREG: Passed her final two parts.

PAUL: You're kidding! . . . Thank goodness.

GREG: How many times has she taken the exam?

PAUL: I shouldn't say. *(Pause.)* That's like her seventh time.

GREG: Seven times, wow.

PAUL: There will be a party at Margaret's tonight.

GREG: You've already passed the exam, right?

PAUL: Yes. Last year I enrolled in a one-week intensive review course in Atlanta and passed all four parts on my first try.

GREG: Impressive.

PAUL: Each part has less than a twenty-five percent pass rate.

GREG: What were your grades?

PAUL: Seventy-five, seventy-five, seventy-five, and seventy-five. The lowest passing grade.

GREG: Hey, you got it over with.

PAUL: Not bad for one week of studying. How do you think you did?

GREG: It's in God's hands.

PAUL: Were you prepared?

GREG: I spent a lot of time in prayer.

PAUL: You studied also, didn't you?

GREG: Yeah.

PAUL: You'll do fine. Besides, very few people pass all four parts on their first try. I was fortunate. I wouldn't worry about it.

GREG: I'll know soon.

PAUL: The firm gives you three years to pass the exam. You have plenty of time. So don't worry.

GREG: I guess Leo's passed.

PAUL: *(Looking at the door.)* Not the law section.

GREG: No way.

PAUL: Oh yes. Margaret and Leo usually go out together and get drunk when the grades arrive.

GREG: He's been here over three years.

PAUL: They're keeping him because we've had a high turnover of senior accountants. But they won't promote him to manager until he passes. Leo will have a cow when he finds out Margaret passed. Especially if he screwed up again.

GREG: If he fails this time, will they let him go?

PAUL: Probably.

GREG: Too bad.

PAUL: But Luther will keep him until he finishes up all the audits he's working on. Bubba, if you passed any parts, I'll buy you a beer.

GREG: We'll see.

PAUL: You want to go to Clancy's around nine?

GREG: Let's hope we get out of here by nine.

PAUL: I'm craving Mexican food.

GREG: I may just stay home tonight.

PAUL: Come on.

GREG: No.

PAUL: I'll drive . . . My treat.

GREG: A Monterey's burrito does sound good.

PAUL: And a couple Margaritas.

GREG: See if Margaret wants to come.

PAUL: I'll give her a call.

GREG: *(Insinuating a sexual relationship.)* Bud, are Margaret and Leo . . .

PAUL: They were.

(Leo enters.)

LEO: Margaret just gave me a copy of the press release. Ladies, the merger is official. Come on, Luther wants to see all of us now.

Scene Two

At Rise: Projected on the conference room's white board: "Mason Industries Audit; Saturday 9:00 AM; August 5, 2000; Deadline: 13 days." Leo and Greg are in the room working.

GREG: You were right about that Ping putter. I tried it out at the putting greens during lunch yesterday.

LEO: I was wondering where you were. If you had gotten lost.

GREG: The putter has a good feel to it.

LEO: Isn't it great on the fast greens?

GREG: Yeah. Hey, I brought it back. It's in my trunk.

LEO: Keep it.

GREG: Let me buy it off you.

LEO: It's yours.

GREG: Are you sure?

LEO: Did the ball feel smooth coming off the club head?

GREG: Yeah.

LEO: Then just say, "Thank you, Leo."

GREG: Thanks, Leo.

LEO: Besides, I just bought an Odyssey.

GREG: I'm ready to play at Crescent.

LEO: We'll see.

(Paul enters with a bag of biscuits. He sets down his audit bag and quickly crosses back to the door. Paul opens the door and looks down the hall.)

PAUL: That was odd. I was walking down the hall and Luther came out of his office. Just as I was about to say, "Good morning," he turned around and went back in . . . Huh. Funny. *(Pause.)* I hate working on Saturdays.

LEO: Are you looking for a job or a career?

PAUL: *(Handing out biscuits.)* One sausage and egg biscuit for Leo. And Greg wanted ham.

GREG: *(Pulling out a dollar.)* How much do I owe you?

PAUL: Dollar and a half.

GREG: All I've got is dollar.

PAUL: We'll call it even.

LEO: I'll catch you later.

PAUL: Don't worry about it. *(Paul takes out his pocket notebook and records the cost of Leo's biscuit.)* Any more news about the merger?

GREG: No.

LEO: So Paul, how are you doing?

PAUL: Great.

LEO: I felt so sorry for you yesterday.

PAUL: Why?

LEO: I'm glad it was you who was up there and not me.

PAUL: My presentation? I thought my presentation went very well.

LEO: Luther understands it was your first time.

PAUL: I covered the topic. What did I leave out? I did a pretty good job.

LEO: Luther can be an asshole.

PAUL: *(With increasing anxiety.)* You think he's disappointed in me? *(Crosses to the door and looks down the hall.)* OK, Luther asked some questions I couldn't answer. I'm going to get back to him on it. All I was supposed to do was present a broad overview. Leo, did he say something to you?

LEO: No. *(Pause.)* I just know Luther.

PAUL: I gave handouts. I used computer-generated special effects in my over-heads. Everyone laughed whenever the cartoon accountant ran across the screen. *(Imitating the cartoon accountant.)* "No more FASBS! No more FASBS . . ."

LEO: Paul, your cartoon accountant resembled Luther.

PAUL: No, it didn't.

LEO: That's what people were saying.

PAUL: No. You're joking.

LEO: Whatever.

PAUL: Shoot. I was just trying to use the right balance of humor. When you're

talking about FASBs . . . it's pretty dry stuff . . . No wonder Luther
didn't want to talk to me this morning.

LEO: Don't fuck up next time.

PAUL: Shoot! I volunteered to go again next Friday.

LEO: Just stick to your damn topic.

PAUL: How bad was it? . . . I didn't embarrass myself, though. Did I?

LEO: Huh.

PAUL: Maybe I should speak to Luther. *(Pause.)* No, I don't want to bother
him. Especially if he's ticked off. I'll let him calm down. *(To Greg.)* How
do you think I did?

GREG: I don't know, I wasn't paying attention.

PAUL: You should pay attention.

GREG: Bud, who cares?

PAUL: Your clients may ask you questions related to those issues.

GREG: Yeah.

PAUL: In a lot of cases, you can save them money.

GREG: What's your topic for next week?

PAUL: Fraud. Preventing and investigating fraud. I'm discussing the "fraud triangle" of opportunity, motivation, and rationalization. I was planning on
using a cartoon character that looks like an accountant dressed as Sherlock Holmes. *(Pause.)* I gave a decent presentation, didn't I?

LEO: GODDAMN IT, FORGET ABOUT IT!

PAUL: OK. Sorry. Anyway, I don't care.

GREG: *(Picking up his coffee cup.)* I need another cup of coffee.
   (Greg walks out of the room.)

LEO: What did y'all do last night?

PAUL: Same as usual. Greg and I went to Clancy's. Half the office showed up.
Where were you and Diane?

LEO: We stayed in.

PAUL: I haven't seen Diane in weeks.

LEO: Who was the band?

PAUL: Doppelganger is playing again this weekend. We didn't leave Clancy's
until after two. We left Margaret dancing on top of a table. Totally
plastered.

LEO: What do you think about Greg acing the CPA exam?

PAUL: WHAT?

LEO: Luther was telling me this morning that Greg made the third highest
grades in the state. High nineties on all four parts. Can you believe that?

High nineties. Ninety-seven on auditing. Law, he made a ninety-eight. *(Trying to recall.)* Accounting and reporting? He made a ninety . . .

PAUL: *(Quickly.)* I've always heard if you make over a seventy-five, you've studied too much.

LEO: Accounting and reporting, he made a ninety-six. He didn't do so well on that one.

PAUL: It really doesn't matter if you make a seventy-five or a hundred. Who gives a darn?

LEO: Luther invited him to lunch on Wednesday.

PAUL: Good for Greg.

LEO: Good for Greg. Luther wants to show him off. They're going to hold on to him. Greg's the next superstar. I just have a gut feeling he is.

PAUL: Greg's a great guy. We're good friends.

LEO: I wouldn't be surprised if he makes partner in less than ten years. He's the next David McClain.

PAUL: Who?

LEO: David McClain is in the Charlotte office. He made partner in only eight and a half years. Yeah, just like David McClain, Greg's a superstar. Super. Star. Third highest in the state. Grades make a big difference.
(Pause.)

PAUL: Are you taking the exam again in November?

LEO: No.

PAUL: You passed. *(Pause.)* Leo?

LEO: I haven't received my grades yet.

PAUL: But everyone else has . . . I'd call the postmaster.

LEO: I don't give a shit.

PAUL: If you didn't pass this time, won't you lose credit for all the other parts? You'd have to take the whole exam over again.

LEO: It's not your fucking concern.

PAUL: You can have my old study guides. I don't need them.

LEO: Has Luther ever taken you to lunch?
(Greg enters.)

PAUL: No.

GREG: Sorry. Luther cornered me again. He wanted to know how the audit was going. Asked about the two of you.

PAUL: What did he say about me?

GREG: He kept calling you Peter.

PAUL: Shoot. . . . Did he say anything else about the merger?

LEO: Yes. When the merger's completed, Peter is the first to be fired.

GREG: Leo, I'm taking a long lunch on Wednesday.

LEO: I don't know. We have a lot of work to finish.

GREG: Luther approved it.

LEO: *(Looking at Paul.)* Did he?

(Paul stands up and crosses to Greg.)

PAUL: *(Shaking Greg's hand.)* Congratulations on acing the exam.

GREG: Thanks.

PAUL: You should have called me.

GREG: It's no big deal.

PAUL: When we go to Clancy's tonight, I'll buy you a couple of beers.

GREG: We'll see.

PAUL: I think it's fantastic.

GREG: *(To Paul.)* Margaret just walked in. Go see how pale she looks.

PAUL: I can't believe she made it in this morning.

GREG: She's making everyone who was there last night swear to secrecy.

PAUL: *(To Leo.)* We were all doing shots. *(To Greg.)* I stopped after what? Three? With Margaret, we quit counting. She was hanging all over one of the guys in the band.

(Margaret enters.)

MARGARET: Good morning, sweethearts.

PAUL: Morning, Margaret.

GREG: *(Overlapping.)* Good morning.

MARGARET: *(Deadpan.)* Hey, Leo.

LEO: Did you have fun last night?

MARGARET: You should have been there.

LEO: Why don't you jump on top of the table and show me what I missed.

(Paul lowers his head.)

MARGARET: Leo, why don't you go fuck a tree. *(Margaret crosses to Paul.)* Big mouth.

PAUL: I'm so sorry . . . I casually mentioned something about last night . . .

MARGARET: *(Fixing Paul's collar.)* Darling, hold still.

PAUL: Sorry. . . . Thank you.

(Leo slams the door shut.)

MARGARET: *(To Paul, rubbing her temples.)* Aspirin, honey. Aspirin.

PAUL: *(Spastically.)* I have a whole bottle. Hold on a second.

(Paul reaches into his audit bag for the bottle of aspirin.)

MARGARET: *(To Paul, referring to his biscuit.)* Mmmm. Something smells good. Let me have a little tiny bite.

PAUL: *(Eagerly.)* Please! Eat! Eat!

(Margaret takes a bite.)

LEO: Would you like a Bloody Mary to go with your biscuit?

(Margaret makes a gesture at Leo.)

PAUL: *(Out of breath, handing the bottle to Margaret.)* There you go.

MARGARET: You're so sweet.

PAUL: I live to serve.

(Margaret takes some aspirin.)

MARGARET: Greg, when are we working together?

GREG: You tell me.

MARGARET: I have an audit coming up next month in Myrtle Beach.

PAUL: I want to go.

MARGARET: Three weeks on the beach.

PAUL: Request me.

MARGARET: I'll talk with Mike and Rob this morning. They're working on the new schedule.

PAUL: We would have so much fun.

GREG: Give me a call.

LEO: Margaret in a hotel room with two boys. That wouldn't be the first time.

MARGARET: *(To Leo.)* Sounds like you're not getting any. Diane cut you off again?

(Leo lets out a slight laugh.)

MARGARET: *(Continues.)* She wouldn't let you come to my party the other night. We had fun without you anyway. *(To Greg.)* I'm glad you were there. *(To Leo.)* What does Diane want this time?

(Leo ignores her.)

MARGARET: *(Continues.)* He's a moody bastard when she cuts him off.

PAUL: Margaret, have you heard anything new about the merger?

MARGARET: Oh God, yes. We're moving into Pierce and Hawthorne's building.

(Leo throws down the audit folder he's reviewing.)

PAUL: They're down on Coulhoun Street.

GREG: When are we moving?

MARGARET: End of next month.

PAUL: We have the prime location.

MARGARET: They have more office space.

LEO: I knew this would happen. They'll have the home-court advantage.

PAUL: Parking is horrible on Coulhoun Street.

LEO: PARKING? You moron, don't you see what's going on. When they start laying off, our office will have the most casualties.

PAUL: You think?

MARGARET: *(To Paul.)* They're not going to fire you. *(Hugging Paul.)* Honey, everyone loves you. You're such a sweetie. *(Indicating a headache.)* Shit, I've got work to do. *(Crossing to the door.)* I'll let y'all know about Myrtle Beach.

GREG: Great.

PAUL: Sounds exciting.

MARGARET: *(Breathlessly.)* Oh God, yes. Call me for lunch.

GREG: I will.

PAUL: *(Overlapping.)* I will.

MARGARET: *(Flirtatiously.)* Bye, Leo. I hope Diane lets you come out and play some time.

    (Margaret exits.)

GREG: Margaret's wild.

PAUL: She's a hoot. Did you see her taking shots of that stuff that looked like cement?

GREG: Yeah.

PAUL: It looked nasty. I wouldn't touch it. . . . She'll drink anything.

LEO: Shoe polish?

PAUL: *(Jokingly.)* If you put in a shot glass.

LEO: Paul, what are saying?

PAUL: What do you mean?

LEO: . . . You think Margaret has a problem?

PAUL: No.

LEO: You just said she'd drink shoe polish.

PAUL: It was a joke.

LEO: Weird sense of humor calling someone an alcoholic.

PAUL: I didn't say that.

LEO: You implied it.

PAUL: *(Frustrated.)* NO! I wasn't implying Margaret's an alcoholic.

LEO: Margaret's not a drunk!

PAUL: I never said she was.

GREG: I agree with Leo, Margaret's not an alcoholic.

LEO: What a thing to say!

PAUL: I didn't—

LEO: Just shut up.

    (Silence.)

PAUL: *(Looking through an audit folder.)* Greg, do you have a second?

GREG: Yeah.

PAUL: Did you go back and investigate any of these differences?

GREG: No.

PAUL: But I thought we talked about this.

GREG: The audit program says to investigate differences greater than ten thousand dollars. If it's less than ten thousand, it's I.N.F.I., Immaterial —

PAUL: Immaterial, no further investigation. I know that. But you have to look at your overall results. There are numerous differences in the eight- and nine-thousand dollar range. That's why I told you to perform additional procedures.

GREG: *(Handing Paul the audit program.)* Read the audit program.

PAUL: I know what the audit program says.

GREG: Well, if you followed the audit program, you wouldn't be going over the time budgets in your areas.

PAUL: But you also have to use your common sense. First of all, Leo wrote the audit program. *(To Leo.)* No offense, Leo.

LEO: What are you girls bitching about?

PAUL: Leo, I have a question. *(Showing Leo the audit program.)* How did you calculate this number?

LEO: I didn't. It's the same figure they used in the prior year.

PAUL: So, who calculated it?

LEO: What's your problem?

PAUL: Look at these work papers. See how many differences there are in the eight- and nine-thousand dollar range.

LEO: So what?

PAUL: Luther is not going to sign off on these work papers. One of us will have to go back on site and perform additional procedures.

LEO: If Luther wants these financials issued in a week and a half, he'll sign off on the goddamn work papers.

PAUL: How can he?

LEO: Luther brought this client in twelve years ago. He and Mr. Gilreath go to church together. They're golfing buddies. . . . This is Luther's audit! And you're not going to fuck it up for all of us.

PAUL: It's still not right.

LEO: You know what your problem is?

PAUL: What?

LEO: You can't see the forest for the trees.

PAUL: Why do we even attempt to audit? We should just write I.N.F.I. on all the work papers. Maybe Katherine can order us an I.N.F.I. stamp. *(Flipping through one of the folders and pretending to stamp the pages.)* Immaterial, no further investigation. *(As he's flipping pages.)* Immaterial. Immaterial. Immaterial. Immaterial. Immaterial. Immat—

LEO: You better remember, I'm giving you a performance evaluation on this audit. I'll remember this when I do.

PAUL: And another thing, I don't like the fact that we've been given an unrealistic deadline.

LEO: Hey . . . I don't give a fuck.

PAUL: Who runs the audit? Us? Or the client?

LEO: *(Holding up an audit folder.)* I still can't figure out what the hell you were doing while you were at Mason Industries. Jerking off?

PAUL: Maybe you should have come on site more than once. *(Pause.)* I'm documenting our conversation.

LEO: *(Lets out a slight laugh.)* Go ahead. I don't give a fuck.

PAUL: According to the audit manual. Both you and Luther will have to sign off on it. *(Pause.)* Leo, I'm serious.

LEO: You're just screwing yourself.

PAUL: I'm following the audit manual. *(Reading from the audit manual.)* "When there are disagreements among the audit team . . . these differences should be documented and signed off by the —"

LEO: No one does that shit! We're in the middle of a goddamn merger. Do you really want to be labeled a troublemaker?

PAUL: You're putting us at risk. *(To Greg.)* I'm not angry with you. I realize you're still learning. I won't mention you in the work paper. *(With increasing intensity.)* But the next time I give you an audit note, you better do it. If you don't understand why, ask me.

(Paul begins typing on his laptop. Leo stands behind him reading over his shoulder.)

LEO: I'll remember this . . . Greg, on Monday you're going back to Mason Industries.

GREG: I was following your audit program.

LEO: *(Throwing the folder to Greg.)* Talk to your buddy! Investigate any differences over $5,000.

GREG: *(To Paul.)* Thanks, Bud!

LEO: *(To Paul.)* Does that get you off? On Monday morning, call the controller and let him know that pretty boy is coming back to blow him one more time.

Scene Three

At rise: Projected on the white board — "Same day, 10:30 PM" Leo and Greg are sitting together chatting. Paul, separating himself from the others, sits at the opposite end of the room and works on a audit folder.

GREG: *(Laughing.)* No way.

LEO: *(Enjoying his own company.)* So my frat brother, Bill, is daring me to fuck her. Hell, it would be a boost for her ego. For me, it's better than beating off. I take her back to the house. We get there. She tells me she's having her period.

(Paul cringes with disgust.)

LEO: *(Continues.)* Fuck! . . . So I fuck her on Bill's bed.

(Phone rings. Leo crosses to phone.)

LEO: *(Continues. On phone.)* Hello. . . . What? . . . Diane, I told you we're working late.

PAUL: *(Overlapping.)* HI, DIANE!

LEO: We have a deadline coming up. *(Pause.)* I don't have time to talk . . . I'm too busy . . . NO. We're not going tomorrow . . . I'm working . . . Diane if you want to go, then go . . . I'll be home in about an hour . . . You know, it's up to you. *(Hanging up the phone.)* Fuck her! *(Pause.)* Diane never thinks about me. It's always what she wants. *(Pause.)* If she goes, I'll never forgive her.

(Paul begins packing up his things.)

LEO: *(Continues.)* When this audit is over, I'm going out and getting me some strange. *(Challenging Paul.)* You coming with me? Get you some strange . . . When's the last time you got laid?

PAUL: I'm going home.

LEO: We still have another hour.

PAUL: We've been here since nine this morning. *(Defiantly.)* Leo, I've finished what I'm working on. I'm tired and I'm going home.

LEO: See if Greg needs any help.

PAUL: Greg, you need any help?

GREG: No.

PAUL: *(To Greg.)* You want to come over and watch a movie?

GREG: No.

PAUL: We could do your laundry at my place.

LEO: Greg wants to finish his work.

PAUL: I bought some Guinness. Your favorite.

LEO: I'm hungry. I could go for a pizza. Greg, I know you could go for some pizza. *(Pause.)* Pizza, pizza?
(Pause.)

GREG: Yeah.

LEO: Paul, go pick up a pizza. *(To Greg.)* Call in an extra large pepperoni.
(Greg picks up the phone and dials.)

PAUL: Where could I charge the time?

LEO: Charge it to miscellaneous.

PAUL: I already have thirty-two hours in miscellaneous.

LEO: Look on the time sheet, there's a category called administration. Put it there.

PAUL: In ADMINISTRATION? . . . No. No. It isn't right. I'll eat the time before I charge it there.

GREG: *(On phone.)* Pick up . . . One extra large pepperoni —

PAUL: And mushrooms . . . Shoot!

GREG: *(On phone.)* And mushrooms . . . Paul. Thanks.

PAUL: *(To Leo.)* Give me the money first.

LEO: Here's a twenty. I want my change.

GREG: About fifteen minutes.
(Paul sits in the corner and pouts. Silence. Margaret enters.)

MARGARET: Come on boys, we're heading to Clancy's.

PAUL: Leo says no.

MARGARET: Leo! Go home and face Diane.

LEO: Fly away. We're working.
(Margaret picks up a folder and glances through it.)

MARGARET: How far along are you?

LEO: Don't touch anything!

MARGARET: OK. I love hard-working men. *(To Paul.)* See you at Clancy's. No wimping out on us. *(To Greg.)* You're still coming?

GREG: I have to get up early for church.

MARGARET: Come on. Stay for thirty minutes. *(Grabbing Greg's hands.)* You're my shagging partner.
(Margaret and Greg begin to dance.)

MARGARET: *(Continues.)* Greg, don't be like Leo. He doesn't like us anymore.

GREG: I'll come down for one drink.

MARGARET: Dip me darlin'!

PAUL: My turn! My turn! My turn!

LEO: Paul, go get the pizza!

PAUL: I'm going! I'm going! I'm going!

LEO: Pauley!

PAUL: WHAT?

LEO: Grab a twelve pack too.

> (*Paul, as he's exiting, pulls out his pocket notebook to write down the beer.*)

GREG: Are we on for Myrtle Beach?

MARGARET: Not yet, goddamnit. I'm still working on it.

> (*Leo let's out a slight laugh.*)

MARGARET: (*Continues. To Greg.*) You and Rob are scheduled for the medical university. Mike has Paul running the Carolina Federal Bank audit . . . Paul is becoming our bank audit specialist.

LEO: Big deal! Banks are basically tick-mark audits.

MARGARET: There's a little more to it than that.

GREG: Sounds boring.

LEO: They're so goddamn regulated. Easy audits.

MARGARET: With the merger going through, Paul has found his niche.

LEO: Whoo wee.

MARGARET: Leo, have you ever been on a bank audit?

LEO: They only assign bank audits to pinheads.

MARGARET: You are so full of shit.

LEO: Darling, that's why my eyes are brown.

GREG: Huh . . . Poor Paul.

MARGARET: What?

GREG: (*Hesitantly.*) Paul was telling me, he really hates auditing banks. Had a real bad experience on the last one. Now he can't stand them.

> (*Leo suddenly stops what he's doing and looks at Greg.*)

MARGARET: Oh, my God.

GREG: He was worried Mike would put him on that audit. . . . Paul already thinks Luther hates him.

MARGARET: Should I say something to Mike?

GREG: Hey, don't get me involved. I'm serious.

MARGARET: I'll talk with Mike. (*Exiting the room.*) Oh well. . . . See you at Clancy's.

> (*Greg continues to work on his folder. Leo stares at him.*)

Scene Four

Setting: Projected on the white board "Mason Industries Audit; Friday 2:45 PM; August 18, 2000; Deadline: 7 Days." The room is empty. An excited Paul enters and dances around the room. A few moments later Leo and Greg enter.

LEO: That was a total waste of time.

PAUL: No, it wasn't.

LEO: Were you wearing that tie as a joke?

PAUL: Hah!

GREG: Bud, if you want to be a partner, dress like a partner.

PAUL: *(To Greg; sincerely.)* How do you think I dress?

LEO: Like a manager at the Piggly Wiggly.

GREG: *(To Paul.)* Work on the image, Bud. God helps those who help themselves.

PAUL: *(Defensively.)* You can't tell me this time Luther wasn't impressed with my presentation.
(Silence.)

PAUL: *(Continues.)* It didn't hurt that I went after Susan. I bet you she didn't read the FASB, until this morning. Totally unprepared. *(Imitating Susan.)* Um. Um. Um. FASB, um. Says um. Um. Um. *(Normal voice.)* I counted. She said "um" fifty-seven times. I didn't say "um" once. *(To Greg.)* So what did you think?

GREG: Luther didn't seem interested.

PAUL: I saw him taking notes.

GREG: He was writing out his schedule for next week.

PAUL: This time I answered every one of his questions.

GREG: You did better last time.

PAUL: I did not! Did you hear Luther try to stump me with, "What should the CPA do to make sure his work remains privileged?" All fraud investigations should be performed at the direction of the client's attorney. Clearly mark the work papers as "attorney work product." Thank you very much.
(Paul picks up a piece of paper and crosses to the door.)

PAUL: *(Continues.)* I hope they fixed the copier. I was incredible! *(Exiting.)*
(Outside the door, Paul sees Margaret. She is carrying birthday balloons. Paul drags her into the room.)

PAUL: *(Continues. To Margaret.)* Did you like my presentation?

MARGARET: You were divine. . . . What a lovely tie.

PAUL: Thanks.

(Paul exits. Margaret turns to leave.)

LEO: *(Calling out.)* Margaret! . . . Margaret.

MARGARET: What?

LEO: Dinner tonight?

MARGARET: *(Taken off guard, awkwardly.)* YES. I'm starving already. Great. . . .
Mike is getting the gang together for dinner at Hyman's Seafood.

LEO: No.

(Pause.)

MARGARET: Where did you want to eat?

LEO: Forget it.

MARGARET: Leo, why are you so . . . YOU? *(To Greg.)* Hey, sweetie.

(Greg looks up and smiles. They exchange hand waves. Margaret exits.)

LEO: *(Reviewing a folder.)* Sweetie, take this folder down to Robin in the tax
department. Tell her I will need the tax return by Tuesday.

GREG: So, what are your plans?

LEO: What?

GREG: Paul was saying that since you didn't pass the law section, you would
probably be leaving soon.

(Margaret enters the doorway.)

MARGARET: Leo, I'm not having dinner with you tonight.

LEO: *(To Margaret.)* I said forget about it! *(To Greg, handing him the folder.)*
Take this to Robin.

(Margaret turns to walk away. Paul appears holding a piece of birthday cake.)

PAUL: *(To Margaret; eagerly.)* What are you working on?

MARGARET: *(Walking away.)* I have a three o'clock meeting with Luther.

PAUL: I just spoke with Luther in the kitchen . . . Tell me if he says anything
about me.

GREG: Was the copier working?

PAUL: It's being serviced again. *(Trying to lighten the atmosphere.)* I wish I could
get serviced as many times a month as the copier does.

(Greg leaves the room. Leo takes Paul's piece of cake.)

PAUL: *(Continues.)* I asked Luther if he would like to have lunch sometime.
He said, "No."

LEO: No?

PAUL: No.

LEO: Just no?

PAUL: Yes.

LEO: *(Laughing.)* The last person Luther hated isn't even in accounting anymore. He's selling life insurance.

PAUL: Shoot!

LEO: If I were you, I would get out. You don't have a future with this firm. *(Handing Paul a business card.)* Here's the number of a headhunter who's a friend of mind. Send him a copy of your résumé. *(Pause.)* You should do it today.

PAUL: But I like it here!

LEO: During my orientation, one of the managers told us to imagine our hand in a bucket of water. Now pull your hand out. Look in the bucket. Is there a big hole where your hand was? NO! Think how quickly the water fills in. That's how important you are to this firm. They don't give a fuck about you. *(Pause.)* Paul, I know for a fact Luther has a list of first- and second-year staff accountants he has to lay off.

PAUL: But I've been given the responsibilities of a senior. I'm moving up. . . . I'm a senior, except for the title.

LEO: Hey, Pierce and Hawthorne dictates what goes on now. They call him up and say, "Luther reduce your staff by blank number." The number is out of his hands.

PAUL: I've already passed the CPA exam. He'll take —

LEO: And you know Luther is going to start with the people he hates.

PAUL: Have you seen this list? *(Pause.)* Leo?

LEO: WHAT?

PAUL: Am I on this list?

LEO: It wouldn't be my place to tell you.

PAUL: But you know?

LEO: I have no idea who's on the list.

PAUL: I don't believe you.

LEO: Hey, leave me out of this.

PAUL: I'll ask Margaret.

> *(Pause.)*

LEO: *(Fatherlike tone.)* Pauley, my friend, let's be honest. You're not partner material. . . . It's not just the suits. You don't have that killer instinct.

PAUL: Yes I do.

LEO: No you don't. You're too goddamn nice to be an auditor.

PAUL: I can be tough.

LEO: Rambo, your clients send you thank-you notes and birthday cards.

PAUL: I maintain a professional rapport with my clients.

LEO: OK. But you're a . . . pinhead. You can't change that . . . One client caught
    you on a security tape dancing alone in the elevator.

PAUL: I was doing morning stretches.

LEO: Luther showed us the tape. You were dancing.

    (Greg enters.)

GREG: Robin's not very friendly.

LEO: She's a bitch.

GREG: I asked her when her baby was due and she —

LEO: WHAT?

PAUL: Oh no! *(Overlapping.)*

    (Leo lets out a hearty laugh.)

LEO: Robin had a little boy about five months ago.

GREG: I thought she was pregnant.

LEO: What did she say? God, I wish I had been there . . . You won't be work-
    ing in the tax department.

PAUL: *(Overlapping.)* I'm so sorry.

GREG: Shut up. SHUT UP! Just shut up!

LEO: When's it due? Goddamn that cracks me up.

    (Paul searches on top of and under the table for his missing pencil.)

PAUL: Who stole my mechanical pencil? *(Still searching.)* I had it this morn-
    ing. It's a blue Berol. Leo, did you take my pencil?

LEO: I don't need your goddamn pencil . . . Greg, did Robin say she'll have
    the tax return ready by Tuesday?

PAUL: *(Becoming more frustrated.)* I bought it! It's my pencil!

GREG: *(Holding up a mechanical pencil.)* Is this it?

PAUL: Yes.

GREG: Don't leave your shit in my space.

PAUL: I'm sorry.

    (Greg throws the pencil like dart at Paul. Paul has to avoid being hit.)

PAUL: *(Continues.)* Thanks!

GREG: *(To Leo.)* Robin will have it to you on Thursday.

LEO: That's unacceptable! Go tell her I want the goddamn tax return on my
    desk, Tuesday morning!

    *(Greg does not reply. Leo crumples up a piece of paper and hits Greg in the
    head with it.)*

GREG: NO!

    (Leo jumps out of his chair and crosses to Greg. Greg immediately stands up.)

LEO: *(In his face.)* You're a pussy!

GREG: We have an assault. Would you like to try for a battery?

LEO: Fuck you.

(Leo walks out of the room.)

PAUL: *(Reviewing a folder.)* Greg, the change in their stock price is not immaterial.

(Paul cautiously slides the folder to Greg.)

GREG: Leo signed off on it.

(Greg slides the folder back to Paul.)

PAUL: I know, but . . . Consider the percentage change in their stock price.
(Paul slides the folder back to Greg. Pause.) Greg.

GREG: You're not my boss.

(Greg slides the folder back to Paul.)

PAUL: Stock manipulation is a possibility here . . . I'm trying to teach you.

GREG: *(Threatening.)* I've already surpassed you.

(Leo enters.)

LEO: WHOO WEE! I LIT A FIRE UNDER HER BIG ASS! Robin will have the tax return to me on Monday morning. That's how a man handles things. *(Laughing.)* "Greg told us you're having twins."

PAUL: *(To Leo.)* The change in their stock price is not immaterial. We should investigate. Look at the equity folder.

LEO: *(Firmly.)* Did I sign off on the work papers?

(Pause.)

PAUL: Yes.

LEO: *(Grabbing the folder.)* I forbid. I fucking dare you to touch any audit folders I don't personally hand you.
(Paul jumps up. Leo places him back in the chair. Paul stands up again. Leo, pushing down on Paul's head, once again places Paul back in the chair. Paul quickly stands up again and moves away. Paul eyes the audit trunk.)

LEO: *(Continues.)* Don't you touch that audit trunk . . . Paul.
(Paul slowly crosses to the audit trunk.)

LEO: *(Continues.)* Don't you touch that audit trunk. *(Pause.)* Paul. Paul. Don't you touch that audit trunk. Paul!
(Paul slams down the top of the trunk. He opens it and slams it again. Paul starts taking audit folders out of the trunk. Leo crosses to Paul. Leo grabs Paul, causing the folders in Paul's hands to go flying across the room. Leo then pins Paul on the top of the trunk.)

PAUL: Get off me. . . . Get off me!

LEO: Poor baby. Go whine to Luther. Be a snitch. That will really help your moron image. *(Releasing Paul.)* I'm working with twiddle dee and twiddle dumb ass.

GREG: *(To Leo.)* Man, you are fucked!

LEO: *(Quickly.)* Greg, who was that girl you were with the other night at Garibaldi's? . . . Girlfriend? She looked like the little girl in accounting at Mason Industries.

PAUL: Pam? *(To Greg.)* You went on a date with Pam?

GREG: We had dinner.

PAUL: ALONE? You can't date the client . . . Oh my goodness, are you SLEEP-ING WITH HER?

GREG: It's not an issue.

PAUL: It violates the rules of "independence." This whole audit is in jeopardy. . . . Technically, we should withdraw from the engagement.

LEO: *(Smiling.)* Luther put together quite a team here. It looks like we're all fucked . . . MAN.

(The phone rings. Leo picks up.)

LEO: *(Continues. On phone.)* Garden club. . . . Hold on, Mikey.

PAUL: *(Overlapping.)* An accountant must also be independent in appearance.

LEO: *(To Paul.)* Princess.

GREG: We went out one time. I'm not seeing her again.

(Leo starts to hand the receiver to Paul and then he pulls it away. He does this several times.)

PAUL: *(To Greg.)* You didn't sleep with her?

GREG: NO!

PAUL: *(To Leo; as he's grabbing for the phone.)* Hand me the damn phone! *(On phone.)* Paul speaking . . . Mike, I love auditing banks. Who said I didn't like auditing banks. She said that? *(To Greg; covering the receiver.)* What did you tell Margaret?

GREG: *(Overlapping.)* I was joking. I was joking.

PAUL: *(On phone.)* . . . No. Please schedule me for that audit. I love banks. I don't know why Greg said that to Margaret. Mike, you know I love audit-ing banks. . . . Thanks for calling. Put me on as many bank audits as you can. Thanks again . . . Bye. *(Hangs up phone; to Greg.)* Why did you say —

GREG: I was joking.

PAUL: I don't understand —

GREG: I WAS JOKING!

LEO: He was obviously joking.

(Paul takes two deep breaths.)

PAUL: Banks are easy.

(Paul screams and then lays his head down on the table.)

LEO: What the fuck! . . . Paul, what the hell are you working on?

(Paul slides all the folders in his area to Leo. Some of them fall off the table.)

PAUL: I need to lie down.

LEO: Get the hell out of here. You're fucking useless!

PAUL: I'll take my name off this audit. I'll take my name off.

LEO: Go home. You look like shit.

PAUL: *(Referring to the audit.)* Yes I will! YES I WILL! I'll take my name off this audit. *(Violently packing his audit bag.)* Banks are easy to audit because they're so regulated. They have to keep everything in perfect order. WHO WOULDN'T WANT TO RUN A BANK AUDIT?

(Paul crosses to the door. Margaret enters.)

MARGARET: *(To Paul; extremely hostile.)* We need to talk!

PAUL: WHAT'S THE MATTER?

MARGARET: WHY ARE YOU TELLING EVERYONE I'M AN ALCOHOLIC?

PAUL: WHAT?

MARGARET: Luther's concerned about me, you little fucker!

PAUL: Who said that I said that?

MARGARET: Do I drink anymore than Mike or Leo? Hell, no!

PAUL: *(Overlapping.)* Margaret . . . I . . . I . . . Let me explain. What ever you heard was taken out of context. I've never said anything against you. They can tell you I haven't.

LEO: *(Enjoying the moment.)* What are you talking about?

MARGARET: *(To Paul.)* You're just like the rest of them. Another little prick.

PAUL: No . . . I'm not. Really, Margaret . . . I'm a feminist at heart. Why don't we go somewhere nice? Just the two of us and talk. We'll work this out. We've always had a special relationship.

MARGARET: "Special"? What do you mean special? . . . You don't? . . . No. You don't think I would ever date you? . . . Oh, my God. *(Laughs.)* You are a dumb fuck.

PAUL: Can we talk?

MARGARET: Go to HELL!

(Margaret storms out. Paul screams.)

PAUL: Margaret, please listen . . .

GREG: *(To Paul; realizing an opportunity.)* Bud, you shouldn't start rumors. *(Hurries out of the room.)* MARGARET! . . . Margaret wait.

LEO: Do you sit down to pee?

PAUL: It's a misunderstanding.

LEO: I'd tell you to turn in your balls, but that would be assuming you had some.

(Paul lowers himself into a chair.)

LEO: *(Continues.)* Madonna, what are you doing over there? *(Picks up the stock folder.)* The equity folder has been completed. *(Throwing it at Paul.)* Now file it back and clean up the mess you've made around here.

(Leo lets out a hearty laugh. Leo exits. Paul picks up the equity folder and looks through the work papers. After a moment, he places the folder in his audit bag.)

PAUL: *(Grinning.)* I'll show them all.

END OF ACT I

ACT II
Scene One

At rise: Greg enters. Projected on the conference room's white board: "Mason Industries Audit; Monday 7:45 AM; August 14, 2000; Deadline: 4 days." Margaret is alone in the room.

MARGARET: Where's the little shit? Paul begged me to meet him here this morning.

GREG: He's late.

MARGARET: This is unacceptable.

GREG: Now that you're a manager, do something about it.

MARGARET: Who told you I made manager?

GREG: I ran into Mike in the hall. Congratulations.

MARGARET: I had to threaten to quit.

GREG: Really?

MARGARET: Friday afternoon I gave my two-weeks notice.

GREG: You were pretty upset.

MARGARET: Damn right I was. Luther called me Saturday morning and offered me the promotion.

GREG: I'm proud of you.

(Greg starts massaging Margaret's shoulders. She abruptly pulls away.)

GREG: *(Continues.)* You're tense.

MARGARET: Greg, you can't be doing that.

GREG: Whoa, OK. Sorry . . . When are we working together?

MARGARET: Soon.

GREG: Let's go out tonight and celebrate.

MARGARET: I'm having dinner with Mike and his wife. *(Pause.)* Why don't you join us?

GREG: You and Mike are managers . . . Are you sure you want to be seen with a lowly staff accountant?

MARGARET: Don't be silly.

GREG: It's just that I don't want to overstep my boundaries.

(Margaret focuses again on Paul. Greg crosses to the table and starts looking through a folder.)

GREG: *(Continues.)* This is not what I expected.

MARGARET: What?

GREG: Nothing, I'm just frustrated.

MARGARET: *(Looking at her watch.)* I'll give Paul five more minutes.

GREG: *(Looking through the folder.)* Fuck . . . Everything is sink or swim. *(Holding up notes.)* Constant criticism. This is bullshit.

MARGARET: They're just jealous.

GREG: Margaret, please put me on your next audit. I could learn so much from you.

MARGARET: I'll see what I can do.

GREG: Leo's no help to me. I hate coming into work.

MARGARET: Things will work out.

GREG: Maybe God doesn't want me here.

PAUL: *(Offstage.)* Did you have a nice weekend? . . . Good to hear it.

GREG: I'm ready to quit.

MARGARET: No, you're not quitting.

GREG: Then let me work with you!

> *(Paul reaches the door of the conference room.)*

PAUL: *(Offstage; opening the door.)* How about them Braves yesterday.

VOICE: *(Offstage.)* They lost.

PAUL: They'll kick butt next time. *(Paul enters with his reinvented look. His glasses are gone. His hair is slicked back and he's wearing a new suit with a red power tie and red socks. His fashionable appearance is not quite appropriate for an accountant.)* Margaret . . . Greg.

> *(Silence. Both Margaret and Greg have to turn away to keep from laughing.)*

PAUL: *(Continues.)* Margaret, I'm glad you came. I was hoping we could talk for a few minutes . . . alone? . . . Please, Greg.

MARGARET: *(To Greg.)* Go on. . . .We're on for tonight?

GREG: Yeah, I guess.

> *(Margaret crosses to Greg.)*

MARGARET: *(To Greg.)* Go to my office. We'll talk.

> *(Greg picks up his coffee cup and exits the room.)*

PAUL: First of all, congratulations! Manager. Wow!

MARGARET: No thanks to you.

PAUL: Luther wasn't going to lose a great auditor like yourself.

MARGARET: Whatever.

PAUL: Can we get past this misunderstanding between us?

MARGARET: Paul, you don't know when to keep your big mouth shut.

PAUL: Did you listen to all the messages I left on your voice mail?

MARGARET: Yes. All fourteen.

PAUL: I come bearing gifts.

> *(Paul pulls out one red rose. Margaret doesn't take the flower. Paul lays it on her lap.)*

PAUL: *(Continues. Reaching into a bag.)* This is to celebrate your promotion . . . It's your favorite. *(Pulling out a large bottle of Absolut Vodka.)* Absolut . . . Not the cheap stuff. *(Realizing.)* Forgive me for being such a poop head.

MARGARET: *(Angrily.)* No.

PAUL: I don't want this to affect our professional relationship.

MARGARET: It won't.

PAUL: Because I really need your expertise right now.

MARGARET: What is it.

(Paul pulls out a typed document.)

PAUL: This is strictly confidential. Leo would freak out if he knew I was sharing this with you. It can not leave this room. Greg doesn't even know about it.

MARGARET: Paul, what?

PAUL: Leo and I have uncovered fraud in the Mason Industry audit.

MARGARET: FRAUD?

PAUL: *(Quieting her down.)* Yes. Yes. Yes . . .

MARGARET: *(Overlapping.)* What kind of fraud?

PAUL: Stock manipulation by Mr. Gilreath and the company's treasurer.

MARGARET: *(Concerned.)* OH MY GOD, does Luther know?

PAUL: *(Nervously.)* Leo and I are meeting with him this morning.

MARGARET: Luther is going to shit!

PAUL: *(Hesitates; handing her the document.)* Here's the draft we're presenting.

(Margaret is reading the document.)

PAUL: *(Continues.)* Please tell me if there's anything I should add.

MARGARET: *(While reading.)* Fuck! So you can definitely tie Mr. Gilreath to this Panamanian company?

PAUL: Yes.

MARGARET: And this company is not listed as a related party?

PAUL: No. It's not mentioned anywhere in the financials.

MARGARET: This is interesting . . . Oh, you misspelled beneficiaries.

PAUL: I'm a horrible speller. Could you cross it out and correct it?

(Paul tries to hand her a pen.)

MARGARET: Let me see the equity folder.

PAUL: Could you make the correction . . . ?

(Margaret looks first on the desk and then in audit trunk.)

PAUL: *(Continues.)* Leo must have the folder . . . Could you make the . . .

(Paul is chasing Margaret around the room.)

MARGARET: You know Luther's daughter is dating Mr. Gilreath's son!

PAUL: Let's finish proofing my work paper. . . . Here's a pen.

MARGARET: I can't believe this.

PAUL: How do you spell beneficiaries?

(Margaret finally takes the pen and makes the correction.)

PAUL: *(Continues.)* Thank you.

MARGARET: Mr. Gilreath would have had to file a report with the SEC explaining his reasons for cashing in a large bundle of stock options. You need to get a copy of that report.

PAUL: Could you write that on the bottom of the page?

(Margaret begins writing.)

PAUL: *(Continues.)* Oh good. Thanks. *(Looking over her shoulder.)* I left the date off. Could you . . . Thanks again.

MARGARET: It's a good thing y'all caught this before releasing the financial statements. The SEC would be all over your asses!

PAUL: Margaret, with Mr. Gilreath being a close friend of Luther's, we really need to keep this quiet.

MARGARET: God, he's going to have a fucking aneurysm.

PAUL: You've been a big help. . . . I hope some day our friendship will be restored.

(Margaret picks up the rose and hands it back to Paul. On her way out the door, she grabs the bottle of vodka.)

PAUL: *(Continues. After she's gone, sarcastically.)* Try not to drink it all before lunch.

(Paul two-hole -punches the top of the document and attaches it into the middle of a folder. Leo enters. Paul is jumpy.)

LEO: I thought you jumped ship.

PAUL: No.

(Leo get his first clear view of the "new" Paul. Leo notices Paul's matching tie and socks.)

LEO: Goddamn. *(Pause.)* Little boy blue. On Friday did you go home and lie down?

PAUL: No. When I got there your wife called. I spent the afternoon with Diane.

LEO: Did Diane sit on your dick and do a 360? That woman is so limber.

PAUL: Surprisingly so.

(Paul picks up a different folder than the one he inserted the new document in.)

LEO: If she wants, Diane can make me come in fifteen seconds or thirty minutes. Total control. She has this trick —

PAUL: Sorry to hear about your separation.

LEO: Who have you been talking to?

PAUL: *(Quickly.)* Diane and I are friends. That's all. Nothing else. Just friends.

LEO: Girlfriends? . . . Stay out of my fucking business.

(Pause. Paul reaches into his audit bag and pulls out a bundle of mail.)

PAUL: *(Handing Leo the bundle.)* Leo. . . . Diane did ask me to give you this . . . It's your mail.

(Leo knocks the mail out of Paul's hand.)

LEO: You flaming little faggot.

(Pause.)

PAUL: I've received all my confirmations. *(Hands Leo the folder.)* You need to sign off on these pages. I've tabbed the first and last page.

(Leo begins initialing the bottom of each page.)

PAUL: *(Continues.)* Aren't you going to review the work papers?

LEO: No. I'm sure you've overaudited. *(Throwing the folder.)* Here.

PAUL: *(Reaching for the folder that he had placed the document in earlier.)* Wait. I also have the accounts-receivable folder.

LEO: Give it to me.

(Leo begins initialing pages. Paul grows increasingly nervous.)

LEO: *(Continues.)* All their major customers responded?

PAUL: Yes.

(Leo stops and examines a work paper.)

LEO: Paul.

(Pause.)

PAUL: What?

LEO: Come here.

PAUL: Why?

LEO: Come over here!

(Paul slowly crosses to Leo.)

LEO: *(Continues.)* This customer has a cash flow problem. They recently laid off a thousand employees.

PAUL: I know. I considered it when I was calculating the allowance for doubtful accounts. They owe a substantial amount for outstanding invoices over hundred and twenty days. Since they are a major customer, I'll also note it in my going-concern evaluation.

(Pause.)

LEO: *(Handing the folder to Paul.)* Here.

PAUL: *(Relieved.)* Thank you, Leo.

LEO: You're welcome, shithead . . . Where the hell is Greg?

PAUL: In Margaret's office.

(Leo picks up the phone and dials.)

LEO: *(On phone.)* Tell Greg to get his ass in here!

PAUL: You should be nice to Margaret now that she's manager.

LEO: Go get Luther's golden boy!

PAUL: You think he's the next superstar?

LEO: Yeah.

PAUL: Hah!

LEO: Jealous of your little buddy?

PAUL: No. Go look at Greg's work papers. Try to make any sense out of them. Ten years from now, you can pick up any of my work papers and you'll know exactly what I did and the results. . . . You sent him back to Mason Industries to investigate those differences. Hah! The explanations he came back with are nonsense! The controller was toying with him and Greg's clueless. *(Pause; looking at the door.)* And Greg doesn't pay attention to anything. Did you ever notice, he's either staring out the window or looking down at his "nice" shoes? Every hour, you're lucky to get ten minutes of work out of him. After ten minutes, he's useless. Unable to sustain. The next superstar. Hah!

LEO: Greg knows how to play the game.

PAUL: Leo. Leo. What about you? When will you become partner? Why aren't you the next David McClain?

LEO: Because I don't give a fuck.

PAUL: Do you have any job offers?

LEO: I receive calls every day.

PAUL: Then why are you still here?

LEO: I'll never work on another audit with you again.

PAUL: That's not an option.

(Greg enters.)

LEO: *(To Greg.)* Don't make me have to chase you down.

GREG: I was busy.

LEO: *(Handing Greg a stack of papers.)* Add this to what you're doing. Proof the footnotes and then I want you to foot the financials.

(Referring to Paul's earlier comment.) . . . Nice shoes.

GREG: Thanks.

PAUL: I have to leave by six.

LEO: I wouldn't make plans.

PAUL: You'll manage without me this one time.

LEO: I'll remember this.

(Leo exits the room.)

PAUL: *(To Greg.)* I have a dinner date.

GREG: It better not be with a client.

PAUL: *(Jokingly.)* Yeah, I'm having dinner with your little girlfriend Pam. *(Paul pulls out a devotional book and opens it to a devotion. In silence, he reads a brief prayer. Closing the book.)* Good. This morning I hadn't had time for my daily devotion.

GREG: What are you reading?

PAUL: *(Handing Greg the book.)* You need to get a copy, *365 Daily Devotions.*

GREG: *(Quickly flipping through the book.)* Not any of that liberal crap, is it?

PAUL: No. No. . . . It's on the Christian Coalition book list.

GREG: Good. Remember Bud, it's got to be the word.

PAUL: I am so blessed to have you in my life.

GREG: Thanks, Bud.

PAUL: You look sharp today. Is your suit tailored?

GREG: No.

PAUL: You're kidding. It's got to be.

GREG: No. Brooks Brothers.

PAUL: I thought it was tailored. It's a perfect fit. Perfect . . . You wear your clothes well. Even Kmart would look great on you! I wish you were my personal shopper.

GREG: I have some catalogs at home I'll bring you.

PAUL: Would you? . . . Why wasn't I born with good taste? You just exude class . . . I can't compete with that. *(Pause.)* Bubba, we're almost finished. Yes! . . . Leo asked me to make an archive back-up of all the computer disks. With most of the audit on computer now, we need to keep an archive copy off-site . . . Can I see your disks?

GREG: In a minute.

PAUL: Sure . . . Leo's in a mood again.

GREG: I noticed. *(Reaching into his audit bag and pulling out two disks.)* Here.

PAUL: Thanks . . . You're welcome to borrow my devotional any time.

GREG: I will.

PAUL: I love your tie. Classy.

Scene Two

At rise: Projected on the conference room's white board: "Mason Industries Audit; Thursday 11:00 PM; August 17, 2000; Deadline: 1 days." Leo is sitting alone drinking. Empty bottles and a food container are visible. Margaret enters.

MARGARET: I got your message. What's up?

LEO: *(Slightly drunk.)* That was quick.

MARGARET: I was just down the street. Greg and I had dinner at Magnolia's.

LEO: Greg, our little boy scout.

MARGARET: Leo, what do you want?

LEO: Heard you bought a new car today.

MARGARET: A white Avalon.

LEO: Take me for a ride.

MARGARET: You really want to go?

LEO: . . . No.

MARGARET: Good night, Leo.

LEO: How's the gang?

MARGARET: We're all wondering who pissed in your water bowl?

(Margaret turns to leave.)

LEO: Congratulations.

MARGARET: For what?

LEO: Your life in general.

MARGARET: Why didn't you study? . . . Leo, I understand how you're feeling right now. I took the fucking exam seven times!

LEO: As Diane put it on my way out the door, "It's not that you didn't pass the exam, you failed."

MARGARET: Be happy she's gone.

LEO: She left behind over nine thousand dollars in Mastercard and Visa debt. Let's not forget Exxon, Chevron, Texaco, Sears, JC Penney's, Belk's, Macy's, Discover . . .

MARGARET: Leo.

LEO: And the fucking American Express card. Aren't you loving every minute of this?

MARGARET: No.

LEO: Mike and Rob came by this morning to offer their support. "Big boy, you'll pass next time. Christ sakes, law is the easiest section."

MARGARET: Don't tell me you wouldn't be doing the same thing if it was one of them and not you.

LEO: Shit, I'd send them a daily reminder. Write it on their goddamn calendar. "August 16th, are you still a loser today?" *(Pause.)* I know my shit! Luther can tell you, I have managed more audits than either Mike or Rob . . . I wasn't originally scheduled for this audit. But when Luther needed someone to step in, I said, "Yes! How soon do you need the financials? Sure! No problem."

MARGARET: Talk with Luther.

LEO: No. . . . Luther hates real men. Any man who threatens his authority.

MARGARET: What are you going to do?

LEO: *(Sarcastically.)* Find another job. *(Holding up a newspaper.)* Look at all these layoffs. Lucent let go another five hundred people today. Do you think their employees had any idea when they walked in this morning? Hell no. That's why there's no loyalty anymore. *(Pause.)* Today I was turned down for the controller's position at a small plastics company . . . I wouldn't have taken it anyway. Not enough money.

(Margaret approaches Leo as if to touch him but backs away.)

MARGARET: What can I do to help?

LEO: *(Mimicking her angrily.)* Ahhhh. "What can I do to help?" *(Pause.)* Forget about it. I screwed myself. Hey, you're pissing with the big boys now. *(Takes a drink.)* I knew they wouldn't let a woman go.

MARGARET: You're beyond salvageable.

(Silence.)

LEO: You're right.

MARGARET: No, I'm not. *(Margaret crosses to Leo. This time she hugs him.)* Leo, I'm sorry.

(Margaret releases the embrace. Leo continues to make advances.)

MARGARET: *(Continues.)* No. Never again.

LEO: Come on, I'm free!

MARGARET: No, Leo.

LEO: Honey, this is your chance.

MARGARET: Honey, I'm not interested.

LEO: *(Pinning Margaret to the floor.)* Then why did you come back here tonight?

MARGARET: I was concerned.

LEO: Come on. We're two of a kind. I know you been trying to make me jealous with Greg. I can read your mind. You're not really interested in that chocolate ice cream.

(Margaret kicks Leo between the legs.)

MARGARET: You're a bastard . . . I will never be alone with you again. *(Margaret storms out of the room. Leo curls up on the floor.)*

Scene Three

At rise: Projected on the conference room's white board: "Mason Industries Audit; Friday 10:45 AM; August 18, 2000; Deadline: This afternoon." Paul and Greg are working.

PAUL: *(On phone.)* I want the details at lunch . . . You better. OK, bye. *(To Greg.)* Another auditor gave their notice.

GREG: Who?

PAUL: Susan "I didn't read the FASB um um."

GREG: Where's she going?

PAUL: Spectrum Plastics.

GREG: Good for us.

PAUL: Did I tell you I had dinner with Pam the other night?

GREG: Did you?

PAUL: After a few drinks, she's extremely talkative. *(Silence.)* Pam said you made her cry. *(Pause.)* Did it excite you? Afterwards did you go home and beat off? . . . Did you? . . . Greg?

GREG: Yes. I did.

PAUL: After you used her, what did you tell her? . . . "Paul says I can't see you again."

GREG: Yeah, something like that.

PAUL: I've been thinking a lot lately about professional skepticism. *(Greg stands up to leave the room.)* Greg, I'm talking to you. Please sit down.

GREG: Fuck off.

PAUL: Pam's threatening to go to Luther.

GREG: So what?

PAUL: . . . It's your career.

(Greg sits down.)

PAUL: *(Continues.)* Good, I got your attention. Let's talk about professional skepticism. You're Greg, the auditor and I'm Paul, the client. We become good buddies. Best buds. You're auditing my books and you find discrepancies. But you think to yourself, Paul's my good friend. Best bud. Your judgment is clouded. You've lost your professional skepticism. This whole time, Paul, the client, is thinking of new ways to screw you . . . I just thought of another example. Look at us. Our company operates under a pyramidal structure. At the bottom of the pyramid are the staff accountants, like you and me. As you move up you have the seniors, then the managers, and finally the partners. At each level there are fewer and fewer. But we all want to be on top. Yet there are very few tops and a lot of bottoms. My question is, should we be friends with one another? Let down our guard?

(Leo enters.)

PAUL: *(Continues. Looking directly at Greg.)* You told Pam you had found my weaknesses and you were trying to make my life miserable.

LEO: Paul, get to work.

PAUL: Leo, please let me finish. It's important to me. Thank you. There are those who believe that to succeed they must destroy other people. They better be careful they don't destroy themselves. *(Pause.)* Back to auditing!

LEO: *(To Paul.)* What are you working on?

PAUL: I'm going through all the final checklists.

LEO: Greg, are the financials proofed and footed?

GREG: Still working on it.

LEO: It's not a semester project. We're binding the financials this afternoon . . . Let me see what you've done.

GREG: Hold on.

(Leo tries to see what Greg is working on.)

LEO: What is that? *(Leo grabs Greg's folder.)* WHAT IS THIS?

GREG: Margaret asked me to do it.

LEO: You're in here working on Margaret's audit? *(Rips apart the folder.)* I want to see your goddamn timesheet. You're not charging this shit to my audit . . . I can't fucking believe this. Get out of my face! GET OUT! GO FIND MARGARET AND STICK YOUR HEAD UP HER ASS!

(Greg exits.)

LEO: *(Continues.)* You want to leave too?

PAUL: No.

(Pause.)

LEO: I'll buy you lunch today.

PAUL: I've made other plans.

Scene Four

At rise: Projected on the conference room's white board: "Mason Industries Audit; One Week Later." The table has been cleared. The audit trunk still sits in the corner. Leo and Greg enter.

LEO: *(Extremely distressed.)* Who locked the goddamn trunk? What's the combination?

GREG: Paul has it written in his daytimer.

LEO: Fuck! Go get Paul.

(Paul enters.)

PAUL: Good morning, Madonna!

LEO: Unlock the fucking trunk!

PAUL: Hold on. Let me find the combination. *(Paul starts going through his audit bag.) (To Leo.)* You're making me nervous. *(Working the combination lock.)* Nineteen . . . Twenty-seven . . .

LEO: Hurry up!

PAUL: I can't work like this!

(Leo backs away.)

PAUL: *(Continues.)* What's going on with the Mason Industries audit?

LEO: Unlock the fucking trunk!

PAUL: I'm trying. Please don't yell at me . . . Nineteen. Twenty-seven. *(Opening the trunk.)* There.

(Leo pushes Paul out the way.)

LEO: Where are the current year work papers? This is all the prior year. *(To Paul.)* Did you file away the current year?

PAUL: No, I haven't had a chance. Leo, what's going on?

LEO: Gilreath at Mason's was arrested yesterday afternoon. It's on the front page of this morning's *Wall Street Journal.*

PAUL: Why was he arrested?

LEO: Stock manipulation. A few weeks ago you said something about their stock price.

PAUL: I don't remember. Greg audited their equity accounts.

LEO: Shit!

PAUL: *(Looking at the* Wall Street Journal.*)* It says here that their stock price rose 600 percent.

GREG: *(Grabbing the paper.)* I would have caught that.

PAUL: Maybe you weren't paying attention. *(To Leo.)* You need to talk with Luther. He probably has the current year's folders in his office.

LEO: I'm sick of this fucking job. Goddamn if I'll take any of Luther's shit.

PAUL: I bet the SEC was waiting for us to issue those financial statements. We acted with due diligence. I doubt seriously they have any grounds for criminal charges against you or Greg.

LEO: I'm giving my two-weeks notice.

(Leo runs out of the room. Paul closes and locks the trunk.)

PAUL: This morning, the SEC will take custody of the audit work papers. Every procedure we performed will be scrutinized. You need to talk to Luther about your relationship with Pam.

(Margaret enters.)

PAUL: *(Continues.)* For legal reasons it's important that he knows what went on during the audit.

GREG: Don't worry, I'll talk with Luther.

PAUL: I'm glad it's you going in there and not me. But then again, you and Luther are tight . . . Of course you probably cost him his job. In a few months, they'll have a nice early retirement party for him. But I wouldn't worry . . . Are you feeling OK?

(Greg crosses towards the door.)

PAUL: *(Continues.)* What is it the Christian Coalition guy said? They don't know they've been beaten until they're in the body bag.

(Greg races to the door.)

MARGARET: Greg.

GREG: Move out of my way.

(Greg exits.)

MARGARET: I thought you weren't going to release the financial statements.

PAUL: It wasn't my decision.

MARGARET: Luther made the decision knowing about this problem?

PAUL: You read my write-up. *(Pulling out a copy of the document.)* Here's a copy. Notice, Leo and Luther signed off on it.

MARGARET: Y'all never talked to Luther. Did you?

PAUL: I did everything I was supposed to do.

MARGARET: Oh, my God. Did Leo even read this?

PAUL: He signed off on it.

MARGARET: If he read it, he wouldn't have released the financial statements.

PAUL: Leo had a lot on his mind.

MARGARET: Because of this, Luther, Leo, and Greg will lose their jobs!

(Silence.)

MARGARET: *(Continues.)* You did it on purpose. You little maggot. If Leo wouldn't listen, why didn't you go straight to Luther?

PAUL: Why didn't we go to Luther? Your handwriting is all over it. As I recall, you told me to let Leo handle it . . . I'm betting you don't want to blow your chance to be partner someday. Are we singing off the same sheet of music? We've always had a *special* relationship.

MARGARET: Why did you do it?

PAUL: Because I can separate business from friendship. Because I'm a winner . . . I gave them the opportunity to do the right thing. I followed the audit manual and you're my witness . . . You know what's funny? Luther actually likes me. This morning we had a wonderful meeting . . . He likes me. He invited me to play golf on Saturday. Can you see me on the golf course with Luther?

MARGARET: I'm talking with Leo.

PAUL: You're smarter than that.

(Leo enters.)

LEO: Luther took my resignation, but didn't accept my two-weeks notice. Asked for my keys and told me to leave within the next fifteen minutes.

MARGARET: Leo?

PAUL: You should have let him fire you. Now you don't even get severance pay.

LEO: Open the trunk.

PAUL: Leo, you can't even apply for unemployment. You quit without cause.

LEO: I'll destroy those fucking files.

PAUL: That's just the prior year.

LEO: I don't give a fuck!

PAUL: I'm not helping you commit a crime.

(Greg enters.)

PAUL: *(Continues. To Leo.)* Do you need anything?

MARGARET: *(To Paul.)* Haven't you done enough? *(Handing the audit folder to Leo.)* He set y'all up.

(Leo stops packing and looks at the folder. Afterwards, he slowly crosses toward Paul. Paul quickly picks up his audit bag and heads to the door. Greg blocks Paul's exit. Preparing for a fight, Leo removes his suit jacket. He then chases Paul around the table before catching him and throwing him onto the table. Leo jumps on top of him and starts to choke Paul.)

GREG: Beat the shit out of him. Fuck him up. Fuck him up!

MARGARET: *(Overlapping.)* No, Leo. No! NO, LEO!

LEO: *(Overlapping.)* I could kill you. I could fucking kill you.

(Leo notices that they are wearing identical ties. Leo releases Paul. Greg storms out of the room. Leo exits.)

PAUL: Margaret. Margaret . . .

(Margaret stops at the door and picks up the equity folder lying on the floor. She stares at the folder. After a moment, she turns and crosses to Paul. Margaret hands him the folder.)

PAUL: *(Continues.)* Margaret.

(She then turns around, puts on her glasses, adjusts her clothing, and exits the room.)

PAUL: *(Continues.)* Margaret . . .

(A bewildered Paul stands there alone. Slowly he smiles as the lights fade to black.)

END OF PLAY

ORANGE FLOWER WATER

By Craig Wright

For Beth and Helen

It is the future generation that presses into being by means of these exuberant feelings and supersensible soap bubbles of ours.

— Schopenhauer

PLAYWRIGHT'S BIOGRAPHY

Craig Wright's plays include *The Pavilion, Recent Tragic Events, Main Street, Molly's Delicious, The Big Numbers, John Dory,* and *Adventures While Preaching the Gospel of Beauty*. Mr. Wright has received several grants and awards over the years for his work, including fellowships in playwriting from the McKnight Foundation and the National Endowment for the Arts. *The Pavilion* was nominated for the American Theater Critics' Association Best New Play Award and has had over thirty productions since its premiere in 2000; *Recent Tragic Events* won an ATCA Best New Play Citation Award in 2002. Mr. Wright holds an M.Div. degree from United Theological Seminary and is a member of the pop-rock band Kangaroo. He currently writes for HBO's "Six Feet Under" and lives in Los Angeles with his wife, Lorraine LeBlanc, and their son, Louis.

INTRODUCTION

In my opinion, this play should be performed as simply as possible, with a single bed for a set, and all the actors on stage throughout. Props should be minimal. As for the ending, the desired effect is one of wonder, humility, and awe in the face of beauty, grace, and the amoral creative power of life.

ORIGINAL PRODUCTIONS

Orange Flower Water premiered at The Jungle Theater, in Minneapolis, on July 12, 2002. It was directed by Bain Boehlke; the set design was by Bain Boehlke; the costume design was by Amelia Cheever; the lighting design was by Barry Browning; the sound design was by Victor Zupanc; and the production stage manager was Elizabeth R. MacNally. The cast was as follows:

DAVID . . . . Brian Goranson
CATHY . . . . Amy McDonald
BRAD . . . . Terry Hempleman
BETH . . . . Jennifer Blagen

The play opened one day later in a production at Contemporary American Theater Festival in Shepardstown, West Virginia, in a production directed by Leah C. Gardiner; the set design was by Markas Henry; the costume design was by Daniel Urlie; the lighting design was by Paul Whitaker; the sound design was by Kevin Lloyd, and the production stage manager was Alison C. Wolocko. The cast was as follows:

DAVID . . . . Jason Field
CATHY . . . . Mercedes Herrero
BRAD . . . . Paul Sparks
BETH . . . . Libby West

CHARACTERS

DAVID: a pharmacist, thirties to forties.
CATHY: wife of David, a choir director, thirties to forties.
BRAD: owner of video rental stores, thirties to forties.
BETH: wife of Brad, thirties to forties.

TIME

The present.

PLACE

The play takes place in various locales in Pine City, a small town in north central Minnesota.

SETTING

The set is a bed and bedside table and four chairs (at the edge of the playing space) on an otherwise bare stage.

Orange Flower Water

Scene One

Music rises in the darkness. Light rises on Cathy.

CATHY: Dear David. Get ready. All three of the kids need to take lunches to school today. I have already made the sandwiches, but the rest needs to be assembled by yours truly. To make matters worse, Gus has early morning math today, as well, so you have to get him there by 7:30, come back and get the girls, and take them later. And try not to fight with Ruthie. If you wake her up early enough, it should all work out, and what I have found works with her is to let her choose the radio station in the car and then shut up. Annie has Brownies after school. As for dinner: You'll be pleased to know I have reached a new state of self-awareness and have not prepared anything, confident that you will be taking the children out for dinner tonight regardless of what the checkbook looks like. Have fun! Don't forget Gus has a soccer game on Saturday and Annie is going to Taylor's birthday party. Maybe you could take Ruthie to a movie? (Can you tell I'm concerned about you two?) Finally, and don't ask me why, the painters are coming on Sunday morning and the fumes are not good for the kids, so either go to church — ha, ha — or take them out somewhere. I should be home by 5:00 PM Sunday afternoon. Please pick me up in the north parking lot of the school. The buses will all be in the south parking lot, but I need to go through the building to divest myself of all the accumulated crap these stupid choir festivals send you home with, so I'll come out the back door and wait for you there. Wish me luck! Cathy. P.S. I stood at the end of the bed this morning, once I was all dressed and ready to go, and the light was angling in from the hall, and you looked very sweet and innocent, very much the same young man who so charmingly and insinuatingly complimented my "nice music" so many years ago. I know we get very busy around here serving the three little Hitlers, but please know, if anything should happen to me this weekend, if for some strange reason, the bus drops through the bridge in Little Falls, or if I'm crushed to death by a mob of anxious sopranos, please know that I love you and feel ever so lucky and proud to be your wife in this strange and way-too-busy world we have procreated ourselves into. Yours more truly than truly can ever say . . . Cathy.
(Light fades on Cathy. She takes a seat in a chair upstage.)

Scene Two

David and Beth rise and come downstage. Beth lies on the bed. David begins walking slowly around three sides of the bed, and as he does so, he sprinkles rose petals on the floor.

DAVID: Now, I want you to put all thoughts of this world out of your mind.

BETH: David . . .

DAVID: Repeat after me: all thoughts of this world out of my mind.

BETH: All thoughts of this world out of my mind.

DAVID: These four walls. The picturesque Holiday Haven Motel. With every step I take, with every petal that drops from my hand, all these things are pixilating, dissolving away . . .

BETH: "Pixilating"?

DAVID: Like the little dots on a computer screen.

BETH: Oh.

DAVID: Shut your eyes.

BETH: But I think it's kinda cute the way you're, doing, you're . . . you're like a little gnome, making a spell.

DAVID: Thank you, that's my gnomish intent. *(Continuing the spell.)* And now the whole town of Pine City — Lake Melissa, Sundberg's Café, The Sandwich Hut, The Voyageur — it's all falling, falling through the clouds, dropping down through miles of clouds until you can't even see it anymore, Beth, it's a speck, and then it's not even a speck, it's gone. Goodbye, Pine City.

BETH: Good-bye, Pine City. *(After a beat.)* So where are we?

DAVID: We're in a bay in a kingdom in the clouds, and it's clear and it's quiet and it's beautiful . . . and it's just us.

BETH: I like that.

(He lets fall the remaining rose petals across Beth's body and the bed. He sits beside her on the bed.)

DAVID: And in the distance . . .

(He begins to unbutton her blouse very slowly.)

BETH: *(Coy.)* What are you doing?

DAVID: In the distance —

BETH: *(Coy.)* I see what you're doing . . .

DAVID: In the distance, we can see huge apples . . .

BETH: Apples?

DAVID: Yes, apples . . .

(He opens her bra, revealing her breasts.)

DAVID: Apples as high as buildings, apples like tall ships, two of them; float-ing on the water, red and then golden near the tops, and the sunlight and the mist, it's all like music, like the sweetest, quietest music, and we're there, and it's all . . . it's all so safe . . . and quiet . . . and cool.

BETH: I'm so sick of this hot summer.

DAVID: Me too.

(Brief pause as he kisses her breasts. Then the conversation continues with inter-mittent kissing.)

BETH: Tell me something.

DAVID: What?

BETH: Do you really love me as much as you *think* you do?

DAVID: I *think* so.

BETH: It doesn't seem possible.

DAVID: Real love never seems possible, it just is.

BETH: I mean it, I worry sometimes . . .

DAVID: *(Attempting to quench the flame of doubt.)* Beth . . . listen to me.

BETH: What?

DAVID: I don't know what's possible or impossible . . .

BETH: I know.

DAVID: I'm *totally* out of touch with reality . . .

BETH: I *know!*

DAVID: All I know is when I'm with you, I feel alive. When I'm with you, I feel like the history of my real life is really happening; and like I'm so lucky to be able to kiss you . . . and touch you . . . and be with you and be your partner, a little while . . . on the way . . . you know?

(He reaches behind her to unzip her skirt.)

BETH: Wait a minute.

DAVID: What? What do you want? Wine? *(Insinuatingly, as a joke.)* Maple syrup? You want to be my little hotcake?

BETH: It's not . . .

DAVID: What? What is it?

BETH: Nothing.

(Brief pause.)

DAVID: Oh shit. It's God again, isn't it?

BETH: No, it isn't!

DAVID: Yes it is, I can see it in your eyes, it's that "There's a God" look. Shit!

BETH: I'm sorry. I can't help it.

DAVID: Beth, there is no God.

BETH: But what if there is?

DAVID: There isn't.

BETH: But what if there is, this, this is a sin, David! Adultery is a sin!

DAVID: You're really gonna use that word?

BETH: Yes, because that's the word for what this is! Adultery's a sin, doesn't that worry you at all?

DAVID: No, because if there is no God, there is no sin, and Beth, there is no God. There's no one watching or judging or remembering anything in this world, there's just us, trying to be happy.

BETH: How do you know?

DAVID: Because!

BETH: David, "because" is not an answer to "How do you know?"

DAVID: Yes it is, because if there were a God, Beth, then the Crusades wouldn't have been allowed to happen, and the Holocaust wouldn't have been allowed to happen. This whole world of shittiness wouldn't have been allowed to happen if anyone who cared was watching. You want to know where God is — if there is one?

BETH: Yeah.

DAVID: God's in us. *If* there is one, which there isn't. But if there is, for the sake of argument, then God's the one who's in love with you, in me; and God's the one who's in love with me, in you; I *think;* I *hope,* anyway; I don't know, I think you love me but then you bring up God all the time as a big excuse —

BETH: It's not an excuse — I don't even want to think about it, it just comes up in my head!

DAVID: Whatever, it's not true! It's a bad dream, it's a lie! God's not up there or *out* there, anywhere, watching, OK! And you know what, here's the clincher, if He is up there watching, and He lets all this other shit happen, lets all these lives get shit down the toilet of history, then fuck him! Let him watch, let him judge! I'll judge the motherfucker right back! *(A brief pause, a little rattled by the gravity of what he's just said.)* Of course, the good news is, He's not *really* there, so everything's cool.

BETH: Well, I guess I'm just not so sure as you.

DAVID: I *know.*

BETH: And you weren't raised in the church and I was, and you have to —

DAVID: I *know* that —

BETH: And I know you think that's stupid —

DAVID: I *don't* think it's stupid —

BETH: But I'm just . . . I just can't be as sure as you about it, OK?

(She pulls her shirt closed, crosses her arms, and sits there. Long pause. David laughs hollowly.)

DAVID: OK, so let me get this straight.

BETH: What?

DAVID: I need to understand what's happening to me, because my penis is kind of asking me a lot of questions right now: three years of being friends; sitting next to each other at soccer games; three years of slowly realizing we're married to the wrong people —

BETH: Don't say that.

DAVID: *(With firmer conviction.)* Three years of getting sicker and sicker, vomiting in our hearts from not being with each other, so you're calling me up in tears from your cell phone in the car at midnight, "Brad did this, Brad did that" —

BETH: I know!

DAVID: And I'm so sad and confused at work I'm filling prescriptions wrong and giving old ladies diarrhea, I'm losing accounts to Wal-Mart, and everybody's telling me I should go in for an MRI? After three years of that, I finally get you in a room with me alone, and it's *God?* This fucking *idea? God* is stopping me now? I don't think so! Let it be . . . cancer! Let me die now of cancer and lose you, but not *God!* Jesus, Beth, after all this time, it has to be something real!

BETH: It's real to me!

DAVID: Sometimes!

BETH: I said that to be honest with you, and just that once —

DAVID: You said, only sometimes!

BETH: Yes, OK, only sometimes! But when it's God, David, sometimes is enough! I'm sorry. I can't change.

DAVID: Beth, I don't want you to change.

BETH: You do, though.

DAVID: No, I . . . look.

BETH: What?

DAVID: I don't want to fight.

BETH: I don't either.

DAVID: I'm here because I'm in love with you, not to fight.

BETH: I know that.

DAVID: And I don't want to make you unhappy.

BETH: I'm not unhappy, I'm just . . .

DAVID: What?

BETH: I'm scared. *(After a beat.)* You don't really want to do this anyway, right? You love Cathy, you love your kids . . .

DAVID: *(A little annoyed.)* Don't tell me what I don't want to do, please —

BETH: Don't be a jerk.

DAVID: Then don't tell me what I don't want to do!

BETH: Well, you *don't, really,* do you? You love Annie and Ruthie and Gus.

DAVID: Annie and Ruthie and Gus are not any happier than I am.

BETH: David, they're the happiest kids I know.

DAVID: Not inside.

BETH: You're weird.

DAVID: No, Beth, they're very uptight. And they know, I swear, they know something isn't right, because they're like always . . . consoling me in some odd way, it's creepy.

BETH: And what about Cathy?

DAVID: Cathy . . . is a mistake that I made, and I am a mistake that *she* made. I don't love Cathy anymore, Beth, I love *you.* I can't help it.

BETH: And when you don't love me anymore?

DAVID: Beth, what do you want me to do? How horrible do I have to feel? Do I wish it was different? Yes! Do I wish I didn't have to make four people miserable in order to follow my heart? Yes! But I can't help how I feel! I love you more than anything I've ever loved in my life!

BETH: Really?

DAVID: Really. I want —

BETH: *Really really?*

DAVID: Yes!

BETH: I mean, if there was ever a time when you have to be honest with me and yourself, it's now —

DAVID: I'm being honest with myself, I want to be with you all the time. All the time. My life when I'm not with you, Beth, is black and white TV with bad sound and no remote. Life *with* you is big-screen color TV, stereo sound, watching *Cosmos* twenty-four hours a day, but not just watching, being in it. Being with you is being *in it.* Gliding through space and the billions of stars . . . what can I say, it's better. It's so much better with you, I don't know how to do without it the rest of the time.

BETH: You're just talking.

DAVID: No, I mean it, I don't know how I ever *did* without it. My whole life growing up would have been so much simpler if, you know, every time I was sad, every time it all seemed hopeless, and people said, "What's the matter," I could have known, I could have said, "Oh, it's just, I haven't

met Beth yet, but I understand that I will, someday, so . . . I'll be OK! Don't worry about me!" That would have been good. But see, I didn't know! I hadn't made it through the jungle yet and found this fountain . . .
(He kisses her abdomen through her clothes.)

DAVID: . . . where beauty sprays up all day in the shape of a woman . . .
(He continues to kiss her, moving lower. A moment passes.)

BETH: You know what? You're in love with being in love, I think.

DAVID: Oh, does that thought comfort you? Does that make it easier for you to not give in and do this?

BETH: No, it doesn't —

DAVID: Look, I'm sorry I have dreams, I'm sorry I wish life was different —

BETH: You're not the only one —

DAVID: Well, you're talking like I'm the only one, "You're in love with being in love . . ."

BETH: I have dreams too!

DAVID: Well, you don't act that way!

BETH: David, I'm scared of how big my dreams are and how much they make me feel, and *that's* why, OK, I'm sitting here trying not to do the wrong thing for any of us, OK?

DAVID: It's not your job to keep me out of hell, or keep me safe or something —

BETH: David, I just don't want to lose you as a friend.

DAVID: You won't. You'll never ever ever lose me as a friend.

BETH: I don't *believe* you said that.

DAVID: What?

BETH: No!

DAVID: Tell me. Come on.

BETH: Every night I lay in bed next to Brad, you know, and I think about *us.* Every night. Even when I don't want to, when it would be easier to just forget, these thoughts come to me from somewhere underneath everything. I think about you and me and . . .

DAVID: And what?

BETH: You're gonna think this is stupid.

DAVID: You think about a baby.

BETH: Yes.

DAVID: I think about a baby too sometimes.

BETH: You do?

DAVID: Yes.

BETH: Why didn't you tell me?

DAVID: I didn't want to seem like . . .

BETH: Like what?

DAVID: Like I wanted you for . . . having my babies or something. I figured you had enough kids . . .

BETH: You should have told me.

DAVID: Yeah?

BETH: Yeah, I wouldn't have minded hearing that.

DAVID: Sorry. I think about our baby.

BETH: Me too.

(They kiss a moment, tenderly.)

BETH: Last night, I was thinking . . . you and I and Lily . . .

DAVID: Lily?

BETH: That's her name, in my head, Lily. She was, like, four years old, with long dark hair and really serious eyes and smart? And we went to the store at Christmastime to get stuff to make cookies —

DAVID: You?

BETH: I know, I can cook, it's a dream! But we all went to the store and it was snowing, those big fat fluffy flakes, and we got stuff to make sugar cookies, and on the way home, she was in her car seat and she reached in the bag and pulled out a little plastic bottle of orange flower water? Which I've read about in, you know, but never seen? And she ended up spilling this orange flower water stuff all over the backseat. And you and I had to roll down the windows, the scent was so strong . . . and the . . .

(Brief pause.)

DAVID: What?

BETH: *(Full of longing.)* And the scent of the orangey air and the coolness rushing into the car and you and me happy and Lily in the back . . . giggling . . . we were so happy. We were *so* happy. And that's just *one* night of laying there thinking in that bed. I do that *every* night. Every night for the past three years. So don't tell me I don't have dreams, OK?

DAVID: I'm sorry.

BETH: I have dreams. What I don't know is whether us taking this forward is gonna make any of them come true, or if it's just gonna make you hate me and I'll lose you as a friend, and then that'll make everything worse. *(She clasps her bra, buttons her blouse, and swings around to sit on the edge of the bed.)*

DAVID: How could it be worse? You're married to Brad.

BETH: David, don't talk about Brad.

DAVID: I'm sorry, that thing you told me the other day, where he was so concerned that you should keep the kids quiet while he watches the game?

"Beth, would you please keep those fucking kids quiet, I'm trying to watch the fucking game!"?

BETH: He's not easy to live with, he takes his work very seriously —

DAVID: Oh come on, videos? And I suppose he "needs his time"?

BETH: He does!

DAVID: You've got to be kidding me! "Keep the kids quiet while I watch the fucking game!"? That's not good! That's like *Bad Father,* that's like one step short of *The Shining!*

(By now, Beth has slipped on her shoes and is standing up.)

BETH: David, do you *really* want to be one of them? You think you could really take being one of them?

(She points outside.)

BETH: You spent all that time trying to convince me the world out there had disappeared. Why? Because it's full of people who do *this,* David. It's full of people who shit all over each other, whose word doesn't mean anything, and whose kids are so screwed up, coming home to no dad or no mom, and it's all sold to us like it's almost normal, are we really gonna be like them? Isn't that what we're asking each other to do?

DAVID: No, we're asking each other for a moment of goodness in a life that is mostly unpleasant and way too short.

BETH: But there are no moments of goodness that don't come with responsibilities.

DAVID: I know that!

BETH: I don't think you do! And I don't think I really do, either! I think we're learning it right now.

(David throws himself onto the bed and screams into a pillow.)

DAVID: *(Into pillow.)* Aahhhhh!

BETH: *(After a beat.)* We should go.

DAVID: *(Looking up from pillow, after a beat.)* You know what my mistake was?

BETH: David, this is not a mistake.

DAVID: You know where I screwed this up?

BETH: David, we're doing the right thing. You have a life. I have a life. Our kids have lives. This is —

DAVID: I never should have talked. Hesitation turns everything into a discussion. And we've been hesitating ever since we met.

(He rises.)

DAVID: I never should have *talked.*

(He goes to her, puts his arms around her. They look at each for a while, and then he kisses her. After a moment, she pulls away.)

BETH: No.

DAVID: *(Giving up.)* OK. OK.

(A moment passes, and then he takes the bottom of her skirt in his hands and pulls it up, and pulls her tightly against him.)

DAVID: Beth, I can't make it seem right, and I can't make the world go away, and I can't even kid myself it's right. I just *want* you, OK? I want to be *with* you . . . and *for* you . . . and *in* you. Right now. OK?

(Brief pause.)

BETH: *(Almost dizzy.)* OK.

(They kiss. After a minute or so, they fall together onto the bed. Music rises. Lights shift.)

Scene Three

David and Beth exit the bed area. Beth takes a seat as Brad stands and meets David in a sunny pool of light downstage left. They gaze out towards the audience, watching a soccer game.

BRAD: Looks like old Arshavir Blackwell's gonna score our only goal again. Christ, he must absolutely hate fucking life being on this team. *(To the field.)* Go! Now take it downfield!

DAVID: Everybody feeds him the ball, that must be kinda fun for him —

BRAD: I know, but the only reason — *(To the field.)* Don't be scared to get in front of him, Carl! *(To David.)* The only reason his parents have him playing rec soccer at all is to teach him a lesson.

DAVID: Yeah?

BRAD: Yeah, he used to be on a traveling team in the Cities, but they thought he was getting a big head. *(To the field.)* Attaboy, Carl, get in his face!, *(To David.)*, so they stuck him with our kids for a season. They live in Albertville so the commute's the same either way. What the hell kinda name is that anyway, Arshavir?

DAVID: I think it's Armenian.

BRAD: If my parents had done that to me, given me a name like that, I woulda taken a shit on the dining room table every night. I woulda crapped 'em out a *great* big bowl of snakes.

(Brad semi-squats and makes a shitting sound.)

BRAD: You played sports? Back in school?

DAVID: Sure. Not soccer, but I, I was on the tennis team —

BRAD: *(Sardonically.)* Yeah, that's a sport. Where's the little woman?

DAVID: Oh, she took, um . . . Ruthie and Annie started ballet today, so —

BRAD: That new place across from the movie theater?

DAVID: Yeah —

BRAD: I thought that's what that might be. I wasn't sure, looking in.

DAVID: Yeah, it's a ballet studio.

BRAD: You seen that babe who runs it then?

DAVID: Mmhmm.

BRAD: Would *you?*

DAVID: Oh sure. Totally.

BRAD: I saw her in there painting the other night, a couple months ago, I guess it was, but she was hot. She had on a leotard and all that long black hair. And she's single?

DAVID: I think so, yeah. But I think she might be the girlfriend of that new guy at the radio station, Wigdahl whatever, but —

BRAD: OK, tell me something.

DAVID: OK.

BRAD: *(After much thought.)* Her or . . . *(He points to a woman nearby.)* Katie Amundson. Desert island, which one do you take?

DAVID: *(A little uneasy.)* I don't know . . . you tell —

BRAD: Come on, have a fucking conversation with me, which one? *(To the field.)* Hand ball! Ref! Ref! That was a hand ball! *(To David.)* Which one? *(To the field.)* Carl, don't let him get behind you like that!

DAVID: Katie.

BRAD: Yeah, I know, I know, for one night, the other maybe, but — you're right — it's very deceptive — *(To the field.)* Don't be afraid to get hurt, Carl! You can't play afraid! *(To David.)* So. Katie.

DAVID: Yeah.

BRAD: Why?

DAVID: I don't know. She's got something.

BRAD: I'll tell you what she's got, she's got that ass. She's got that undeniable ass. *(To the field.)* Hey, Gus, nice D! *(To David.)* Did you see that?

DAVID: Yeah. *(To the field.)* Way to go, Gussie!

BRAD: He's a good kid.

DAVID: Thanks.

BRAD: OK. Katie "A for Ass-licious" Amundson or . . .

(He surreptitiously points to another woman nearby.)

DAVID: Elena?

BRAD: Yeah.

DAVID: Are you serious?

BRAD: You getting picky all of a sudden?

DAVID: No, it's just . . .

BRAD: See, I *like* that eye.

DAVID: It would drive me crazy, I think —

BRAD: If it went *out,* yeah, like a walleye, yeah, but *in* a little like that is kinda sweet. It's kinda helpless-looking, like you could catch her. Like she'd be at the back of the herd, dawdling.

(Brad crosses his eyes.)

DAVID: No.

BRAD: *(Still with eyes crossed.)* You don't see any charm in this at all?

DAVID: No.

BRAD: See, I'm taking Elena on that one. Does Katie know you feel this way about her?

DAVID: No.

BRAD: You want me to get her over here and you two could set up some time maybe? You could meet at a motel?

DAVID: No. Thanks.

BRAD: Cathy would bite your balls off, wouldn't she?

DAVID: Oh, yeah.

BRAD: So what about Beth? *(To field.)* Go! Go! Go! Go!

DAVID: Your Beth?

BRAD: Yeah. My Beth. Katie or my Beth?

DAVID: *(Bewildered.)* I don't know, what about Cathy?

BRAD: Cathy or Katie?

DAVID: Yeah.

BRAD: For me?

DAVID: Yeah.

BRAD: That's easy, I'll take Cathy. Doggy style. Just kidding.

(Brad winks at David and then shifts his focus to the field and starts clapping.)

BRAD: *(To the field.)* Good game, you guys! Good game! Way to hustle out there! Good hustle, Arshavir! Good hustle, Carl! *(To David.)* Wouldn't you take Beth?

DAVID: Over Katie?

BRAD: Over Cathy. *(To the field.)* Nice game, Gus! Get your stuff together!

DAVID: Uhh . . .

BRAD: I'll see you next weekend, and hey, by the way, Beth told me to ask you, she knows her insurance won't let her refill her pills until the end of the month, but Oscar got into her purse and ate 'em.

DAVID: Is he OK?

BRAD: He doesn't seem any sicker than usual. He ate her lipstick and blush and everything.

DAVID: Christ.

BRAD: Yeah, he eats her old tampons if she doesn't cover the bathroom trash tight enough. *(With too much edge.)* It's fucking disgusting.

(Brad puts out his hand to shake.)

BRAD: Nice talking to you, I'll see you next week.

(They shake hands. As Brad exits, he calls upstage, in a joking sotto voce . . .)

BRAD: Hey, Katie, I think David over here wants a word with you! No, I'm just kidding, bye!

(He exits upstage, followed by a disconcerted David. Music rises. David sits down. Lights shift.)

Scene Four

Beth stands, goes to the bed area and pulls a suitcase out from under the bed, sets it on the bed, and opens it. She removes several articles of clothing and sets them beside the suitcase on the bed. She changes blouses. Meanwhile, Brad has put on an apron that says "World's Greatest Dad" and he enters the scene carrying a large spatula and a container of charcoal lighter fluid as Beth begins putting the clothes carefully back into the suitcase.

BRAD: Have you seen the other one of these?

BETH: No.

BRAD: I thought I asked you to buy two, we're always running out —

BETH: Gosh —

BRAD: This one's hardly got enough to —

BETH: *(Tense and falsely.)* Gosh, honey, I'm sorry, I must not have gotten around to it.

BRAD: What are you doing? What are you doing?

BETH: What does it look like I'm doing, Brad? I'm leaving.

BRAD: What?

BETH: You heard me, I'm leaving.

BRAD: *(Gesturing to where he entered.)* Because of that down there? Because —

BETH: I'm not stupid, Brad!

BRAD: No, this is funny . . .

BETH: The boys aren't stupid and I'm not stupid, and to say something like that —

BRAD: I didn't mean you were stupid, it was just a . . . comment, for Christ's sake —

BETH: In front of *my* friends.

BRAD: Beth, they know —

BETH: That you think you can say something like that is so scary to me —

BRAD: Beth, they know I'm a prick, they don't listen to what I say.

BETH: They know you're a prick.

BRAD: Yeah, everybody knows I'm a prick!

BETH: And you're able to live with that?

BRAD: It's who I am! Look, I'm sorry, I — I say things! I don't mean them, I just say them! You know that!

BETH: No, what I know is . . . I'm really not happy . . . and I haven't been happy for a long time, and that's . . . just . . . I gotta go. *(She closes the suitcase.) I* gotta go.

BRAD: No.

BETH: What does that mean?

BRAD: It means no, I won't let you go. You can't —

BETH: Do you want me to scream? Do you want to make a big scene with Denny and Sonya downstairs?

BRAD: Go ahead.

BETH: Brad!

BRAD: Denny and Sonya can go fuck themselves for all I care, my wife isn't walking out the door!

BETH: Like I'm some character in a story!

BRAD: What the hell does —

BETH: You say it like I'm some little character in a story, "my wife's not gonna . . . " *I'm not some little character in a story!*
(As she picks up the suitcase and attempts to exit past him, he touches her. She drops the suitcase and screams at the top of her lungs.)

BETH: DON'T TOUCH ME! DON'T TOUCH ME!
(He backs off.)

BRAD: Sorry!

BETH: Every time you touch me, it's like being raped!

BRAD: Jesus Christ, you're a fucking freak!

BETH: No, I'm not.

BRAD: Just tell me where you're going.

BETH: No! It's none of your business!

BRAD: You're gonna run to what's his name, your little boyfriend?

BETH: I'm going to the cabin, you don't know what —

BRAD: You're gonna go run to your little fucking boyfriend.

BETH: I don't know what you're talking about.

BRAD: Oh, fuck you!

BETH: No, you think I need someone to run to, like I need somebody, like living in the same house with you for fifteen years isn't enough to make me sick to my stomach? I don't need another reason to be miserable, Brad! You're all the reason anyone would ever need!

BRAD: Beth, I know you and that pharmacist have been fucking around behind my back. I wasn't gonna do anything about it —

BETH: *(Overlapping.)* You are so wrong about —

BRAD: *(Overlapping.)* — because I didn't want the boys to find out their mother was a whore!

(She picks up the suitcase.)

BETH: You know what, I'm going. You obviously have some idea in your head that is totally of your own creation and —

(He reaches to stop her.)

BETH: *(Like an animal.)* I SAID DON'T TOUCH ME!

(She starts to go.)

BRAD: *(A little unnerved.)* So, so, so right in front of Denny and Sonya . . .

BETH: Everyone knows you're a prick, Brad! I'm sure they'll take it in stride!

BRAD: He won't leave Cathy, you know that, don't you?

BETH: I'm not even gonna have this discussion because, you know what? I don't know what it's about!

BRAD: He won't!

BETH: *(Suddenly shifting.)* Look, he knows what he wants and I know what I want and we've been very clear with other —

BRAD: Aha! So you *are* fucking this guy!

BETH: Yeah, Brad, I guess I am, I'm "fucking this guy!"

BRAD: Oh, maybe I shouldn't use such bad language, you're right. It's such a beautiful thing when two people who are married to other people can put their stinky little parts in each other, I'm sorry if I made it sound cheap! Fuckin' A!

BETH: I know it's cheap.

BRAD: Oh, you do?

BETH: Yes, I *know* it's not good —

BRAD: But you *don't* know there's no way he's leaving those three little kids? Come on! You've gotta know *that,* right? He's never gonna leave those kids. That bitch wife of his has him wound around her finger tighter than a Duncan fucking yoyo. Have you ever seen him with her at the store picking out movies? It's Merchant Ivory, Jane Austen, Merchant Ivory, Jane Austen, English every single fucking time, he's not going *anywhere!* You *must* know that, Beth. You're not stupid, you *must. (After a beat.)* So look, let's go downstairs and have a beer and —

BETH: No!

BRAD: Come on, you can bitch to Sonya, Denny and I'll take the boys to the lake for a swim or something —

BETH: NO!

BRAD: Do you want me to just send 'em home?

BETH: No. I don't know!

BRAD: Look, let me go down there and tell 'em we need a little time —

BETH: No!

BRAD: Yes, I'll let them get the coals started, maybe Denny can figure out how to use that thing of yours where it works without fluid and we'll . . . I'll be right back up.

(*Brief pause.*)

BETH: (*Resignedly.*) Whatever.

(*Brad exits and sits in his chair. Beth carries the suitcase back into the room and sets it down. She sits on the edge of the bed and bursts into tears. She cries for a minute or two; then stands and looks around the room at all the things she'll be leaving. Then, Brad rises and enters the scene again, having taken off his apron.*)

BRAD: They decided to go home.

BETH: I'm sorry. I'll call Sonya later and explain —

BRAD: No, they understand, it's not a big deal.

BETH: It's a big deal, Brad.

BRAD: You know what I mean.

BETH: What did you tell them?

BRAD: I said you're fucking the pharmacist at Sundberg's and we gotta talk.

BETH: You did not.

BRAD: No, I didn't, I just said we had to talk, that's all. And they took the boys.

BETH: Where?

BRAD: I don't know, they'll go to Perkins or somewhere and have some dinner I guess.

(Brief pause.)

BETH: God.

BRAD: What?

BETH: Everything actually has to happen, doesn't it? You think in your mind things can happen without happening, but in the end, they always have to actually happen. Actual kids have to get driven away by actual friends . . . and actual people have to sit there and actually . . . live.

(Brief pause.)

BRAD: So you know for a fact he's leaving Cathy?

BETH: *(Beaten down.)* God, I don't know, Brad. And I don't care, we're . . . this is not about that. That's as much of a mistake probably as this was, I'm the queen of romantic mistakes —

BRAD: You and me.

BETH: What?

BRAD: A mistake?

BETH: Yeah!

BRAD: It wasn't a mistake for me.

BETH: What am I supposed to say to that?

BRAD: Nothing, but that's . . .

BETH: All of a sudden you have feelings . . . ?

BRAD: *(Honest.)* No, it's just what I'm saying. Is it perfect all the time? No way. But it's not a mistake. But you, you really think —

BETH: Look . . . do you really want to have this conversation? Because, truthfully, I just want to go.

BRAD: Then go! Fuck it! *(He screams fiercely, right in her face.)* Go! Go! Go! Go!

BETH: *(Overlapping.)* Don't you understand, you stupid idiot, this doesn't make me happy?

BRAD: *(Overlapping.)* Go! Go! GO! GO! GO!

BETH: Don't you understand that? If I felt like I had a choice, I'd . . . I'd have one!

(A pause. He steps away from her. After a moment, Beth rises.)

BRAD: *(Still angry.)* You're going up to the cabin?

BETH: Yeah.

BRAD: Is he gonna be up there?

BETH: No.

BRAD: *Yes.*

BETH: I don't know! Does it matter?

BRAD: Yes, it's my fucking cabin! I built it! I don't want some shit-for-brains pharmacist fucking my wife in that cabin!

BETH: Then he won't come up!

BRAD: I'm just asking for the common courtesy of not having him spray *his* come all over *my* pillow!

BETH: I said he won't come up, shut up about it already! I wasn't planning on it anyway, but —

BRAD: Thank you!

BETH: God! You're such a pig!

BRAD: Does Cathy know?

BETH: *I don't know!* I told you, that's not what this is about! This is you and me, Brad! David or no David —

BRAD: Fuck, don't you say that name in my house . . .

BETH: David or no David —

BRAD: *Don't say that motherfucker's name in this house, Beth!*

BETH: He doesn't know what I'm doing, I haven't told him about this. It's not like we're on walkie-talkies all the time, it's not that serious.

BRAD: So you don't know if Cathy knows?

BETH: No, I don't, and I don't care.

BRAD: Because the minute you walk out the door, I'm gonna call over there and tell her her husband is fucking my wife.

BETH: Is that supposed to make me stay? You want me to stay with you for his sake?

BRAD: I don't know, Beth! You're the one who said this shit has to actually happen! All I'm saying is, walk out the door and things will start to actually fucking happen!

BETH: And you have to hurt everybody else?

BRAD: Yeah, I do!

BETH: This is not about them!

BRAD: Bullshit! Bull-fat-fucking-bull-*shit!* We were happy —

BETH: We were never happy, Brad, like people are supposed to be —

BRAD: Bullshit! We were happy for fifteen years —

BETH: I was never happy!

BRAD: Is that what he tells you, that you've never been happy?

BETH: No!

BRAD: This *wonderful* guy —

BETH: It's the *truth!*

BRAD: He takes half your fucking life and pisses all over it just so he can get in your pants, getting you to believe you've never been happy? We've fucked in this bed, shit, how many times, Beth? A thousand times? Two thousand times? And you're fuckin' telling me you've never been happy? What, that you fuckin' faked it *every* time? Just tell me you faked it every time! Every time you said you loved me, every time you pushed that pussy of yours in my face and said you loved me —

BETH: There's more to life than sex, you *idiot!*

BRAD: *(A sudden rush, a new thought.)* And you *owe* me nothing?

BETH: What?

BRAD: I made a promise to you and I've kept it all these years and you owe me *nothing?*

BETH: I've cleaned your house and fed you and fed your kids and made sure everything —

BRAD: I'm talking about a *promise* —

Beth: If anything, you owe *me* —

BRAD: I'm not talking about housework, I'm talking about a *promise!* I took my life, I could have done whatever I wanted to with it, but I chased you down — stupid fucking me — and you never let me forget that — "oh, he had to chase me down" — "I wasn't really ready, but he was *so persistent*" — and stupid me, I chased you down because I thought you were the most beautiful woman I'd ever seen in my life and I thought "Shit, Brad, you *are* an idiot, but maybe, just maybe, she'll see something in you that you don't even see, you know?"

BETH: I know, I'm the worst thing that ever happened to you, I know that!

BRAD: *Nobody*, none of my friends thought you'd go out with me, I remember Slick said it was a "logical impossibility" —

BETH: And it still is, that's the problem!

BRAD: So why did you say yes? You bitch! Why did we have kids? Why did you waste my time for the past fifteen motherfucking years?

BETH: Because I didn't know what else to do! And I didn't think I would ever be good at anything! And I didn't think it would last this long!

BRAD: Oh, should I have died? Did I miss my cue?

BETH: No, it's just . . . *life gets long sometimes!*

BRAD: You know, you're full of shit!

BETH: I am not full of shit, Brad, I'm just tired of being married to you, and that's all it is! It's nothing as complicated as you seem to want to make it.

BRAD: You loved me!

BETH: I didn't love you, I was scared to live!

BRAD: No, you loved me, you did! And when this whole thing turns to shit on you, you're gonna know that too, in the pit of your fucking heart, you're gonna know it like you never knew anything!

(He picks up the phone.)

BRAD: What's his number?

BETH: Don't call him.

BRAD: What's his fucking number?

BETH: Brad, if you wanna be mad at somebody, be mad at me!

(She tries to hang up the phone.)

BRAD: Don't touch that fucking phone again!

BETH: Look, you want me to stay, I'll stay, but —

(Again, she tries to hang up the phone.)

BRAD: I said, don't touch this fucking phone! *(He pushes her away.)* You think it feels like being raped every time I touch you? I'll throw you down and fuck you right now, you fucking cunt!

BETH: I'm leaving. Before you do something that gets you locked up in prison. Because that wouldn't be good for the boys.

(She picks up the suitcase.)

BRAD: *(Yelling.)* Oh, do us all a favor!

BETH: I am!

BRAD: *(Yelling.)* Save me from *myself!* What a fucking joke!

BETH: You can stop yelling, Brad, I'm leaving!

BRAD: *(Top of his lungs.)* Go ahead! And I'll tell the boys when they get back all about their mother the fucking whore!

(Beth goes upstage and sits down in her chair. Brad yells in her direction. Even louder, so all the neighbors can hear.) I oughta screw you right through this bed and straight down to Hell where you came from, you fucking cunt! You motherfucking cunt! *(Music rises. He dials the phone, waits. Still rattled, his voice hoarse.)* Hi, Audrey. Pull up David Calhoun on the computer. What's his number? Thanks. *(He waits. He hangs up. He dials. He waits.)* Hi, is this Cathy? Yeah, this is Brad Youngquist. Yeah, from the video store. No, I know, there's, it's not overdue yet, listen, I just thought you should know your husband's fucking my wife. *(He slams down the phone, sits on the bed. Lights shift as music rises.)*

Scene Five

Brad rises slowly from the bed and moves into a pool of light downstage.

BRAD: Dear Beth. The boys are staying at Denny and Sonya's tonight, the house is a mess, and I'm a little drunk. ("No, you're a big drunk," I can hear you say in my mind.) As you of all people know, I'm not very good with words. And I know I'm not easy to live with. But I hope you'll give me another chance. I'm willing to put all of this shit behind us if you'll give me another chance. I want another chance. I need another chance. You're the best thing that has ever happened to me in my life, and I can't believe I'm sitting here on the edge of losing you forever. If you're really happier with the pharmacist, then I guess you should be with him, but I really hope that after a few days up there at Chez Youngquist, you'll want to come home to me. I'll build you your own bathroom up there, if you want. I love you, Beth. I'm not perfect, but I do love you the best I know how, and I can learn and change and be better, if you'll just come home. You are so pretty. Looking around right now, I see you are the pretty part of everything here. Without you here, this place is really a dump. And I don't mean cleaningwise. You know what I mean. Please come home if you want to and we will be lovers again. From the bottom of an ocean of that awful beer your brother makes and which I finally got desperate enough to take a crack at . . . your biggest fan . . . Brad.

(Brad turns and exits upstage and sits down in his seat. Music continues.)

Scene Six

David and Cathy are on the bed. The atmosphere is one of grim, slightly absurd resignation. Note: this entire scene should be done quietly enough to indicate that neither participant wishes to wake the children.

CATHY: I'm not going to tell the kids for you.
DAVID: I wouldn't ask you to.
CATHY: Oh, I think you would. I think you were just about to.
DAVID: I wasn't.
CATHY: It's going to seriously mess up Gus.
DAVID: I'll work it out with him.

CATHY: The girls I can handle, I can train them not to hate men — I would have had to do that anyway — but Gus, I don't have access to him.

DAVID: I don't either, really —

CATHY: *That's* an excuse.

DAVID: Look, I said I'll talk to him! I'll talk to them in the morning.

CATHY: Then I'll leave the house, because I don't think I can take it.

DAVID: Look, do you want me to go?

CATHY: No.

(Long pause.)

CATHY: You know what I want?

DAVID: What?

CATHY: You want to do what I want? You want to console me? Make yourself feel better?

DAVID: What?

(She crawls on top of him, clearly trying to initiate sex. Brief pause.)

DAVID: I can't.

CATHY: Why? Because you don't "love" me anymore? Your license to say shit like that has been permanently revoked.

DAVID: Cathy, this won't stop me from leaving.

CATHY: Oh, stop being so vain. Did it ever occur to you that maybe I'm glad to be rid of you? You're such a shit to the kids lately anyway, David, it's probably all for the best.

DAVID: Honey, I think you're a little confused.

(She slaps his face hard.)

CATHY: No. I'm not. I know exactly what I'm doing. OK?

DAVID: OK.

(Straddling him, she begins slowly moving her hips up and down. Just a little.)

CATHY: Give me your hands.

DAVID: No.

CATHY: Come on, hold me up a little.

(After a moment, he offers his hands. They link hands.)

DAVID: I can't get it up. I won't. I can't.

CATHY: You're so noble. It's touching. Let's get Beth on the phone and tell her how you're enduring this trial so gallantly by refusing to get an erection.

DAVID: This really doesn't seem like you.

CATHY: David, you're so self-involved, I don't think you really know what seems like me or doesn't seem like me anymore.

DAVID: You might be right.

CATHY: Hold me around the back.

DAVID: No! Just . . . get off me . . .

CATHY: David, if you want to go stay somewhere else, then do it, but if you're gonna stay here, then . . .

DAVID: What?

CATHY: *(After a long beat.)* Get on the team!

DAVID: "Get on the team."

CATHY: Yes! Get on the team . . . you jerk.

(Brief pause. He laughs a little, she laughs back, and he relents, puts his hands on her behind, beneath her nightgown. She continues moving above him. After a while, she leans down and kisses him. He does not respond. She begins kissing his face, shoulders, and chest every now and then.)

CATHY: How is it with Beth?

DAVID: What?

CATHY: The sex.

DAVID: You don't want to know.

CATHY: Yes I do.

DAVID: It's great.

CATHY: It's easy for it to be great when you don't have to watch the person pee every morning.

DAVID: So I should wake up and realize Beth won't do it for me once I've got her all to myself, twenty-four hours a day.

CATHY: That, and the self-hatred for what you've done to the kids. And Brad showing up every morning to take a shit on your porch.

DAVID: Did he tell you that?

CATHY: Yeah.

DAVID: That guy is fascinated with shitting on things. I think he must hold his tension in his ass, that's why he's always got prostate problems.

CATHY: And where do you hold yours?

DAVID: My tension?

CATHY: Mmhmm.

DAVID: The obvious answer is my dick, I guess, I don't know, you obviously have a plan —

CATHY: I think you hold it in me.

DAVID: I hold *my* tension in *you*. That's a trick.

CATHY: Isn't it? See, I think, in little ways you ask me to hold it for you, and I do, and then you hate me for helping you, so you run off and generate passionate feelings for other women.

DAVID: There are no other women, it's just Beth. It's always been just Beth.

CATHY: Katie Amundson.

DAVID: Did you and Brad have dinner or something together?

CATHY: We had coffee.

DAVID: Where?

CATHY: At Sundberg's.

DAVID: You shit!

CATHY: It wasn't my idea. It was Brad's, he said he wanted to infiltrate the enemy camp.

DAVID: Right in front of everybody at Sundberg's?

CATHY: David, it's a free world! You've proved that. It's a great, big, ugly, free world.

(Long silence. Suddenly they kiss with real abandon, tinged with anger, for the first time. After a while, she pulls back.)

CATHY: Today in class, I was handing back tests . . .

DAVID: Yeah?

CATHY: I'd given them this very simple ear-training test, just for fun, and little Jason Pearson, he said, "Mrs. Calhoun? I got nine out of twenty-five. Is that good?" So I sent him down to Ed's room, I said, "Go ask your math teacher."

DAVID: You still like teaching?

CATHY: I do. It's . . . you know what it is, ultimately? I think it's as simple as I enjoy the company of kids. *(After a moment.)* You know who doesn't like school, though . . .

DAVID: Ruthie.

CATHY: She was complaining to me today about how all her teachers expect her to be perfect. She said, "The more I do better, the more they expect me to do better. It's too much." She said that about twenty times, staring into the rearview mirror like this total drama queen: "It's too much. It's too much."

DAVID: Are you trying to make me sentimental about the kids? It's working.

CATHY: I'm just telling you about your children, David. I'm not as cagey as you think.

DAVID: You're the smartest person *I* know.

CATHY: No, I'm not. I don't like all that noodly crap you read, all that poetry and philosophy and stuff —

DAVID: No, you know what I mean, you're smart about bullshit.

CATHY: So why do you want to be with her? You want somebody dumb?

DAVID: She's not dumb. She's just a little more naïve than you.

CATHY: She'd have to be, to think you could actually love her.

DAVID: I do love her.

CATHY: Uh, huh.

DAVID: I do!

CATHY: David, can you please reach a little inside me and do your part?

(He's nonplussed.)

CATHY: What?

DAVID: I don't know, you've never been this direct before.

CATHY: Well, our marriage is essentially over, right?

DAVID: I think so, yeah.

CATHY: You're leaving me for Beth, right, you two are gonna go be boyfriend and girlfriend?

DAVID: I hope so.

CATHY: Then do I really need to waste my dignity on you?

DAVID: OK.

(He does something beneath her nightgown which registers a nonverbal response.)

CATHY: Thank you.

(A few moments without words pass.)

CATHY: I thought you said you couldn't get it up.

DAVID: Honey, this is just making me sad.

CATHY: Look, unless you want me to start screaming . . . at the top of my lungs . . . and have the children come running in here . . . and watch you pack your bags right now, you'll shut up, OK?

(Brief pause.)

DAVID: OK.

(Brief pause.)

CATHY: I want you inside me.

(David sighs.)

CATHY: Shit, David, would you please stop pretending to care? Picture *her*. Or Katie Amundson.

DAVID: I don't have to picture anybody else.

CATHY: Don't do me any favors.

DAVID: I do think you're pretty.

CATHY: *(Quoting* The Rainmaker.*)* "You're pretty, Lizzie. You're pretty."

DAVID: Shut up!

CATHY: You shut up!

(A moment passes. Through a silent agreement, over the course of ten seconds or so, they work together to get him inside her.)

CATHY: There. Isn't that better?

DAVID: Better than what?

CATHY: Fighting.

DAVID: It feels like fighting to me. I feel like I'm getting the shit beat out of me.

CATHY: Good.

> (Brief pause. As the scene continues, the pace of their physicality accelerates slightly, their words more and more broken up by breaths and silences. This acceleration is gentle, however, and the volume is never loud enough to wake up the kids.)

CATHY: It was actually fun . . . having coffee with Brad. He's such a palooka. He's kinda sweet.

DAVID: He's not very sweet to Beth.

CATHY: Poor her. But he's not as dumb as you think, David. He's known about you two for a long time, long before he called.

DAVID: She told him?

CATHY: No, don't worry, your little sweetie didn't betray your confidence. He just knew. He told me . . . he told me the day he figured it out, he was driving by Warehouse Foods . . . and he saw a man and a woman loading groceries into the back of a car. One was lifting them out of the cart and then handing them . . . handing them to the other one to put into the trunk. And he said it suddenly occurred to him, "I bet they think they're two different people."

DAVID: What the hell does that mean?

CATHY: That's what I said. He said for one second, it looked to him like they were really one person, but with two bodies. But one person. Connected. By invisible threads. And that's when he knew.

DAVID: Brad said this.

CATHY: Yeah.

DAVID: The video-store guy.

CATHY: Yeah, I know. But what it made *me* think was . . . what I didn't tell *him* . . . what it made me think was . . . maybe we're *all* the same person.

DAVID: How so?

CATHY: Maybe all of us . . .

> (Their lovemaking escalates.)

DAVID: Are you OK?

CATHY: I'm OK. Are you OK?

DAVID: I'm OK.

CATHY: OK. Maybe all of us . . . sometimes it feels like we all know we were together once . . . we all *were* one person . . . and things were better. But for some reason, it's all gotten broken up somehow, it's all splintered and broken up . . . how it all was. And even though we know . . . we're destroying everything . . . by imagining we're not connected . . . even though we know it's a lie to break the promises and . . . do the harm we do . . . to each other . . . maybe we *have* to.

DAVID: Why?

CATHY: You tell me. That's why I'm asking.

(Brief pause.)

CATHY: What could be worth hurting someone else this much? *What?*

DAVID: Love?

CATHY: See, that's too disgusting to even think about. I'm gonna come.

DAVID: Me too.

(After a few minutes of wordless intercourse, they both have orgasms. She collapses onto him. A long time passes in silence.)

DAVID: I'll tell the kids in the morning.

(Brief pause.)

CATHY: *(With great sadness but no tears.)* Fine.

(After a moment or two, she begins to cry. He moves to put his arms around her. She sits up a little, still on top of him, and pushes his arms away.)

CATHY: *(Still crying.)* No! I don't want any sympathy. I don't want any of your shitty little sympathy.

(Brief pause. He wipes her tears away as they fall on his face.)

CATHY: Sorry.

(She settles back down onto him. He does not embrace her; his arms lie stretched out impotently at his sides. A moment. Then music rises. Lights shift.)

Scene Seven

David and Cathy rise from the bed and get dressed. Once dressed, David goes upstage to his seat. Beth rises, wearing a raincoat and carrying an umbrella, and meets Cathy downstage in a pool of gray light. Sounds of rain and periodic thunder can be heard; nothing too threatening. They are both focused on the soccer field. Cathy is eating candy from a small bag.

CATHY: That Arshavir is something else, isn't he?

BETH: *(Uncomfortable.)* Uh, I just thank God, for Carl's sake, he's on the team.

CATHY: Gussie, too.

BETH: He's a natural.

CATHY: *(To the field.)* Get in there, Gus! Good man!

(Brief pause. Thunderclap and the sound of intensified rain.)

BETH: Do you want to get under here?

CATHY: Sure. Thanks. You want some Sour Skittles?

BETH: No, thanks.

CATHY: Gus tells me they're the biggest thing to happen to candy since Gushers. They're not bad.

BETH: *(After a beat.)* I'll try one. I've seen the commercials, I was wondering. *(Cathy gives her some candy. They eat a moment in silence. After a beat, Beth holds out her hand for some more.)*

BETH: Just, like, two.

CATHY: See what I mean?

BETH: Yeah.

(Brief pause as they chew.)

CATHY: So look, what am I doing here with candy, I'll tell you, I'm the one who's going to be taking over your "Meals On Wheels" route.

BETH: You're joining First Lutheran?

CATHY: Well, David doesn't believe in God, as I'm sure you know, but now that he's out of the house, I don't care, I'm gonna at least get 'em baptized. So they don't rot in Hell.

BETH: Yeah, I think that's good.

CATHY: You can tell him, too.

BETH: I don't . . . whatever. You can tell him if you want.

CATHY: Anyway, I just wanted to warn you, I'll be the one showing up at the church to get trained-in, so don't freak out.

BETH: Thanks. I could get someone else to do it, if you want — I mean — it's pretty much nothing —

CATHY: No, I think this is what church is for, right? Breaking down the barriers we put up in the world? Between people?

BETH: Are you serious?

CATHY: In a funny kind of way, yeah. I mean, it should be. That's the point, right?

BETH: In theory.

CATHY: Well . . . here's a barrier.

BETH: Yes, here is one, you're right.

CATHY: *(To the field.)* You have to run, Gus! You have to actually run! *(Cathy offers Beth more candy. She takes a few.)*

BETH: Thanks.

CATHY: *(To Beth.)* But you, you're quitting.

BETH: Yeah, who told you that?

CATHY: Pastor Ed.

BETH: Why did he tell you that?

CATHY: Why are you quitting?

BETH: *(After a beat.)* Are you really asking me?

CATHY: Yeah.

BETH: Why?

CATHY: Because I want you to know you don't have to quit because of me and the kids, that's all. I wouldn't want that.

BETH: Wouldn't you?

CATHY: No.

BETH: I'm quitting because . . .

CATHY: David's making you.

BETH: No. No, I'm quitting because when I try to pray now . . . I feel stupid.

CATHY: I think everybody feels that way. It's a stupid thing to do.

BETH: *(Very absently, with an eye on the soccer game.)* When I was really little, you know, I thought God was like my dad, only bigger. And, uh, just like it felt to walk through our house where my dad had built all the furniture, that's how it felt to walk through the whole world. Everything seemed like it had a little note taped to it: "Thought you might like this tree!" "Thought you might like this sunset!" "Thought you might like this cute boy! I made him just for you!" You know what I mean?

CATHY: I do.

BETH: I told my guidance counselor in high school, you won't believe this, I told her I didn't need to choose a career, because God had a plan for my life. But she said she was part of how God let people *in* on His plans. And I believed her. And *that* was the beginning of the end . . . because after that, it was so easy to see everything that way. Making out in the back of Jeff Kosternople's VW bus seemed like God's way of letting me *in* on something; and drinking too much in college was God's way of letting me *in* on something. And now, just when I would really love to look out over those trees and see a little note: "Hi Beth! Thought you might like this world" — I look around and there are no notes on anything, anywhere. *(After a beat.)* Cathy, I'm really sorry about what's happened. If it ever felt like a choice, I'd have chosen differently, but it never did. I'm sorry.

CATHY: Are you going to keep the kids?

BETH: Not if Brad has his way. His lawyer's really good, it's kinda scary.

CATHY: So it'll just be you and David.

BETH: Looks like.

CATHY: You should know, he's had a low sperm count the past few years.
(Beth laughs hollowly.)
CATHY: What?
BETH: (As if having heard a death sentence.) Nothing.
CATHY: We were trying up until two years ago to have one more. He blamed
me until we went to a doctor in the Cities and did the tests. But who
knows, if he's happier with you, maybe that'll bring it back up. It works
that way sometimes. In which case, if it does, let me tell you, he's very
good with babies. Loves babies. But once they're no longer helpless, he
blames them for everything. He can be very petty when it comes to —
BETH: Cathy?
CATHY: What?
BETH: I really don't want to have this conversation.
CATHY: Oh. OK. But I'll see you on Wednesday.
BETH: Yeah. I'll show you how to feed the old people.
CATHY: Beth, I hate to tell you this, but I think we are the old people.
(Thunder claps as Cathy exits upstage to her chair. Music rises. Lights shift
as Beth enters the bedroom area and joins David there. Lights shift.)

Scene Eight

David and Beth are standing in the bed area, both fully dressed, wearing
jackets.

BETH: It's a nice house.
DAVID: I like the trees. I killed every tree at our house within about three years
of moving in. It'd be fun to have trees again.
BETH: Something to kill.
DAVID: No, I'd be better to these trees.
(Brief pause as they look around the room.)
BETH: It would be nice to have a few more bedrooms.
DAVID: (A little edgy.) I know, but it's all about what we can afford at this point —
BETH: I just —
DAVID: What? (Referring to the realtor.) Just say it, she's downstairs staring into
that pager of hers. Say it. I know what you're gonna say.
BETH: (Whispering.) I can't have Carl and Kevin thinking they don't have their
own room at Mommy's house.
DAVID: And what about my kids?

BETH: I feel the same for them.

DAVID: Oh, you do?

BETH: Yes.

DAVID: The exact same.

BETH: David, don't start that again —

DAVID: Look, we both know, this is how much house we can afford right, did we have the conversation or not? Did we sit there and add it all up or not?

BETH: David, if Carl and Kevin don't feel at home here now, if we don't make it a welcoming place for them now, they'll never feel like they belong.

DAVID: So what do you want me to do?

BETH: I don't know!

DAVID: If you know this is how much house we can afford, then what are you asking me to do?

BETH: I'm not . . . asking you to do anything!

DAVID: It seems like you are!

BETH: No, I just said I wish there were more bedrooms!

DAVID: Which is an indictment of me.

BETH: No, it's a fact.

DAVID: No, it's not, it's an indictment of me.

BETH: Would you stop? We're choosing to do this and it's . . . it's just hard to face the limits of it, that's all.

DAVID: And the limits are set by the fact I don't make enough money to buy a house with six bedrooms, or however many you think would be enough for everyone to feel "at home!" It's an indictment of me!

BETH: If you want to see it that way, for some sick, self-destructive reason —

DAVID: There's no other way to see it!

BETH: That's not true!

DAVID: Yes it is! You don't want to work, so my salary is it, my salary is the border of what's possible —

BETH: I have told you I'm willing to work if it's —

DAVID: No! I don't want you coming home every day, tired and miserable, and blaming it on me! He didn't make you work, I'm not gonna make you work. I won't have you hating me for that. Shit. *(He sits on the bed.)* Isn't this fun. *(Brief pause.)* My kids would like their own rooms too, you know.

BETH: I know.

   (Brief pause.)

DAVID: Shit shit shit.

BETH: I'm sorry I brought it up.

DAVID: To have to . . . to have to be at this kind of point in my life . . . is really discouraging sometimes, you know?

BETH: I think it's sort of fun.

DAVID: Then why do you bring up impossible things I can't do anything about? If it's so fun?

BETH: I wasn't —

DAVID: You don't think it's fun, anyway, that's a shitty patronizing thing to say.

BETH: If I can't be honest with you about what I care about, David, then who can I talk to about it? Who?

DAVID: You can talk to me, but I'd appreciate it if you did it without accusing me of keeping your kids from feeling at home!

BETH: I never said — *(Brief pause.)* Forget it. *(Longer pause.)* Look. Do you like this house?

DAVID: I like it OK. I wish we could get something bigger too, something closer to the lake, like your place —

BETH: But given all that, do you like this house?

DAVID: Yeah, I like it. I like the trees.

BETH: Then let's buy it.

DAVID: No, it doesn't have enough bedrooms.

BETH: David. We'll have a summit meeting with the kids. And we'll let them decide together how to decorate that other bedroom, we'll get two bunkbeds, we'll let them divide up the drawers, we'll put them in charge of everything. What we can't give them in terms of space, we'll give them in terms of autonomy.

DAVID: Don't try to make it better.

BETH: I'm not.

DAVID: Yes you are, you're being like a prairie wife.

BETH: And you're being kind of a jerk.

DAVID: No, I'm not. Look, I didn't fall in love with you so you could be brave and resourceful. I wanted to give you things and treat you better than your asshole husband, not . . . force you to make excuses for why we can't treat your kids like members of the family.

BETH: Your kids, too.

DAVID: I know, but I can carry that, I've been disappointing my kids ever since they were born. Disappointing you is a new feeling. And I don't like it. *(She goes to him.)*

BETH: You want to go back to our kingdom in the clouds.

DAVID: I wouldn't mind.

BETH: With the apples like tall ships, sailing . . .

DAVID: It was better. It was simpler.

BETH: No it wasn't. We were lying all the time and sneaking around.

DAVID: I didn't mind the lying.

BETH: I did.

DAVID: You would've gotten used to it.

BETH: No, I was nervous all the time, and rushing around trying to fit you into my schedule . . . I never got the grocery shopping really totally done the whole time we were seeing each other . . . it was hell.

DAVID: But now you get it done.

BETH: Yes!

DAVID: That's great. Christ, I can feel it starting all over again.

BETH: What does that mean?

DAVID: Just what you said, Beth, it's exactly what you said. We've done it, we've become like them. We're the ones who break up families and buy shitty furniture to fill up ugly houses, we're the ones who ruin the world all for the chance to have sex with someone we want to have sex with. *(Brief pause.)* Don't look that way.

BETH: Is that what you think this is?

DAVID: Isn't it? I mean, what else is it?

BETH: It's love, I thought —

DAVID: "Love."

BETH: I thought that's what it was anyway.

DAVID: Love that tears everything in its path apart. Love that deprives innocent children of their parents.

BETH: Oh, my God . . .

DAVID: Don't get that tone in your voice, please. It's so fucking dramatic.

BETH: I knew this would happen . . .

DAVID: Beth, would you please spare me your fragility just this once, just this once?

BETH: I have left my children —

DAVID: I've left mine too!

BETH: Don't tell me I can't have feelings about that, about how much I've set aside!

DAVID: See, this is how it starts, we're not even in the goddamn house and it's "how much you've set aside" . . .

BETH: David, if you're not comfortable with thinking you're worth it —

DAVID: Don't make it about me!

BETH: Then what —

DAVID: It's what we have together, if it's anything, but I can't take it being about me!

BETH: Then what we have together —

DAVID: Which it might not even *be* —

BETH: If you can't live with what it costs me to be with you, then we shouldn't do this!

DAVID: *(Loud.)* Maybe you're right, maybe we shouldn't! *(Long silence. Quieter.)* Maybe it's all a big mistake. *(Brief pause.)* When I sat Gus down and told him I was moving out . . . you know what I felt? I felt . . . this is terrible to even say . . . I felt . . . I enjoyed making him sad.

BETH: No, you didn't —

DAVID: Yes I did, that's who I am now, I was being all sympathetic but inside I was saying, "See, you little shit, this is how hard it's been for me ever since the day you were born and cemented me into this marriage; now you live with it for a while and see how it feels." I felt that feeling behind the words; behind all the sadness and sympathy, there was just . . . smallness.

BETH: I don't believe that.

DAVID: You don't feel any resentment at all . . . towards them?

BETH: Of course I do, David, they're my kids! But it's been . . . I know you don't want to hear things like this, because I'm not supposed to feel anything that makes you feel guilty, but . . . living without those guys is breaking my heart, resentment and all, it's breaking my heart! I thought I knew what heartbroken was —

DAVID: But being with me has taught you.

BETH: That's not what I'm saying —

DAVID: But that's what the situation *is!*

BETH: You know, *you're* the one a person can't say anything around, you're the one who's fragile —

DAVID: I'm the one who's realistic!

BETH: *Then it's too late to be realistic!*

DAVID: No it's not! You can go back to Brad.

BETH: I don't want to go back to Brad!

DAVID: You want to go back to your boys!

BETH: Yes I do! But I can't!

DAVID: Why? Just go back! Suck it up! Deal with it! I certainly don't want to spend the rest of my life with someone who's this unhappy!

BETH: Neither do I!

DAVID: Then go back! Why don't you just go back?

BETH: *(Whispering fiercely, full of hate and desperation.) Because I'm pregnant, you fucking jerk, you selfish selfish selfish fucking jerk! Because I'm pregnant. (Brief pause. He reaches out to her.)*

BETH: Don't. Don't touch me. Don't you ever . . . ever . . . ever touch me again. *(She wipes her eyes as she cries.)* God. I'm so alone.

(Brief pause. They both look up suddenly toward where the door to the room would be.)

BETH: *(Pulling herself together.)* Here she comes.

Scene Nine

Lights rise on David, downstage.

DAVID: Dear Lily.

(Music rises.)

DAVID: Life goes by so quickly I thought I would take a moment today to sit down and write you a letter. You can't read yet, but I am going to put this in the box Mommy keeps all your pictures in, and you can read it when you're older. Long before you were born, Mommy used to have dreams about you. And she would tell them to me, and we would have so much fun sitting quietly, talking about what you'd be like. It was almost as if you were our friend before you were ever really here! Of course, we didn't really know you then. We didn't know your first word would be "purple," or that you would like eating lamb so much, or that you would be such a great singer! It has been a real treat to find out all the ways we were wrong about you and right about you, and you continue to surprise us every day. Lately, when we put you to bed, you make us say, "Tweety tweety, co-co-coconut, ga ga goo goo, bo bo bo bo, I love you, see you in the morning, sleep well, good night, sleep tight, don't let the bedbugs bite, that's right, that's all, sweet dreams, work well, think twice!" And we don't know where you came up with this from!

Today is a very special day, because it is Christmas Eve! You are so excited! You have asked Santa for a Barbie doll, a puppy, and a tiger — we'll see what happens! But the best news is, today one of Mommy's dreams about you came true. We went to the store this afternoon, and the traffic was very busy and it was snowing, and we got flour and butter and sugar to make cookies. And we got something very strange called orange flower water, to make the cookies smell pretty. In Mommy's dream, you spilled the orange flower water in the backseat — we didn't know then that you would be a good girl who wouldn't do that — but we rolled down the windows anyway as we drove back to our apartment and poured out some of it on the seats, and we were all so happy our hearts almost flew out of us and took off.

What also was different today from Mommy's dream is it was a little sad. Because Mommy and Daddy hurt a lot of people's feelings, and made your half-brothers and half-sisters very sad, just for the chance to be together. And they all visited us this morning, and you cried when they left, because you love them so much and they are very sweet to you. And this is one of life's great mysteries, Lily, my dear little pumpkin seed, and I cannot explain it, but somehow people are always hurting each other and love keeps happening. It just keeps happening. And the longer you live and the more you notice this, the harder it gets to know what's right and wrong. Sometimes it almost seems impossible. All I know is I would not change anything that ever happened, ever, because I am so excited to know you and Mommy and we can't wait to see what you are going to do with your amazing life.

So. That's all. I am wrapping this letter around this little bottle of orange flower water — Mommy's cookies didn't really turn out so good — so you can smell it again when you are bigger and you want to remember all the mixed-up reasons that go into making a miracle like you. Whatever happens to you ever in this life, always remember we love you, Lily, and you are worth *everything*.
(Lights out.)

END OF PLAY

ABSOLVING BUCKNER

by Liam Kuhn

This play is dedicated to those for whom hope springs eternal,
even if success remains elusive (i.e., Red Sox fans everywhere).

PLAYWRIGHT'S BIOGRAPHY

Liam Kuhn is a 2002 graduate of Dartmouth College, where he majored in creative writing and English literature. His short stories have been published in a number of literary magazines and earned him both the Sydney Cox Memorial Prize and the inaugural Richard Eberhart Literary Fiction Award. *Absolving Buckner* was selected by a panel of judges from the Dartmouth faculty as a winner in the 2002 Eleanor Frost Playwriting Competition. In December 2002, Mr. Kuhn was awarded a grant to attend the Vermont Studio Center in Johnson, Vermont, as a writing resident. While staring into the void that is life after college and giving himself an ulcer worrying about things like graduate school and gainful employment, Mr. Kuhn is currently at work on a novel and a full-length script. *Absolving Buckner* is his first play.

ACKNOWLEDGMENTS

For their ceaseless support, advice, and encouragement, I owe a world of gratitude to my family: Liz, Bill, Devin, and Erin. Many thanks also to the original cast and crew whose dedication and enthusiasm showed me how much fun playwriting can be. I'm especially indebted to the judges and producers of the Frost Festival, Professors Joe Sutton and Paul Gaffney, Marisa Smith, Laura Tepper, and my drinking buddies.

INTRODUCTION

I wrote this play when I was in college. I got the idea for it in much the same way that I got all my bright ideas in college — I was procrastinating, half-asleep on a couch with a beer in my hand and sports on the television. The next day, I was due to present a ten-page scenario to Joe Sutton's playwriting class. I had scribbled some vague notes about a bank-robbery-gone-awry-romantic-comedy thing, but it wasn't working out, and my heart wasn't in it. Then I saw (for the hundredth time) a clip from Game Six of the 1986 World Series. The Mets' announcer, Vin Scully, gave the play-by-play, "Little roller back of first . . . and it gets by Buckner! It gets by Buckner and the Mets win! The Mets win the ball game, the Mets win!" The image of Bill Buckner, wobbly legs and all, walking off the field at Shea Stadium, head bowed in shame, is one that's haunted me most of my life.

I grew up in New Jersey, but was not a Mets fan, nor (God forbid) was I a Yankee fan. I liked the Red Sox. Which is to say I liked having my heart broken every year. For a lot of American men, sports are more than mere pastimes. They are self-contained languages, bridges of communication, dreams kept alive. They are therapy. Unless you're a Red Sox fan. Then it's nothing but modern-day Greek tragedy and sadomasochism and endless frustration, but in a weird way, that can be therapeutic, too.

The characters, the setting, the issues of love, friendship, masculinity, and forgiveness all evolved organically into *Absolving Buckner.* It was a fun play to write and I was lucky enough to write it at an immensely fun time of my life. I was a senior in college with very few worries of my own, so I got to make some up for a bunch of fictional people I'd never met.

ORIGINAL PRODUCTION

Absolving Buckner was originally produced at the Bentley Theater in Hanover, New Hampshire as part of the Seventy-fifth Annual Eleanor Frost Playwriting Festival. The play, which opened on May 23, 2002, was directed by Mark Orsini. The set design was by Dan Soule; the lighting designer was John Paul Reid; the costume designer was Sarah Tonnesen; and the stage manager was Abigail Goodhue. The cast was as follows:

BRENDAN . . . . Andrew Dahl
FRANK . . . . Thomas Pasculli
MARTY . . . . Philip Mone
SEAN . . . . Thomas Dickie

CHARACTERS

BRENDAN MALONE: early thirties, a stout, hearty man in comfortable, well-worn clothes.

FRANK SULLIVAN: late twenties, an overeducated, slightly pretentious mailman riddled with insecurities.

SEAN GARRITY: late twenties, with a tired, run-down look.

MARTY NOLAN: early forties, a thin, graying bartender with a slight Irish brogue and an acerbic wit.

TIME

This play takes place on an October night in 2001.

SETTING

The dim interior of O'Shaugnessy's, an Americanized version of an Irish pub, set in a small and fairly remote New England town, not unlike Bellows Falls, Vermont. The bar is an absolute dive. Its shabby, wood-paneled walls are covered with old Bushmills Whiskey mirrors, pub towels, Celtics pennants from their glory days in the 1980s. A poster bearing the slogan "Guinness for Strength" hangs prominently on a back wall. There are a few empty tables scattered about the room, creating a sense of crowded isolation, if that's possible. The most important thing about this bar is that it is anything but a clean, well-lit place. It is dirty and dim, and while it might not be a "tough" bar per se (There are exactly zero Harley Davidsons parked outside), it is a bar where at least an adequate facade of toughness is necessary, despite whatever infirmities lie beneath the surface of its patrons. It is a male-dominated space, and as such, the conversations that take place within O'Shaugnessy's rarely stray from sports, work, sexual exploits (real and imagined), and the type of good-natured mockery and belittling that takes place among men in the absence of women.

Absolving Buckner

As the curtain rises, we see the bartender, Marty Nolan, wiping down a table in the center of the room. Standing behind Marty, waiting to sit down in the center chair at the table, is Brendan Malone. They are alone in the bar and as the lights come up, Marty is in the middle of telling Brendan an old joke.

MARTY: . . . and so then the Pope says to the Rabbi, he goes, *"Tip* her? I don't even *know* her!"
(Laughs.)

BRENDAN: Marty, you're priceless. That's like the fortieth time I've heard you tell that joke and it just keeps getting funnier.

MARTY: *(Missing the sarcasm.)* Come on now, Brendan, don't get all soft on me. This isn't that type of bar, you know. *(Beat.)* Want me to start you off with a pint of the usual?

BRENDAN: Ah, no. Let's hold off on that for now. Just bring over a pitcher when the boys get here.

MARTY: Yeah, where are they anyhow?

BRENDAN: *(Checks his watch, frowns.)* Dunno. They're probably running a little late.

MARTY: No shit they're running a little late. Didn't I just say that? I'm not asking if they're on time, jackass, I'm asking where they're at.

BRENDAN: Maybe they found a place that doesn't water down the beer so much.

MARTY: Yeah, or maybe they finally made some other friends.
(Brendan is genuinely hurt by this comment, despite its good-natured, all-in-fun tone.)

BRENDAN: Jesus, Marty, that's a low thing to say.

MARTY: Loosen up a bit; I was only joking. Here's your man, anyway.
(Marty ambles off exiting stage left as Frank Sullivan enters from stage right. Frank is an intense (but not unhandsome), troubled-looking man, twenty-seven years of age. His clothes suggest a lower-middle class background, and nothing about the way he looks is flashy or ostentatious. His speech patterns, however, don't seem to jibe with his appearance or environment; he makes the fact that he is of above average intelligence and fairly well read quite apparent through the seemingly endless stream of quotes and references that spring from his mouth. His verbosity, considering the type of world he lives in, reflects a certain arrogance. It is important to note, however, that this arrogance is not borne out of a genuine love-of-self, but out of an attempt to counteract

and cover up a deep-seated insecurity and sense of inferiority that has plagued him since his early teenage years. His friends put up with Frank's apparent arrogance because they are used to it — and because that's what friends sometimes have to do.)

(Frank's entrance to the bar, ordinarily so routine a thing, is anything but ordinary or routine tonight. He looks utterly shocked and terrified by something and instead of walking directly to his usual seat at the table, he waits at the side of the stage with great trepidation.)

FRANK: *(Whispered loudly and frantically.)* Brendan!

BRENDAN: What?

FRANK: Brendan! Are you alone?

BRENDAN: Do you *see* anyone else around?

FRANK: Where's Sean?

BRENDAN: I don't know. Not here yet. Quit the fucking shenanigans and sit down.

(A small flush of relief washes over Frank, although not nearly enough to wipe out the look of fear. He hurries over to the table and sits in the chair to the stage left of Brendan.)

BRENDAN: What the hell's wrong with you?

FRANK: I need to talk to you.

BRENDAN: Well, you've come to the right place.

FRANK: This is *very important.*

BRENDAN: What's the matter, Frankie, get bit by a dog on your mail route today?

FRANK: Brendan, something happened. Something happened that might change all of our lives. I'm in no mood for your fucking jokes right now.

BRENDAN: *(His mood changes here, — his needling Frank is no longer entirely good-natured.)* Well maybe I'm in no mood for your fucking stories, Frank. You ever think of that? You ever think of how *old* it gets for me and Sean to sit here every night and listen to you and your self-aggrandizing tales of woe? You ever think of what a drag you can be sometimes?

FRANK: *(Screams.)* Listen to me! *(Softer.)* Please.

(Brendan is shocked by Frank's explosiveness and begins to realize that the atmosphere in the bar tonight is far more charged with emotion than it has ever been. This realization scares Brendan, and he takes a second or two to think before he speaks.)

BRENDAN: OK . . . OK.

(Trying to turn the intensity down a notch with some playful ribbing.)

But if this is going to be another one of your marathon parables, let's get some beer, first. *(Calls offstage.)* Marty!

FRANK: *(Screams.)* SHUT UP! *(Softer.)* We don't have time for that.

BRENDAN: What do you mean, "We don't have time for that"? We're in a fucking bar, Frank. We're practically required to drink.

FRANK: He could get here any minute.

BRENDAN: Who?

FRANK: Sean!

BRENDAN: What the hell are you talking about?

FRANK: I'm trying to explain!

BRENDAN: You're not *saying* anything!

FRANK: You're not letting me talk!

BRENDAN: *(Beat. Softly.)* Talk.

FRANK: *(Sighs, tries to compose himself.)* OK. *(Beat.)* Look, I'm not sure how to tell you this, but . . . I mean, there's no easy way to . . . *(Tails off.)* *(Pause, defeated.)* Fuck it. You were right, let's get a beer.

BRENDAN: *(Calls offstage.)* Marty!

(After a moment or two, Marty enters from stage left carrying a full pitcher of beer and two stacked pint glasses. He places them on the table and exits stage left. Brendan fills the two glasses and hands one to Frank, who grabs the pint and drinks half of it in a gulp, as if he's just crossed a desert. Brendan sips his beer and looks at Frank with concern, worry, and a little fear.)

BRENDAN: So you were saying . . .

FRANK: Something very bad's happened, Brendan. Something horrible. *(Beat.)* I don't know any good way to say this, so I'm just going to start from the beginning.

(Just as Frank is about to launch into his story, Brendan catches something in the corner of his eye offstage left, turns his head and nods in greeting to someone still offstage.)

BRENDAN: Here's Sean anyway.

(An irate Sean Garrity enters from stage left. Sean is a regular-looking guy, — maybe his hair's getting a little thin on top, maybe he's put on a few pounds since his college days, but he still retains a certain undeniable handsomeness. He's the only one wearing a tie, a long gray one that accentuates his pale blue Oxford dress button-down shirt, which looks somewhat wrinkled and has the sleeves rolled up. Despite the fact that he is more formally dressed than his two drinking buddies, Sean somehow manages to look more disheveled and haggard than either of them.)

FRANK: *(Quickly.)* Brendan, I gotta go. I'll go call you later.

(As Sean storms in, Frank quickly drains what's left of his pint and gets up to go.)

FRANK: *(To Sean, who is blocking his path.)* Oh, hey, Sean. I was just leaving.

SEAN: Well, now you're not. Sit down.

FRANK: *(Obviously lying.)* Yeah, I'd love to stay but I just remembered I promised my nephew I'd go to his Pee Wee League Hockey game tonight.

SEAN: *(Screams.)* SIT DOWN!

(Frank sheepishly retreats to his chair. Sean takes off his coat and sits in the chair on the other side of Brendan.)

BRENDAN: Jeez, Sean, you look ready to kill someone.

SEAN: *(Sighs.)* You don't —

(Sean's anger is so consuming that he can't articulate his thoughts. As he stumbles through these false starts, his fists are clenched on the table and his knee is bouncing frantically up and down as his body tries to burn off some of the nervous energy. Finally, he freezes himself and looks down at the table.)

SEAN: *(With quietly smoldering rage.)* I'm gonna need a fucking beer to get through this.

(Sean bounces up from his chair and heads towards the bar, exiting stage left.)

BRENDAN: Wonder what's eating him.

FRANK: Brendan, I *need* to tell you something *right away.*

BRENDAN: Is it a full moon or something? Why the fuck is everyone behaving so goddamned weird tonight? You show up late and start acting all spooked and shit, and now Sean rolls in looking like an irate Mike Tyson hopped up on amphetamines.

FRANK: Brendan, I think I can explain if you'd just —

BRENDAN: I mean, whatever happened to acting normal? It's not like we don't do this every night. You'd think you guys would have the routine down by now. It's not that complex: come to the bar, drink beer, watch the game, shoot the shit, drink more beer. Simple.

FRANK: Stop joking around and *listen* to me!

BRENDAN: Fine.

FRANK: *(Sighs heavily, composes himself.)* Here goes. *(Long pause as he searches for the right words.)* For the past three months, I've been —

(Sean returns from stage left, carrying an empty pint glass. Frank makes a gesture of defeat, — the frustration he feels at not being able to talk to Brendan before Sean returned is clearly evident. Sean walks over to the table and sits down. He fills his glass from the pitcher and takes a long sip of beer.)

SEAN: Well, it's over.

BRENDAN: What is?

SEAN: Everything. You name it, it's over. My marriage, my family, my life.

BRENDAN: What's this all about, you and Shannon get in another fight?

SEAN: Oh yeah. But this time was for real. This wasn't some fight over me getting drunk and puking all over the usher at her sister's wedding or leaving the seat up on the john. This *was serious* . . . Honestly, I think it might be over between us.

FRANK: Why, what happened?

SEAN: Guys, I only tell you this because you're my best friends. Hell, you're my only friends. You've been there for me in the past and you know how much Shannon means to me . . . meant to me. And I know this is the kind of thing that happens all the time in a lot of marriages and some actually get stronger because of it, but —

BRENDAN: Jesus, boy, out with it already. What happened?

SEAN: *(Exhales, then, with somber gravity.)* Shannon's cheating on me.

BRENDAN: *(With genuine shock and disbelief.)* What?

SEAN: Yeah, she —

FRANK: *(With the slightest hint of defensiveness.)* How can you tell?

SEAN: I found — Look, I just fucking know, OK? It doesn't matter how I can tell, all that matters is that she would do something like that to me. She's cheating on me. What more do you need to know?

BRENDAN: *(Soothingly.)* Calm down there, Sean. I'm sure that there's a perfectly rational expla —

SEAN: Don't tell me to calm down! This isn't some junior prom date who has too much spiked punch and winds up jerking off the guy next to me in the limo. This is my wife. This is *Shannon. (Begins to break down a little.)* I loved her. She was the only woman I ever really . . . *(Voice trails off. Almost inaudibly.)* You have no clue . . . no fucking clue.

(*Unused to such unabashed displays of genuine emotion, the men attend to their pint glasses to lessen the tension and fill the awkward silence that has descended upon the bar.*)

FRANK: Sean, buddy, c'mon. Maybe she's not cheating on you. Sometimes people do things that could easily be misconstrued as . . . *(Tails off.)* I mean, if you didn't catch her in the act, how can you be absolutely positive that she —

SEAN: What the hell is wrong with you? What fucking difference does it make if I caught her in the act or not?

FRANK: *(Rather feebly.)* It's just that —

SEAN: I told you Shannon's cheating on me. There's nothing to debate. End of story. And I told you this shit because I thought you were my friend and would understand. And now you drop this Inspector Clouseau crap on me? What is that, Frank? I know you read a lot of books and like to pretend that you're some big fucking genius, but keep your goddamned hypotheses to yourself, Columbo, or I swear to God I'll ram my fucking shoe night through your teeth.

BRENDAN: Sean, there's no need for that. We're here for you. I think what Frankie was trying to say was that maybe things aren't quite as bad as you think. If you don't have any solid proof, any real evidence that she was —

SEAN: This is absurd. Whose side are you guys on? Jesus Christ, if I knew this was the kind of shit I'd get from my so-called friends, I never would have opened my mouth in the first place.

FRANK: We're just trying to help you look at things objectively.

SEAN: That's not what you're supposed to do!

BRENDAN: What *are* we supposed to do?

(*Sean's frustration has reached a breaking point. His anger turns in on himself and he becomes very small. His answer sounds as if it is coming from deep within some repressed part of him, as if spoken by a small, defeated, pouting child.*)

SEAN: You're supposed to tell me that it's all right. That I'm better without her. That I don't need her. You're supposed to tell me that it'll all be OK.

FRANK: It will be OK.

SEAN: (*Irate again; explosive.*) You don't know that! You don't fucking know that. How do you know?

FRANK: I'm only trying to —

SEAN: This is bullshit! I don't know why I'm here. I don't know what I thought I could gain by coming here, by telling you . . . (*Tails off.*) I can't fucking stand this!

(*Sean pounds most of his pint, slams the glass on the table, gets up, throws down some crumpled dollar bills, and turns to leave.*)

BRENDAN: Sean, wait, don't go.

FRANK: Where are you going?

(*Brendan makes a move to get up and go follow after Sean, but Frank puts a hand on his arm to stop him, pulling him back into his seat. Sean continues to leave, without looking back, and finally exits stage left. Both Frank and Brendan watch him go, then sit in silence, stunned, for a few moments.*)

FRANK: Holy shit.

BRENDAN: I've never seen him like that before.

FRANK: (*Beat, shaking his head.*) That's what I was trying to tell you about before he got here.

BRENDAN: *(Confused.)* What are you talking about? You knew about it?
(*Frank is silent. He looks down at his beer. Pause.*)

BRENDAN: Frank?
(*Frank slowly looks up from his beer but does not speak.*)

BRENDAN: *(Incensed.)* You fucking knew about this and you didn't say anything, Frankie?

FRANK: *(Long pause.)* *(Softly and with a great deal of anguish.)* Brendan, it was me. I'm the one. I've been sleeping with Shannon.

BRENDAN: *(Flatly.)* That's not funny, Frank.

FRANK: I know.

BRENDAN: *(Pauses, frowns incredulously.)* Are you . . . *(Tails off.)* You're serious, Frankie?

FRANK: *(Quietly, with great shame, almost whispered.)* Yes.

BRENDAN: Jesus.

FRANK: I didn't want you to find out like this. I mean, I wanted to let you know . . . I wanted to own up to it before you heard it from Sean.

BRENDAN: How could you do it?

FRANK: Look, I know what I did was wrong. Unconscionable. Sometimes I still can't even believe it ever happened. But it did. *(Beat.)* I — I don't need you to judge me. I need you to help me. I need you to *forgive* me.

BRENDAN: You expect me to just sit here and — and . . . *(Tails off.)* Frank, I'm *Sean's friend.* I'm your friend, too, but I'm not your confessor. And this . . . this is some major league shit, Frankie. This changes everything.

FRANK: I know. *(Beat.)* It's just . . . it's eating me up inside, Brendan. I feel awful. I don't know what to do.

BRENDAN: *You* feel awful? How the hell do you think Sean feels?

FRANK: I know —

BRENDAN: *(His shock begins to turn to anger.)* I don't think you do, Frank. If you did, there's no way you would have done what you *did*. *(Beat.)* I can't believe you.
(*Frank takes a long sip of beer followed by an equally long pause.*)

FRANK: Look, I'm not trying to condone my actions . . . but, in my defense, it's not like he's been treating Shannon right lately.

BRENDAN: Frank, you're missing the point!

FRANK: *(Missing the point.)* Am I? So they're married. So what? Maybe they shouldn't be. Sean's a good guy and all, but can you imagine being his fucking wife? Shannon deserves more. She *needs* more. *(Realizes Brendan's not buying it, pauses, tries different approach.)* Look, she confides in me. She tells me things. The woman has dreams, Brendan. She doesn't want to spend her whole life trapped in this piece-of-shit town, stuck in a dead-end marriage. Sean can't offer her a way out like I can.

BRENDAN: You pathetic little piece of shit! How can you sit here and try to bullshit me like that? You make yourself out like some knight in shining armor — Frank, you're a fucking *mailman.* You're no savior. Sean's not a monster. He doesn't mistreat Shannon. He doesn't hold her back. You're his friend, Frankie. How could you do this? You've been his friend since like grade school.

FRANK: *(In a tone of far-off reminiscence.)* Second grade. I can still remember when we first met. Mr. Dempsey's gym class. I was the kickball captain and Sean was the kid nobody wanted on their team. It's not that he wasn't good, he just never seemed to care about the game, he never seemed to try at all. And one day, when I had to choose between him and Herbert Snodgrass —

BRENDAN: Frank, as touching and heartwarming as I'm sure this story no doubt is, now is not the time for a leisurely stroll down memory lane.

FRANK: Fine. *(Beat.)* But my point is, even back then Sean never really tried hard, never really gave anything a hundred percent. I think Shannon senses that. A marriage needs total commitment; it needs an investment that I don't think Sean's willing or capable enough to give it. Nietzsche called marriage "the will that moves two to create the one which is more than those who created it."

BRENDAN: Shut up! Just shut the fuck up with that crap! I don't give a rat's ass what Nietzsche or anyone else has to say. None of that matters! The only thing that makes any difference now is what you think . . . and what you're prepared to do about all this.

FRANK: What do you mean? I think I've already done enough.

BRENDAN: You little prick. Don't you get it? You can't just stay friends with the guy whose wife you're boning. It doesn't work that way. Something's got to give.

FRANK: Well, what if he never finds out it was me?

BRENDAN: He's gonna find out.

FRANK: What if he doesn't? What he doesn't know can't hurt him. This way, instead of being his enemy, I can be there for him. I can support him, help him get things back on track, back to normal . . .

BRENDAN: *(Explosive.)* No you can't! *You've fucked it all up!* Don't you see? It can't be like it *was,* not now, not after this shit.

FRANK: *(Pathetically.)* Trust me, Bren, it'll never happen again.

BRENDAN: *(Sneeringly.)* Well that's fucking typical, Frank.

FRANK: What is?

BRENDAN: You pick now as the time to bail out. You couldn't have quit before this really got started. You couldn't have ended it before you slept with her. No, you pussy out now, when you might get hurt. You're not a man, Frank, you're a little chickenshit boy who's in way over his head.

FRANK: Brendan, I don't need this from you. I told you because I thought you could help.

BRENDAN: *(Snaps.)* You don't need this from me!? I don't need this from *you!* Do you ever think of anyone besides yourself? Don't you see the position you've put me in?

FRANK: *(Pleading.)* Brendan, stop it, please, I didn't mean to —

BRENDAN: *(Even louder.)* Hold on there, lover boy. I'm just getting started. *(Maliciously.)* I mean, to think that you not only had the nerve to sleep with Shannon, but to also think that you could somehow still be friends with Sean? Like he'll just forget about this? And now you expect me to choose sides here? *(Very loudly and maliciously.)* God, Frank, why don't I just go over there, into the bathroom, and pull my pants down around my ankles and bend over for you? Wouldn't that make it a whole lot easier for you, since you're so fucking intent on screwing over all your friends! *(At this point, Marty enters from stage left, wiping his hands with a bar towel. He walks quickly, but quietly, over to the table where Brendan and Frank sit.)*

MARTY: *(In an embarrassed, friendly tone.)* Guys, guys, please. If you could just keep it down a bit.

BRENDAN: *(Snaps at Marty.)* What?

MARTY: All I'm saying is that you guys are getting a little loud. Maybe if I brought you another pitcher —

FRANK: Marty, we're just having a conversation.

BRENDAN: Yeah, this is a bar, not a library.

MARTY: I know, fellas. I'm just asking that you tone things down a notch. If it gets too loud, then the other customers — *(Frank, rather suddenly, starts to lose it. All the anger that he feels at Brendan and himself he channels toward Marty.)*

FRANK: Look around, Marty . . . what other customers!? *(Rises from his chair. Stresses each word, gestures around the room.)* Look around you! There is NO ONE ELSE HERE! Can't you see that? Can't you see? WE ARE ALL ALONE! Goddamnit! *(Frank breaks down and collapses in his chair, with his head in his hands, sobbing. Brendan and Marty exchange confused, surprised glances. They are silent for several seconds before Brendan moves toward Frank and puts a comforting arm around him. The impact of this outburst is enormous, it is enough to make Brendan believe, at least for the time being, that Frank is the more tortured of his two friends.)*

FRANK: *(Muttering, barely audible.)* Can't you see?

MARTY: *(Weakly.)* I'll, uh . . . I'll leave you guys alone for now.
(Marty exits stage left.)

BRENDAN: *(Soothingly.)* Frank, it's OK. Calm down.

FRANK: *(Very softly.)* I'm sorry . . . I'm sorry.

BRENDAN: I know, Frankie. Come on, now. Calm down. Here, have a drink.
(Brendan pours the remaining contents of the pitcher into Frank's pint glass and slides it towards him.)

BRENDAN: Come on. Pull it together . . . *(Beat.)* Things'll work out somehow.
(Frank lifts his head from his hands and stares at Brendan.)

FRANK: No. No they won't . . . It's worse than you think.

BRENDAN: What are you talking about?

FRANK: Brendan, she's going to leave him. Permanently.

BRENDAN: *(Dismissively.)* No, I don't think so. They'll get through this. They'll work something out. You'll see.

FRANK: No, you don't understand. She *told* me.

BRENDAN: She told you she was going to leave, for good?

FRANK: Yeah. She meant it, too. And it's my fault. It's all my fault. *(Beat.)* She loves him. She really does. It's just, I put all these thoughts in her mind. About getting out of here, about following her dreams, living a new life, all that shit. I told her she would never become anything with Sean. I said all these awful things. He was *my friend,* Brendan.

BRENDAN: *(Softly.)* Why'd you do it, Frank? I mean, do you love her?

FRANK: *(Long pause.)* No. *(Beat.)* No. That's the worst part. I don't even love her. I just said all that stuff to see what would happen. To see what I could do . . . to see if it was in me . . . if I had the power to make a woman just . . . *(Tails off.)* She's throwing it all away.

BRENDAN: Maybe not. Maybe it's not too late. Talk to her. Tell her the mistake she's about to make. It's not too late. She'll understand. If she loves Sean, they'll work things out.

FRANK: It's too late.

BRENDAN: *(Slight pause while he considers something.)* It can't be. *(Beat.)* Look, Sean doesn't know it was you, does he? Well, it's like you said: what he doesn't know can't hurt him. Just convince Shannon to go back to Sean and make her swear to never tell him that it was you. That'll work.

Things'll go back to normal and he'll just think she had some meaning-less fling with some guy he's never met. Happens all the time.

FRANK: *(Quietly.)* Brendan, stop. I know what you're trying to do and I appre-ciate it, but it can't go on. You were right, it doesn't work like that.

BRENDAN: *(With growing conviction.)* No, really, it might work. I mean, if you could convince Shannon to leave her husband, you could talk her into going back to him. And Sean himself said that these things sometimes make marriages stronger. The damage doesn't have to be permanent; noth-ing's irrevocable.

FRANK: *(Sternly.)* Forget it. It won't work.

BRENDAN: *(Like an angry child throwing a temper-tantrum.)* But it *has* to! Don't you see? It *has* to work out. If it doesn't, then where does that leave me? If Sean leaves Shannon and you and he aren't friends anymore, then I'm all alone.

FRANK: *(A little taken aback.)* What are you talking about?

BRENDAN: I need this. *(Indicates his surroundings.)* I need to be able to come to this bar and have a few drinks with my friends. I don't have a perfect life, Frank, but up until tonight it's been a pretty good one. I love my wife and I love my daughters and I have a decent job, but Jesus, Frankie, it wears you down. You need a place to unwind, you need people you can *talk* to. And this shit tonight . . . I don't know . . . I just feel every-thing spinning out of control.

FRANK: *(Beat.)* *I* don't know what to say, Brendan.

BRENDAN: Forget it. Just forget I said anything about it.

(There's a long, embarrassed silence that Frank finally breaks, tentatively.)

FRANK: She's telling him tomorrow. At dinner. That's why I needed to say some-thing tonight. They've had this dinner planned for weeks. It's like the anniversary of when they first met or something like that. She's going to wait until dessert and then she's going to tell him she wants a divorce. He's been suspicious of the affair for a couple weeks already, but he's always thought it was just something they could work through, just some minor flaw in the relationship that they could fix and make everything OK again.

BRENDAN: Well wasn't it? I mean, wasn't that why she turned to you?

FRANK: It wasn't even that. She loves him. She never stopped loving him. It's just — she has dreams for bigger things. Things that I convinced her Sean would never be able to provide.

BRENDAN: And that you could give her?

FRANK: Oh, no. The girl's not stupid, Bren. She knows I can't offer her shit. I'm a fucking post office pedagogue . . . a mailman moralist. I'm no ticket out of here . . . I'm about as phony as they come and I'm pretty sure she senses that.

BRENDAN: But if she still loves Sean and she knew you couldn't offer her anything better —

FRANK: *(Finishing Brendan's thought.)* Then why would she throw it all away? Good question. I guess I don't really have a good answer to that one. It's kind of like that story about the dog with the bone.

BRENDAN: *(Sarcastically.)* Great, Frank, another fucking parable.

FRANK: Do you get what I'm saying or not?

BRENDAN: As usual, I've got no fucking clue.

FRANK: Man, you *must* have heard this one before. There's a dog with a bone and he's walking near a lake or something and he stops to look at his reflection in the water. He's got this big bone in his mouth and he sees his image reflected off the lake, but since he's a dog and dogs don't know any better, he thinks he's looking at *another* dog with another bone in *its* mouth. So he leans over the lake and opens his mouth to try to get the bone from the reflection and of course his bone — the real one — drops down into the water and the poor son of a bitch is left without any bones at all.

BRENDAN: That's the dumbest story I've ever heard.

FRANK: That's not the point.

BRENDAN: I mean, he's a dog, why didn't he just jump in the lake and get the bone back? Dogs know how to swim.

FRANK: Brendan, shut the fuck up and *listen* to me. The point is, there didn't have to be any other bone in Shannon's case. All she needed was a reflection, an *image* —

BRENDAN: Lemme get this straight. First, you sleep with Shannon. Then, you break up her marriage. Now you're calling her a dog? That's messed up.

FRANK: I'm ignoring you. *(Beat.)* Anyway, what I'm saying is, for someone like Shannon, it was just the idea of something better, even if there wasn't really anything behind it; that was enough. And tomorrow night, she's going to drop her bone, the real one, into the water and never see it again. *(Beat. Sadly.)* And it's all because of me.

(Brendan realizes that Frank is serious and deeply upset. A strange, awkward silence hangs in the atmosphere for a while before Marty reemerges from stage left with another pitcher of beer and brings it over to their table.)

MARTY: Here, guys, I noticed you were running a little low. It's on the house.

BRENDAN: *(With at least feigned cheerfulness.)* Nonsense, Marty, just put it on my tab.

MARTY: So either way, I'm never seeing a single dime for this one.

BRENDAN: *(A little more cheerfully.)* That sounds about right.

FRANK: *(To Marty.)* Hey, I'm sorry about before.

MARTY: Forget it.

FRANK: No, really. I kinda went apeshit on you and I didn't really mean to . . . It's just, I've had a lot on my mind lately.

MARTY: Nah, we all have days like that, Frank. It's just part of being human.

FRANK: *(Beat.)* Yeah. I guess you're right. Thanks, Marty.

MARTY: Don't mention it. Anything else I can get for you guys, just give a holler.

BRENDAN: Hey Marty, you're married, right?

MARTY: *Was* married. Not anymore.

BRENDAN: What, she left you?

MARTY: *(Ominously.)* That's one way of putting it.

FRANK: Tell us about it.

MARTY: *(Pauses, considers.)* I'm not trying to sound rude or anything but I just don't feel like talking about it.

BRENDAN: C'mon, Marty, we're all friends here.

MARTY: No disrespect, fellas, but you come in here all the time and you do a lot of talking and that's . . . that's good, that's what this place is here for . . . *but (Sighs.)*, there are just some things that you know not to talk about. All those words, all that talking . . . it doesn't get you anywhere . . . it doesn't *change* anything. *(Pause.)* Look, I gotta get back to watering down the beer.

(As Marty exits stage left, Sean enters from stage right.)

BRENDAN: *(Whispers to Frank.)* Oh shit, heads up.

(Sean makes his way over to the table takes his coat off and drapes it over the back of his chair and then takes his seat. His empty glass from earlier is still on the table, and he fills it from the pitcher and takes a long sip. Brendan and Frank, unsure of what mood Sean's in, wait for him to speak first.)

SEAN: Well, that did no good.

FRANK: What?

BRENDAN: Where'd you go?

SEAN: Nowhere. I just took a walk, that's all. Tried to sort some things out in my head.

(Pause. Brendan and Frank aren't sure how to react.)

BRENDAN: Yeah? And?

SEAN: I was thinking about what you guys said. About how I should give Shannon the benefit of the doubt and not jump to conclusions.

FRANK: That's right, you can never be too sure about these things.

SEAN: The question is, what happens when even the benefit of the doubt isn't enough?

BRENDAN: What do you mean?

SEAN: *(Pause . . . sighs.)* I didn't want to say this before because . . . *(Tails off.)* I guess I didn't want to seem weak in front of you. I guess I wanted to be able to come in here and hear that things weren't as bad as I thought. But they are. They're worse. I know Shannon's having an affair because I have proof. I — I had it the whole time. I just didn't want to admit it to you . . . I didn't want to admit it to myself.

FRANK: What are you talking about?

SEAN: Well, it's not like there were used condoms strewn across the pillowcase or anything like that, if that's what you had in mind. But there are things — little things, stuff I should have noticed earlier but didn't. She was acting real weird a few days ago when I came home early from work. Sort of hovering near the phone. And then tonight, right before I got here, I found a belt that doesn't belong to me under the bed and an almost empty bottle of chardonnay in the back of the fridge.

FRANK: Maybe she drank the wine alone.

SEAN: Shannon hates that stuff. I don't drink it, either.

FRANK: *(Persistently.)* Well, maybe some of her friends brought it over as a gift . . . or, or maybe she had a glass with some of the girls from work. It doesn't prove anything.

BRENDAN: *(Quietly.)* Frank, enough.

SEAN: Yeah, pal, I know what you're trying to do but it's not really working. This is why I left before.

FRANK: Sean, maybe if you —

SEAN: *(Changing the subject, getting angry.)* Honestly, what did I do wrong? Why wasn't I good enough? *(Beat.)* The fucking bitch.

FRANK: Sean, don't say that; she's your wife.

SEAN: Not anymore. Not after this shit.

BRENDAN: You don't mean that. You still love her. If you didn't, then it wouldn't get to you like this.

SEAN: Like what?

BRENDAN: Well, you know —

SEAN: No, Brendan, I don't. Like what?

FRANK: What he's saying, Sean, is that Shannon still means something to you. A lot. Otherwise, what she did to you wouldn't hurt so much. And I have a pretty good feeling that you still mean something to her. This doesn't have to be the end of anything.

SEAN: I can't go back. Not after this. I could never go back. Even if she still loves me — which I kind of doubt, what with her fucking other men and everything — I could never forgive her.

FRANK: You *have* to.

SEAN: Why? Why do I have to? I can't forgive *this.* (*Shakes his head . . . beat.*) You can't comprehend it, Frank . . . you're not married. You don't know what it's like. But when your wife does something like that, when the woman you love . . . (*Tails off.*) There are just some things that can never be forgiven.

BRENDAN: Sean, don't be thinking like that.

SEAN: (*Loudly.*) How am *I supposed* to think? What am I supposed to do, Brendan?

BRENDAN: (*Beat. softly.*) I don't know, Sean. I don't . . . (*Tails off.*) I'm sorry. (*Brendan's struggle to articulate an answer, to come up with a solution that will turn everything back to normal, drains him, and a silence hangs in the air like another cloud of cigarette smoke suspended in the bar. Slowly, Frank looks up from the table and speaks softly.*)

FRANK: Let me tell you guys a story.

SEAN: What? No.

FRANK: Come on. It'll help.

SEAN: (*Angry.*) It'll help!? What the fuck's the matter with you? This isn't story time, Frank. You're not on Romper Room. This is my *life* we're talking about.

FRANK: (*Louder.*) I know. (*Softer, more composed.*) Believe me, Sean, I know. But it is *very* important that you hear this.

SEAN: I don't really see how another one of your fucking parables could be at all important after the shit I laid on you guys tonight. (*Over enunciating each word.*) My — wife — is — sleeping — with —

FRANK: (*Desperately.*) Just *listen, please. I need to* —

SEAN: You know, I'm getting sick and tired of your stories. I'm *really* not in the mood for this.

FRANK: (*Loses it, irate.*) Just let me tell my story! LET ME TELL MY FUCK-ING STORY!
(*Beat.*)

SEAN: (*Shocked by Frank's outburst and responds flatly.*) Fine. Tell your damn story. (*Sensing that Frank's story is going to be a characteristically long one despite, or perhaps because of the seriousness of the situation, Brendan grabs the pitcher and tops off everyone's beer. Frank takes a deep breath, composes himself, and begins.*)

FRANK: OK. So you say you'll never be able to forgive Shannon for what she did. Fine. That's understandable. But before you do something you'll regret, before you walk away from something that's important to you, let me remind you of one thing.

SEAN: What's that?

FRANK: The 1986 World Series.

BRENDAN: Jesus.

FRANK: Game Six. For the first time in eighty years, the Red Sox are going to win it all. I mean, it's a *fait accompli;* they're one strike away. They have the champagne on ice over in their clubhouse, Doc Gooden's in the Mets' dugout, crying his eyes out like a little girl.

BRENDAN: Maybe he just ran out of crack.

SEAN: *(Impatiently.)* Can we get back to *me,* here?

FRANK: *(Shoots an angry glance at Brendan.)* I'm trying to. Anyway, this is it. Finally, the curse of the Bambino will be broken, all of New England's on the edge of their seats, parents are holding newborn babies up to the TV set so that when they grow up, they'll be able to say they saw the Sox finally win a World Series.

SEAN: Right, but then Buckner misses the ground ball and the Sox lose. What's your point?

FRANK: Let me finish! Please. Sean, think how enormous Buckner's error was. He was run out of town. He got death threats, his wife couldn't go to the grocery store without some asshole rolling an orange at her feet to see if she'd miss it, he had to take his daughter out of school because the other kids wouldn't stop pelting her with erasers.

SEAN: Frank, what the hell does this have to do with my situation?

FRANK: Listen to me! I'm trying to tell you. So what happens to Buckner? His career's pretty much over. He can't stay in Boston, and no other team wants to take a chance on the biggest goat in World Series history. So he's essentially done with baseball. Because of that one little error. I heard he runs some concession stand at a bowling alley out in Jersey now.

SEAN: *(Bitterly.)* Great fucking story. In other news, my wife is cheating on me and my life is ruined!

FRANK: Right, and like you said, you can't forgive her.

SEAN: No, Frank, I don't think I can. *(Beat.)* Wait. What are you saying? That I should forgive her because she made an error? Is that what this is all about?

FRANK: Well —

SEAN: Please tell me you're not trying to equate my wife's marital infidelities with a misplayed grounder.

FRANK: No, I'm not saying that what she did was —

SEAN: Because that's what it sounds like to me, Frank, and that's some fucked-up shit that I can't believe I'm hearing, even from you. You think I should just forgive and forget because people overreacted to the Buckner thing?

FRANK: No, that's not what I mean at all. Don't feel sorry for Buckner. This isn't about Buckner. Fuck Buckner.

SEAN: Then what the hell are you saying?

FRANK: Everyone blames Buckner, right? The thing is, they're *wrong*. It's not his fault the Sox lost.

BRENDAN: Sure it is. I've seen the replay a hundred times. He let Mookie Wilson's grounder go right through his legs!

SEAN: All right. *(Slight beat.)* You know what, guys? I don't care. I love the BoSox as much as the next guy, but I really don't give a shit about whether Buckner lost the game or not. You wanna know why? *Because my wife is sleeping with other men!* That's a little more important to me right now.

FRANK: Sean, I know. That's what I'm trying to —

SEAN: Brendan, honestly, help me out here.

BRENDAN: I'd let him finish, Sean.

SEAN: This is bullshit! You know what? If you guys want to sit around here and shoot the shit about some stupid World Series game that happened fifteen years ago, fine. Fuck it. I'm leaving.

(Sean gets up as if to leave.)

FRANK: *(Loses it.)* Shut up! Shut up and *listen* to me! Sit down.

(Sean is shocked, and he sits down again.)

SEAN: *(Shaking his head.)* Fine. But get to the fucking point.

FRANK: All right. Here's my point. When the ball gets to Buckner, he's at least a dozen feet away from the bag. There's no way he beats Mookie Wilson in a foot race to first, so no matter what he'd have to flip the ball to the pitcher covering. But — and you can see this on the replay — the pitcher, Bob Stanley, was nowhere near first. He's not even in the picture. *(Slight beat.)* Maybe everyone's got it wrong. Maybe it's Stanley's fault. Maybe Buckner's just unlucky.

(There's a very slight pause while the men let this new information sink in.)

SEAN: *(Sarcastically.)* Well, I'm glad you guys cleared that up. Now what the hell does it have to do with me?

FRANK: What I'm trying to say, Sean, is that . . . well, maybe it's not Shannon's fault.

SEAN: *(Defensively.)* So whose fault is it? Mine?

FRANK: What Shannon did was wrong. There's no doubt about that. And you're right, you can't equate missing a grounder with sleeping around, but as much as you blame Shannon for what's happened, maybe it's not entirely her fault.

SEAN: What are you saying? I did something wrong so it's my fault she wasn't faithful?

FRANK: *(Irritated.)* This isn't about you, Sean!

SEAN: What's that supposed to mean?

FRANK: *(More composed.)* Sorry. What I mean is, *you* might have done nothing wrong; *Shannon* might have done nothing wrong. Someone could have come along and, I don't know, made Shannon think the wrong things.

SEAN: I don't understand what you're saying.

FRANK: I'm saying it's the other guy's fault. It's Bob's fault.

BRENDAN: Bob who?

FRANK: Bob Stanley.

SEAN: *(Confused beyond belief.)* My wife is sleeping with Bob Stanley?!

FRANK: Jesus, Sean, no. *(Pause.)* I don't know. Maybe I'm not saying this right. All I know is that you should talk to Shannon. You should work things out with her. Give her a chance.

BRENDAN: I think he's right, Sean.

SEAN: *I gave* her a chance. You don't know what this feels like, to have the woman you love do this to you. It's not the kind of thing where you can just snap your fingers and get over it. It's not something I'll ever be able to forget.

FRANK: You don't have to forget it, Sean, but you do have to forgive her. She loves you —

SEAN: *(Getting angry.)* You know, I don't even know why I'm listening to this shit.

FRANK: All I'm saying is —

SEAN: Who the fuck are you to talk? Honestly, this has nothing to do with you. You have no investment in this either way, so you can just sit there and cook up little stories that don't mean shit, but you seem to forget the unending hell I'm going through here.

BRENDAN: Sean, he's just trying to put things in a different perspective for you.

SEAN: I can't fucking stand it, though. It's like listening to some deaf kid talk about what his favorite Bob Dylan album is; who gives a shit? The kid's deaf. He doesn't have a clue what he's talking about.

FRANK: It's not like that at all, Sean.

SEAN: No? It's not? Then tell me, oh-infinitely-wise-one, what *is* it like? 'Cause all I'm hearing *is you telling* me how I should deal with *my* wife.

FRANK: If you would actually *listen* to what I have to say, instead of automatically dismissing it —

SEAN: I'm not *dismissing* it, Frank. I'm just a little confused as to why anyone should take relationship advice from *you,* of all people. I mean, when was the last time you even got laid?

BRENDAN: *(Trying to defuse the situation.)* Now, guys . . .

SEAN: I'm serious, that's why you do this shit. Why you always quote other people, always tell other peoples' stories; it's 'cause you've got nothing going on in your own life that's worth hearing about, so you just throw out some obscure quotes or bring up some old ballgame and think you're actually fooling people.

FRANK: Sean —

SEAN: *(Unrelenting.)* You're a smooth one, though, Frankie. You do fool a helluva lot of people, I'll give you that. Even Shannon's said *(Girlish voice, mockingly.),* "Oh, that Frank, he sure has a different way of looking at things. He's soooo smart." Well, you ain't fooling me, not anymore, you arrogant piece of shit.

FRANK: *(Defensively.)* Sean, there's really no need to —

SEAN: Honestly, Frank, here's what I don't get. If you're so intelligent, if you're such a fucking expert on how to keep a marriage together, then why are you the only one here who isn't married? Huh? I mean, before you start telling me what I need to do to get my marriage back on track, why don't you actually go on a couple of dates? Get a little *pussy* once in a while before you hang out your shingle as a marriage counselor, Frank.

BRENDAN: *(Sternly.)* Sean, that's enough.

FRANK: *(To Brendan.)* No, no. He's right. *(To Sean.)* You're right. Who am I to talk? I can't imagine how hard these last few days must have been for you. How difficult your situation is. *(Slight beat.)* That's why I didn't want what I'm about to tell you to come out like this.

BRENDAN: Frank, don't. Not like this.

FRANK: I've no other choice, Brendan. I can't sit on this any longer. It's tearing me apart inside and if he wants to be an asshole about things, let him. I can stoop to his level.

BRENDAN: Don't do it, Frank. It won't help anyone this way.

SEAN: *(Genuinely worried.)* Whoa, hold on here . . . what the hell are you guys talking about?

FRANK: *(With pure evil in his voice.)* Hey, Sean, you wanna know when the last time I got laid was? Do you wanna know the last time I got a little pussy?

BRENDAN: *(Disgusted.)* Jesus, Frank.

FRANK: Last Tuesday night, Sean. From 8:35 to 9:47. In the Radisson Inn on Route Ten.

SEAN: *(Confused.)* God, Frank, I didn't need the *exact* time and place.

FRANK: *(Snidely.)* I believe it coincides nicely with your wife's "poetry class" at the college. The time before that was two Fridays ago, while you *happened* to be in Boston on business.

SEAN: *(Not allowing himself to believe what he's hearing.)* What — what are you saying?

FRANK: What I'm *saying*, Sean, is that it's Sauvignon Blanc, not Chardonnay in the back of your fridge. And you're wrong, Shannon *does* drink it. And that's just the tip of the iceberg of what you don't know about her.

(Sean sits there, stunned as the information begins to sink in. After several seconds, and without warning, he lunges across the table, grabbing at Frank's throat. In the skirmish, a glass falls from the table and shatters. Brendan quickly gets between both men and separates them. Marty comes running from stage left and restrains Sean while Brendan holds Frank back.)

SEAN: *(Yelling at Frank.)* I can't fucking believe you.

MARTY: *(To Brendan.)* What the hell is going on here?

BRENDAN: Just hold him, please.

(Brendan pushes Frank back with one hand and grabs his chair with the other. He drags the chair a few feet to stage right and sits Frank down in it. Sean struggles to break from Marty's hold, but Marty has experience in barroom brawls, and Sean quickly realizes he won't be able to break free.

MARTY: *(To Sean.)* Calm down or I'll throw you out.

SEAN: Let go of me. *(To Frank.)* How the fuck could you do that to me?

MARTY: *(Soothingly.)* Calm down.

SEAN: It's not my fault.

MARTY: I don't give a shit whose fault it is. You guys are friends, knock this crap off.

SEAN: *(Composes himself.)* Fine, Marty, you're right. I'm fine now.

(Marty tentatively loosens his grip on Sean. Seeing that Sean seems to have calmed down, he lets go of him. Sean brushes himself off and slowly returns to the table. Once he's a few feet out of Marty's reach, however, he rushes at Frank. Frank's chair topples over and Sean gets one or two good blows in before Brendan and Marty pull him off.)

SEAN: *(Seething.)* I swear to God, I'll get you for this shit!

BRENDAN: *(To Frank.)* Are you OK?

> *(Frank stands up slowly, with his hands covering his face. He lowers his hands and is bleeding from just above his left eye. He looks past Brendan and stares at Sean with a look that expresses more emotional anguish than physical pain.)*

BRENDAN: It's just a scratch, you'll live.

> *(As the following lines are spoken, Marty retrieves a dustpan and broom from behind the bar, offstage left. He reenters and begins sweeping up the broken glass.)*

FRANK: *(To Sean.)* I didn't mean it to be like this.

SEAN: *(With venom.)* Don't talk to me.

FRANK: Sean, I'm sorry. I didn't want things to turn out like this.

SEAN: Fuck off.

FRANK: She loves you, Sean.

SEAN: *(Screams.)* What do you know about love? *(Pause . . . softer, but with no less hatred in his tone.)* You're a fucking disgrace. *(To Brendan.)* You knew about this? You knew about this shit and you didn't say anything?

BRENDAN: *(Quietly.)* Sean, I —

SEAN: You're just as bad as he is.

BRENDAN: Sean, you don't understand. How could I choose sides?

SEAN: *(His anger is so intense he is near tears.)* How could you choose sides? He slept with my wife, Brendan! *(Beat. Sean summons up all the rage that is left in him and directs it towards Brendan and Frank.)* You're all fucking cowards! I wish I'd never met you.

> *(Sean grabs his coat from the chair and begins walking offstage left, with Marty following close behind him.)*

FRANK: *(Calling after Sean.)* Sean, she does love you. You have to understand. She loves you. *(Sean exits. Sound of door closing.)* I'm sorry.

> *(Brendan slowly returns to his seat, clearly exhausted and stunned by what's happened tonight. Frank picks his chair up, drags it back to the table, and sits down. He finishes what's left in his pint glass, runs a hand through his hair, then refills the glass with what's left in the pitcher. He looks like shit.)*

FRANK: *(In a sad, distant voice.)* Brendan, what's going to happen?

BRENDAN: *(Angry.)* I don't want to talk about it.

FRANK: Will it ever be the way it was?

BRENDAN: *(Sternly, as if reproaching a child.)* Frank, I'm going home now. I suggest you do the same.

FRANK: What happened? What have I done?

BRENDAN: You fucked everything up, Frank, that's what you did. *(Softer.)* But look, there's nothing more you can do about it tonight, so just go home.

FRANK: *(Suddenly defiant.)* No. I'm not going home.

(Frank runs to the wall near stage left and crumples to the ground, slouched against the wall underneath a "Guinness For Strength" poster.)

BRENDAN: Jesus, Frank, stand up.

FRANK: No.

BRENDAN: Quit acting like a little kid.

FRANK: I knew he wouldn't understand. I said it all wrong. It wasn't supposed to be like that. I let him get to me.

BRENDAN: I'm leaving, Frank.

FRANK: I — I don't even know who I am anymore. I've done all these awful things . . .

(Brendan prepares to leave. He begins to put on his jacket. Frank looks around on the floor and finds a shard of the broken glass lying next to him. He grabs it and holds it daggerlike against his throat.)

FRANK: Brendan!

BRENDAN: Frank, you're drunk. Just put the glass down and let's get the hell out of here.

FRANK: I don't deserve to live.

BRENDAN: You're being ridiculous. Now put the glass down before you hurt yourself.

FRANK: That's the point!

BRENDAN: *(Irate.)* Are you that fucked up, Frankie? Are you that fucked up that after all the shit you caused tonight, all the pain you brought everyone else, you can roll around on the floor and wallow in self-pity?

FRANK: This is serious, Brendan.

BRENDAN: Is it, Frank? Or is this just like all those stories you tell? Is this just another way for you to get attention?

FRANK: You never take me seriously. You always treat everything like it's a big fucking joke. I'm not a joke, Brendan!

(As if to illustrate his point, Frank pushes the glass harder against his throat. As earlier when Frank screamed at Marty, Brendan realizes just how close to the edge his friend really is.)

BRENDAN: OK, Frankie, I know. Now come on, put down the glass.

FRANK: I need to know something. With all the shit I've done, all the awful things . . . do you forgive me?

BRENDAN: *(Sighs as he struggles to find an answer that won't betray his own disgust with Frank's behavior, but also one that won't push his friend over the edge.)* It's not that I don't —

FRANK: *(Screams.)* DO YOU FORGIVE ME?

BRENDAN: Jesus, Frank, yes. Yes, I forgive you.

FRANK: Will Sean forgive me?

BRENDAN: Yes. Frank, we understand. We forgive you.

FRANK: *(Suddenly enraged, pushing the glass harder against his throat.)* It's not enough! It's not enough to be forgiven. It doesn't do anything. Everything's still the same. I still have to live with what I've done.

BRENDAN: *(Slowly, soothingly.)* You have to forgive yourself, Frankie. And you will, . . . over time.

FRANK: *(Still irate.)* Nothing's *changed,* Brendan! I'm still *me.* When I wake up tomorrow everything will be exactly the way it is now. I'll still have to look at myself in the mirror.

BRENDAN: It'll be OK. You made a mistake. That's all. We all make mistakes.

FRANK: A mistake, Brendan? Jesus Christ! I slept with my best friend's wife! That's not exactly something you can chalk up to common human frailty. I slept with Shannon and then I lorded it over Sean tonight. I fucking *bragged* about it, Brendan.

BRENDAN: You're not a bad person, you just did something bad.

(Frank slowly drops his arm to his side, but still holds onto the glass. After a moment, his face contorts in torment and he brings the glass up to his throat again, drawing a thin trickle of blood down his neck.)

FRANK: *(Louder, more forcefully.)* What is wrong with me?

BRENDAN: *(Panicked, desperately.)* Jesus, Frank, don't . . .

(Still holding the glass against his neck, Frank looks up at the ceiling, as if addressing God.)

FRANK: *(Frantic, irate, shouting each word separately.)* WHAT IS WRONG WITH ME? *(Frank collapses in a heap and drops the shard of glass. He begins sobbing. Softly, barely audible.)* Forgive me . . . forgive me.

(Brendan moves in. He slides the piece of glass away from Frank and puts his arm around him. The two sit there in silence for a moment, and slowly Frank's crying abates. The full weight of what has happened tonight and what has almost happened hangs in the air for quite some time before Brendan speaks.)

BRENDAN: *(Softly.)* Hey, Frank?

FRANK: *(Very softly.)* Yeah?

BRENDAN: You forgot something.

FRANK: What?

BRENDAN: In your story. About Buckner. You forgot the most important part.

FRANK: What's that?

BRENDAN: When it happened, when he missed the ball . . . it was only Game Six. The season wasn't over. They still had to play the seventh game. Buckner still had to go home that night. He still had to wake up the next day, see himself in the mirror, put on his uniform, and face his teammates, the press, the crowd . . . He still had to find a way to go out there and keep playing.

(The two men slowly get up and walk off, exiting stage left. A few seconds later, the lights go out. Curtain.)

END OF PLAY

COPYRIGHT AND CONTACT INFORMATION